Freedom and Rights

A.J.M. MILNE

Ph.D., B.Sc. (Econ.)

Reader in Philosophy at The Queen's University, Belfast

Freedom and Rights

LONDON · GEORGE ALLEN AND UNWIN LTD

NEW YORK · HUMANITIES PRESS INC.

TO ANITA MILNE

B
824.4
. M5

PRINTED IN GREAT BRITAIN
in 11 point Bell type
BY C. TINLING AND CO. LTD
LIVERPOOL, LONDON AND PRESCOT

Preface

The idea of this book began to take shape in my mind during the summer of 1961. But more than six years were needed to work it out. I spent the academic year 1963-64 in the University of California at Berkeley on a research fellowship from the American Council of Learned Societies. Throughout July '64 I was a member of a seminar on freedom of speech at The Center for the Study of Democratic Institutions at Santa Barbara, California. It was time well spent, especially in what I gained from informal discussion. I should like to thank the A.C.L.S. and the Santa Barbara Center. I am also grateful to The Queen's University of Belfast for giving me leave of absence.

Readers familiar with Collingwood's work will recognize what I owe to it, in particular to his *Essay on Philosophical Method* and to certain parts of *The Idea of History* and *The New Leviathan*. But I have many other intellectual debts. They are too numerous to acknowledge individually but I would like to mention my colleagues, past and present, in the Philosophy Department at Queen's and also the students I have taught over the past ten years or so. Both, without perhaps realising it, have helped me to clarify many of the ideas which have gone into this book. I am most grateful to my friend, Mr. E. D. Phillips of Queen's, for his invaluable help with the proofs. Finally, I must mention the contribution of my wife, to whom this book is dedicated. She has certainly earned it, for she undertook the thankless task of pruning my manuscript and licking it into some sort of literary shape, all too often in the face of a stubborn rearguard action by the author. It was a job which only a wife could have done but by no means every wife. The blemishes which remain are my fault, not her's, and I am truly grateful to her.

A. J. MILNE

Belfast, August 1968.

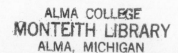

Contents

Contents

Contents

A*

Introduction

In his senatorial days, President Johnson once described himself as: 'First, a free man; second, an American citizen; third, a United States Senator: and fourth, a member of the Democratic party.[1] In giving pride of place to being a free man, he was echoing a widely held sentiment. In the Western world today, we are officially in favour of freedom. We think that the good life is that of a free man and that the good society is a free society. Any movement of social or political reform which claims to be promoting freedom in some form or other is guaranteed at least a measure of respect. No one among us wants to be identified as hostile to freedom. It is much the same with the idea of rights. If the old doctrine of natural rights no longer has quite the prestige it once had, its place has been taken by the idea of human rights. We take pride in the claim that in Western societies basic human rights are respected and believe that in this matter we are superior to other societies. We think that rights and freedom go together, and that in a free society, the protection of rights is of the first importance. The twin values of freedom and rights are the corner-stone of our modern Western civilization, or so we profess to believe.

It was not always so. In Classical Antiquity and in the Middle Ages, freedom and rights occupied less exalted positions in the scale of human values. Freedom was important as denoting social status, that of the free man in distinction to the slave and the serf. Value was attached to rights long established by law and custom. But our ancient and medieval ancestors did not equate the good society with the free society. They did not think about freedom in general terms apart from particular social, moral and political contexts. Nor did they attach much importance to the idea of basic human rights in the abstract apart from the laws and customs of particular societies. It was not

[1] In a radio interview broadcast during the American Presidential Election campaign October, 1960, by the Voice of America.

until the seventeenth century that our modern ideas of freedom and rights began to influence European thought and action. Nor do they command the same respect outside the Western world today. In the Communist world, they are dismissed as typical cases of bourgeois ideological rationalization. While lip service is sometimes paid to them elsewhere outside the West, they are in fact invariably more honoured in the breach than in the observance. Few Asian, African or South American nations even pretend to attach the importance to them which we do.

Does this matter? Are these non-Western peoples missing something? Are there good reasons for placing freedom and rights so high in the scale of human values? What can count as good reasons? What, in any case, is it to be a free man? What can be meant by a free society? Are they good, and if so, why? What is it to have a right? In what sense, if any, can there be natural or basic human rights? What justifies the claim to a right? Can there be unrecognized rights? If so, how can the claim to them be justified? These are the questions with which this book is concerned: questions about justification and reasons, as well as those about freedom and rights themselves. It is an inquiry into freedom and rights, to discover what importance should be attached to them, and at the same time an inquiry into the rational grounds for attaching importance to anything in human life. My aim is to try to discover what the proper perspective is and to see freedom and rights in that perspective.

If history and tradition are reliable guides, these questions fall within the domain of philosophy. This book may accordingly be described as a philosophical exploration, being concerned in particular with a cluster of problems in moral, social, and political philosophy. In the last generation, academic philosophy in Britain and America has been pre-eminently analytic in character. This book is a partial return to a more traditional approach. It is an essay in philosophical synthesis rather than merely philosophical analysis. There is a good deal of analysis in what follows, but it has been undertaken in the interests of eventual synthesis, that is of relating and integrating concepts, and has therefore been carried only as far as that interest requires.

INTRODUCTION

In exploring any philosophical topic, it is a wise policy to begin by examining the work of predecessors. Accordingly Part 1 of this book is devoted to a review of the work of a number of philosophers past and present on the subjects of freedom and rights. The review is in no way exhaustive. It is not intended to be a history of modern philosophical thought about freedom and rights. But it is intended to pave the way for what is to follow, and I have confined attention to those philosophers whose work has appeared to me to be most useful from this point of view. Part 2 begins the task of investigating the perspective and, after carrying the discussion a certain way, turns back to freedom and rights to see what light is thrown upon them. Part 3 is devoted to completing the discussion of the perspective, and in particular to dealing with a fundamental problem disclosed in Part 2. Finally in Part 4, the discussion of freedom and rights is resumed, and they are set in the completed perspective.

According to Aristotle: 'It is the mark of an educated man not to look for more precision than the subject matter admits of.'[1] This has been my governing principle throughout this book, and more especially in investigating the problems of the perspective. I have not tried to be more exact, or for that matter more complete, than the task in hand required. But I have at least aimed at that much exactness and completeness. One topic has not been expressly raised at all, although by implication a good deal has been hinted. This is the old topic of the freedom of the will. This omission may be defended by the precedent of John Stuart Mill who in his essay 'Liberty' excluded it from his discussion. Finally, I should like to emphasize the exploratory character of this book. The conceptual synthesis which it offers is put forward as a contribution to what should be a continuing debate: how best to understand ourselves and the social, moral, and political values to which we profess allegiance.

[1] *Nicomachean Ethics.* Book 1.

PART 1

Freedom and Rights:
A Preliminary View

Chapter 1
Some Theories of Freedom

1. NINETEENTH-CENTURY PHILOSOPHERS

A. *John Stuart Mill*

In the hundred years since its first publication, John Stuart Mill's essay 'Liberty' has become a classic. We can hardly do better than begin with it. Like Hobbes and Bentham before him, Mill thinks of freedom in negative terms. You are free or at liberty to the extent that you are not subject to constraint in the shape of compulsion, coercion or interference by any other human being. When, if at all, is such constraint justified? This is the problem of freedom as he sees it. 'The object of this essay,' he writes, 'is to assert one very simple principle as entitled to govern absolutely the dealings of society with the individual in the way of compulsion and control, whether the means used be physical force in the form of legal penalties or the moral coercion of public opinion. That principle is that the sole end for which mankind are warranted individually or collectively in interfering with the liberty of action of any of their number is self-protection; that the only purpose for which power can be rightfully exercised over any member of a civilized community against his will is to prevent harm to others.'[1] Mill insists that interference with someone else's liberty for his own good is not justified. 'His own good, either physical or moral, is not a sufficient warrant. He cannot rightfully be compelled to do or forebear because it would be better for him to do so, because it would make him happier, because in the opinions of others to do so would be wise or even right.'[2]

But having stated his principle, Mill goes on immediately to qualify it. 'It is perhaps hardly necessary to say that this doctrine is meant to apply to human beings in the maturity of their faculties. We are not speaking of children or of young persons

17

below the age which the law may fix as that of manhood or womanhood. Those who are still in a state to require being taken care of by others must be protected against their own actions as well as external injury.' [3] He adds that the same qualification applies to uncivilized peoples. 'For the same reason we may leave out of consideration those backward states of society in which the race itself may be considered as in its non-age.' [4] Then summing up, he writes: 'Liberty as a principle has no application to any state of things anterior to the time when mankind became capable of being improved by free and equal discussion.' [5]

But why should the principle of self-protection be accepted? Why is it wrong to constrain an adult for his own good? Answering this question Mill writes: 'It is proper to state that I forego any advantage which could be derived to my argument from the idea of abstract right as a thing independent of utility. I regard utility as the ultimate court of appeal on all ethical questions. But it must be utility in the largest sense, grounded on the permanent interests of a man as a progressive being.' [6] Explaining the bearing of utility in the largest sense upon the problem of freedom, he writes: 'The only freedom which deserves the name is that of pursuing our own good in our own way so long as we do not attempt to deprive others of theirs or impede their efforts to obtain it. Each is the proper guardian of his own health, whether bodily or mental and spiritual. Mankind are the greater gainers by suffering each other to live as seems good to themselves than by compelling each other to live as seems good to the rest.' [7] For a fuller exposition and defence of utility as an ethical principle, the reader must be referred to Mill's essay 'Utilitarianism'. Here it is enough to notice the general character of the moral theory on which he bases his solution of the problem of freedom. In 'Liberty', after stating his general principle of self-protection, he goes on to consider its bearing upon certain topics, especially freedom of speech and freedom for what he calls 'individuality'.

His argument in support of freedom of speech is probably the best known part of the essay. The foundation of his case is the great disutility of censorship in any form. 'But the peculiar evil of silencing the expression of opinion is that it is robbing the human race, posterity as well as the present generation, those who dissent from the opinion still more than those who uphold it. If the opinion is right, they are deprived of the opportunity of exchanging error for truth; if wrong, they lose what is almost as great a benefit, the clearer perception and livelier impression of truth produced by its collision with error.' [8] All human opinions are fallible. The truth can never be known with absolute certainty. The only rational ground that we can have for believing any opinion to be true is that it has survived the test of criticism. 'The beliefs that we have most warrant for,' he writes, 'have no safeguard to rest on but a standing invitation to the whole world to prove them unfounded. If the challenge is not accepted, or is accepted and the attempt fails, we are far enough from certainty still, but we have done the best that the existing state of human reason admits of, we have neglected nothing that could give the truth a chance of reaching us. If the lists are kept open we may hope that if there be a better truth it will be found when the human mind is capable of receiving it and in the meantime we may rely on having attained such approach to truth as is possible in our own day. This is the amount of certainty attainable by a fallible being and this is the sole way of attaining it.' [9]

Mill agrees that for practical purposes we are justified in assuming the certainty of many of our opinions. But he points out that: 'There is the greatest difference between presuming an opinion to be true because with every opportunity for contesting it, it has not been refuted, and assuming its truth for the purposes of not permitting its refutation. Complete liberty of contradicting and disproving our opinion is the very condition which justifies us in assuming its truth for purposes of action and no other terms can a being with human faculties have any rational assurance of being right.' [10] If then it is granted that it is desirable that action should, so far as possible, be guided by true opinions, an admission which is clearly warranted by the ethical principle of utility, it follows that complete freedom of speech is desirable as a necessary condition for reaching such opinions. Such in essentials is Mill's case.

What he means by 'individuality' and why he thinks it important may be gathered from the following passage. 'As it is useful that while mankind are imperfect there should be different opinions, so it is that there should be different experiments in living, that free scope should be given to varieties of character short of injury to others and that the worth of different modes of life should be proved practically when anyone thinks fit to try them. It is desirable in short that in things which do not primarily concern others, individuality should assert itself. Where not the person's own character but the traditions or customs of other people are the rule of conduct, there is wanting one of the principle ingredients of human happiness and quite the chief ingredient of individual and social progress.' [11] A person achieves individuality to the extent that he determines his own life in his own way in the light of his judgement of what is best for him. That there should be freedom to pursue individuality subject to the principle of self-protection is desirable because people are no more infallible about ways of living than they are in their opinions. Mankind are the gainers from being free to experiment in ways of living just as they are from being free to experiment in the pursuit of knowledge. Being free to pursue individuality is simply being free to pursue our own good in our own way subject to not impeding others in their efforts to do the same.

According to Mill, the idea of a free society is the idea of a society with certain definite characteristics. In the first place, it will be a civilized society, i.e., a society whose adult members are capable of being improved by free and equal discussion. Secondly, it will be a society in which the exercise of constraint is limited to the preventing of harm by anyone to anyone else. Thirdly, and as a consequence of these first two characteristics, it will be a society whose adult members all enjoy freedom to pursue individuality subject to the limits of the principle of self-protection and to express whatever opinions they have come to hold without being subject to any penalty. Only to the extent that these characteristics are present, can any actual society be regarded as a free society.

B. *T. H. Green and Bernard Bosanquet*

Some twenty years after the publication of Mill's 'Liberty', T. H. Green wrote a short essay entitled; 'The Different Senses of

Freedom'. He agrees with Mill to the extent of holding that the literal meaning of 'freedom' is negative. 'As to the sense given to "freedom",' he writes, 'it must of course be admitted that every usage of the term to express anything but a social and political relation of one man with others involves a metaphor.' [1] He then goes on: 'Even in the original application the sense is by no means fixed. It always implies indeed some exemption from compulsion by others but the extent and conditions of this exemption as enjoyed by the free man in different states of society are very various. As soon as the term "freedom" comes to be applied to anything else than an established relation between a man and others its sense fluctuates much more.' [2] But what interests Green is the use which a man who is exempt from compulsion makes of his freedom. It is in this connection that the various metaphorical senses of the term are significant. He maintains that: 'Freedom means very different things according to the nature of the object which the man makes his own or with which he identifies himself.' [3]

He goes on to contrast the man who directs his life on the basis of rational moral convictions with the man who is content to allow his inclinations of the moment and his desire for personal enjoyment to be his guide without considering his personal well-being on the whole or his responsibilities to others. In one sense both are equally free for each is equally the author of his actions and is free from compulsion by others. But in another sense the former is free while the latter is not, for he is at the mercy of his inclinations and desires. As Green puts it: 'He may be considered in the condition of a bondsman who is carrying out the will of another, not his own.' [4] According to Green; 'from his bondage he emerges into real freedom' by becoming a rational moral agent, or as Green expresses it, 'by seeking the satisfaction of himself in objects in which it should be found and seeking it in them because he believes it should be found in them.' [5]

This doctrine, according to which there is an important sense of freedom in which only a rational moral agent is really free, has come to be known as the positive theory of freedom in contradistinction to the negative theory of Mill according to which freedom is simply the absence of external constraint. Versions of it were put forward by Rousseau, Kant and Hegel, and it was re-

21

stated some twenty years after Green's essay by Bernard Bosanquet in *The Philosophical Theory of the State*. Bosanquet thinks that the negative theory reflects the view of freedom held by the plain man, for whom to be free is simply to be free from constraint by other people. But what is constraint? Bosanquet answers: 'It is constraint when my mind is interfered with in its control of my body, either by actual or threatening physical violence under the direction of another mind. A permanent and settled condition of such constraint, by which I become in effect the instrument of another mind, is slavery.' [6] He then adds that: 'It will not lead us far wrong if we assume that the value put upon liberty and its erection into something like an ideal comes from the contrast with slavery.' [7] But while acknowledging the importance of this sense of freedom, Bosanquet holds that it is seriously defective as an exhaustive account of the idea. 'It is obvious,' he writes, 'that the above definition will be wholly inadequate to the simplest facts respecting the demands which have through all history been asserted and achieved under the name of political freedom. A man may be a long way more than a slave and yet a long way less than a citizen.' [8]

Bosanquet thinks that Rousseau provides the key to a more adequate conception of freedom. 'Liberty no doubt is, as Rousseau has taught us, so far agreeing with Mill, the essential quality of human life. It is so, we understand, because it is the condition of our being ourselves.' [9] It follows from this that we can exist without being ourselves, namely when we are unfree. Selfhood is something to be achieved rather than a merely empirical phenomenon. Now this is one of the central tenets of the Idealist ethical doctrine of self-realization, of which both Green and Bosanquet were exponents. According to Bosanquet, in our every-day unreflecting moments: 'What we mean by "ourself" is the given self, the group of will and wishes, of feelings and ideas, associated from time to time with my particular body, in short the actual uncriticized mind as we experience it all day and every day.' [10] But as the result of self-critical reflection: 'We know that the given self, the mind from day to day, is not satisfactory and we throw the centre of gravity outside it and place the true self in something which we rather want to be than actually are, although at the same time it is clear that to some extent we are this something or we should not want to be it.' [11]

On this view, each of us in our day to day activities is a self in the making rather than a fully formed and complete self. In order to become fully ourselves, we must become all that we have it in us to be. But what this is, each of us can find out only in the practical experience of actual living. The life of each of us is an adventure in self-discovery in which we succeed to the extent that we find ways of exercising and developing our various gifts and capacities. But this process of human self-development is not one which any of us can carry out in isolation. None of us is self-sufficient and we can become what we have it in us to be only by sharing in a common life with others. The true self of each of us, however different in other respects, is a social self. 'We realize indeed,' Bosanquet writes, 'that to be ourselves is a principle at once of distinction or position among others, and a thorough-going transition into and unity with, the life which is at the root of theirs.' [12] According to this doctrine of self-realization, which might be described as one of immanent teleology, rational moral conduct is the pursuit of true self-hood through a life of intelligent and responsible social co-operation.

Exploring the implications of the doctrine for the idea of freedom, Bosanquet writes: 'But now that it occurs to us that in order to be ourselves we must always be becoming something which we are not, in other words we must always recognize we are something more than we have become, liberty as the condition of our being ourselves cannot simply be something which we have, still less something which we have always had, a *status quo* to be maintained. It must be a condition relevant to our continued struggle to assert the control of something in us which we recognize as imperative upon us or as our true self but which we obey only in a very imperfect degree.' [13] Bosanquet here seems to be saying that freedom, rational moral conduct and self-realization are co-extensive. You are free to the extent that you achieve real selfhood and you achieve real selfhood to the extent that you are a rational moral agent. Freedom properly under-stood is therefore something more than merely not being subject to constraint by other people. It has an internal as well as an external side. On its internal side it is the condition of mind and character of the rational moral agent, the rational moral agent being the self-determining autonomous agent who achieves genuine human selfhood. Such an agent, being emancipated from subjection to his natural impulses and inclinations, is free so far as his empirical self is concerned to become what he has it in him to be.

This line of thought leads Bosanquet to reaffirm one of Rousseau's most controversial contentions. Not only is freedom something more than the absence of external constraint; such constraint can actually contribute to freedom. 'Thus it is,' he writes 'that we can speak without contradiction of being forced to be free.' [14] He was to be severely taken to task for this opinion by later critics but before passing judgement it is important to see how he continues. 'It is possible for us to acquiesce as rational beings in a law and order which on the whole makes for the possibility of asserting our true or universal selves the very moment when this law and order is constraining our particular private wills in a way which we resent or even condemn.' [15] What in the heat of the moment we condemn as an invasion of our freedom because it interferes in some way with our private self-interest, we may come to see on reflection to be socially desirable and may therefore be glad that we complied with it although at the time we did so most unwillingly. This seems to be Bosanquet's point. Whether it rebuts his critics is a question which must be deferred until later. He goes on: 'Such a law and order maintained by force which we recognize as on the whole the instrument of our better self-affirmation is a system of rights and our liberty, or to use a good old expression, our "liberties", may be identified with such a system considered as the condition and guarantee of our becoming the best that we have it in us to be, i.e., of becoming ourselves.' [16]

This is to recognize that the external side of freedom is important although subordinate to the internal. A man's rational moral conduct and therefore his achievement of selfhood may be impeded by interference from other people. He ought to be free from such interference. What is important, that is to say, is not the absence of constraint as such but its absence in the form of interference by anyone with anyone else's rational moral conduct and hence with his self-realization. Such external freedom can be secured by a system of rights maintained by law and a society in which it is secured is a free society. To be compelled to obey a law which secures one of these rights is not to suffer any deprivation of internal freedom. It is only to be made to do what as a rational moral agent you ought to be doing anyway. You are being forced to be free in the sense that you are being compelled to do what you really know you ought to do and in your better moments want to do, but which owing to temporary weakness or laziness you cannot bring yourself to do voluntarily.

Looking back over the preceding account of the negative and positive theories, it is clear that to regard them as mutually exclusive alternatives would be a mistake. The positive theory claims to include the negative theory but to go beyond it, making good its shortcomings. These arise out of the negative theory's failure to recognize that freedom has an internal as well as an external side. It takes the external side to be the whole of the matter. Green and Bosanquet are in effect saying that they are not so much rejecting Mill's argument as improving upon it while retaining what is valuable in it. In support of this, they might point to Mill's qualifications to his own principle and especially to his reference to human beings 'capable of being improved by free and equal discussion' as evidence that latent in his argument are considerations pointing in the direction of a tacit recognition of the internal side of freedom. But all this does not of itself show that the claim of the positive theory to be an improvement on the negative theory is justified. As we shall see, two contemporary philosophers who on this point at least may be taken as spokesmen for the present generation, have not been convinced, and have rejected the positive theory and have come down emphatically on the side of the negative theory.

2. CONTEMPORARY PHILOSOPHERS

A. *Maurice Cranston*

In *Freedom, A New Analysis*, a book which was first published in 1953, Maurice Cranston endorses the negative theory of freedom and rejects the positive theory. He does so on linguistic grounds, in this reflecting a characteristic approach of post-war British philosophy to philosophical problems. The idea behind this approach, at least as it is exemplified by Cranston, may be summarized as follows. Philosophical problems are the outcome of conceptual ambiguity or confusion. They are not really problems, i.e., not like scientific problems, but are rather perplexities or puzzles. They must be 'dissolved' rather than solved, by conceptual analysis and this should take the form of a careful study of the language in which the relevant concepts are expressed, special attention being paid to the conventions governing the use of the words which embody the concepts. This should disclose the source of the conceptual ambiguity or confusion which, it is held, always arises from a breach or misobservance of linguistic conventions. Cranston begins his task by giving an extended lexicographical definition of the term 'freedom'. 'The more familiar sort of definition', he writes, 'takes the form of a report in which, e.g., an English word is used by English speaking people in ordinary conversation'. He then goes on; 'Definitions which report what words mean conventionally, what people commonly mean when they use them, may be called lexicographical definitions.' [1]

Cranston has little difficulty in showing that the meaning of 'freedom' lexicographically defined, is negative. 'Consider how much, or rather how little you say if you say you are free.' He writes: 'Imagine a meeting with a stranger; you know nothing about him or his predicament. He approaches you and says: "I am free". You are baffled. Has he just escaped from prison, from his debts, from his wife, from his sins? He has told you that he is free but he has not told you what he is free from. He has confided remarkably little.' [2] Although we often speak of being 'free to . . .' as well as being 'free from . . .', Cranston does not think that this shows that 'freedom' has a positive as well as a negative meaning. 'I may say: "I am free to dine with you this evening", or, "I am free to leave London tomorrow".' He writes: 'I mean when I use these words that I am free from anything which would prevent me doing what is mentioned. "I am free to dine with you this evening". is another way of saying "I am free from any sort of engagement or impediment that might have stood in the way of my dining with you this evening". It is shorter but it is not more positive.' [3]

What then is to be said about the positive theory? Cranston

gives an account of it, based on his interpretation of the ethical doctrine of self-realization. 'But we cannot understand this conception of freedom,' he writes, 'unless we keep in focus the picture of man as such philosophers see him. They see him as a rational creature but not wholly rational. Besides his rational will, man is subject to the solicitations of impulses and desires which are not rational.'[4] According to Cranston, this view of man leads to a distinction being drawn between 'liberty' and 'licence'. 'Such philosophers insist that in speaking of freedom with regard to human persons, we are concerned with something which stands in marked contrast to what they often call with Milton "licence" or the indulgence of non-rational desires and passions. Applying the word "licence" to the indulgence of the non-rational element, they reserve the words "freedom" and "liberty" for the unfettered exercise of the rational will.'[5] Cranston calls this view the 'theory of rational freedom'. The distinction between 'licence' and 'freedom' leads its advocates to give a positive meaning to the latter term. 'Freedom, they say, is something to be realized. The frustration by the rational faculty of the non-rational usurpation of the human will is realized in self-discipline, in the maintenance of reason's proper authority, and this is how certain philosophers have come to say that freedom is government, government by reason, conscience, *Geist*, intellect.'[6]

There is also what Cranston calls 'a more stringent version' of the same doctrine, to which he gives the name of 'compulsory rational freedom'. Philosophers have been led to this view through reflection upon the implications of rational freedom. He summarizes their argument as follows: 'Rational freedom is realized in rational control. The study of history and of human behaviour teaches us what are the external conditions most favourable to and those most antithetical to, the exercise of rational control within the individual. Hence in so far as favourable conditions can be established, indeed forced, by those in authority in the community, such enforcement will promote the freedom of each individual.'[7] Cranston points out that those who advocate 'compulsory rational freedom' are propounding a doctrine markedly at variance with ordinary ways of thinking and speaking. 'Whereas in ordinary usage, the word "freedom" stands opposed to "constraint", this philosophical conception of freedom calls for the presence of constraint, first to assist the rational faculty in each individual to secure mastery over his non-rational faculties, and secondly to clarify non-rational ends for people of limited intelligence.' [8]

Cranston proceeds to criticize the doctrine of 'rational freedom', asking what it is that those who advocate this doctrine are really doing. In maintaining that freedom is government by reason, they cannot be offering a lexicographical definition for this is not how the word 'freedom' is ordinarily used. He suggests that what in fact they are doing is to give a stipulative definition. 'It often happens that a speaker or a writer makes an announcement of the way in which he proposes to use a certain word, stipulates what the word is to stand for when he uses it. This may be called "stipulative definition".' [9] Cranston allows that stipulative definitions are often useful, especially in the sciences but he does not think that advocates of 'rational freedom' can strengthen their case by resorting to them. Their point is that the rational part of the self ought to direct conduct and that the non-rational animal part ought to be under its control. According to Cranston, the rational part of the self is regarded by such philosophers as the real or true self. 'Accept this picture of the bi-focated man,' he writes, 'and you do not have to make a case for rational freedom. If "I am free" means "My real self is free", and my real self is the rational reflective part of my being, no further revision of the concept of freedom is necessary, for it is clear that if your animal desires are not really yours, i.e., do not originate in your real self, you will not be free if their satisfaction is unimpaired.' [10]

On this view of the self, the rational reflective part of human nature will be subject to constraint by the animal desires and passions if the latter are allowed to determine conduct. But to the extent that the rational reflective side takes charge, in so far in other words as he is governed by reason, a man is free from constraint by the animal desires and passions. Hence the ordinary negative meaning of freedom suffices. There is no need to re-define the term. To attempt to do so, to suggest that a man who is governed by reason is free in some new sense different from the ordinary meaning of the term, is to introduce confusion into what is already quite straightforward. Such a man is free in the ordinary negative sense of the word, namely free from constraint by animal desires and passions. To say that he is free in some new positive sense is false and betrays a failure to understand the ordinary meaning of the word.

But the position of advocates of the more stringent version is worse. According to Cranston: 'The doctrine of compulsory rational freedom involves a complete repudiation of the conventional antithesis between freedom and compulsion, and this can only be done by a complete repudiation of the lexicographical definition of the word "freedom" and the stipulation of another definition to take its place.' [11] But he argues that exponents of 'compulsory rational freedom' do not in fact intend to repudiate the lexicographical definition completely. 'Evidently what they wish to do,' he writes, 'is to use the word as stipulatively defined only in some of the cases in which they use it.' [12] But this is bound to lead to confusion. 'If a man uses a word in one sense at one time and in a profoundly different sense at another, his hearers will never be sure what he means when he uses it.' [13]

In addition to perpetrating this confusion, exponents of 'compulsory rational freedom' violate the principles of good stipulative definition in another way. They define 'freedom' to mean what an existing English word lexicographically defined already means. ' "Discipline" stands in ordinary English usage,' Cranston writes, 'for what the theorists of compulsory rational freedom propose that the word "freedom" shall represent.' [14] But why should they try to redefine 'freedom' as 'discipline'? According to Cranston: 'The answer is a simple one. It is because "freedom" is a laudatory word and "discipline" is not, except for the responsible minority.' [15] Advocates of 'compulsory rational freedom' are thus guilty of confusion doubly confounded.

So much for Cranston's criticism of the positive theory; how convincing is it in the case of Green and Bosanquet? Green is careful to distinguish between the literal meaning of 'freedom', which he takes to be exemption from compulsion by other people, and various metaphorical senses in which the term may be used. His point is that 'freedom' may be used metaphorically to bring out the difference between the rational moral agent and the man of impulse and inclination. In order to be a rational moral agent, it is not enough to be free from constraint by other people, although this is certainly necessary. One needs also to be free from subjection to those tendencies and forces within oneself which interfere with rational moral conduct, to be free, in other words, to live and act as one ought. In making these points, Green is not offering a stipulative definition of 'freedom' to replace its lexicographical definition. He is trying to throw light on freedom as an important human value and is arguing that the central question is: what ought one to be free for? His answer is that one ought to be free for a life of rational moral conduct and that for this, the absence of external constraint is not enough. It is also necessary to know what such conduct is and why it is desirable, and to be able and willing to pursue it. Unless you know what you ought to be free to do and to become, you cannot know what you ought to be free from. If and when you know the former, you may come to see that in addition to being free from constraint by other people, you need also to be free from certain tendencies and forces within yourself. While this internal freedom is still negative, there are two respects in which it has a positive reference. The first is the necessary knowledge of what you ought to be free to do and to become. The second is, that what frees you from internal subjection is something positive within yourself, namely the development of your mind and character as a rational moral agent. Green's version of the positive theory is intended not to exclude but to include the negative theory, while going beyond it and taking account of what it overlooks.

Bosanquet is explicitly cited by Cranston as an exponent of 'compulsory rational freedom', no doubt because of his endorsement of Rousseau's dictum about being 'forced to be free'. But Bosanquet is not saying that anyone can be forced to be a rational moral agent. His point is that someone who is capable of achieving rational moral conduct may be kept up to the mark in a moment of weakness by external constraint. He must already be capable of rational moral conduct on his own before he can be prodded by an external stimulus to do what on reflection he knows he ought to do. Like Green, Bosanquet is trying to throw light on the importance of freedom as a human value. His version of the positive theory is fundamentally the same as Green's but it is filled out by an account of what rational moral conduct is, based on the ethical doctrine of self-realization. Cranston misrepresents this doctrine on an important point. Bosanquet contrasts the empirical self with the self which the rational agent is trying to become, arguing that the latter is always something more than the former. He speaks of the latter as the 'true' or 'real' self, but he does not say that the empirical self is altogether different from and alien to it. His fundamental point, which admittedly is not always expressed with the force and clarity that it might be, is that the 'true' or 'real' self includes the empirical self suitably modified and adapted to the life of rational conduct. In trying to become what one has it in one to be, the empirical self must not be repudiated or disowned but moulded, adapted and developed in the light of the standard which one is trying to achieve. To be liberated from subjection to those forces and tendencies within oneself which interfere with rational moral conduct is not to annihilate them but to direct and harness them rather than being directed and driven by them.

All this is not to deny that there may be serious objections to the positive theory. It is only to point out that Cranston has failed to make them. His preoccupation with purely linguistic considerations seems to have prevented him from seeing what Green and Bosanquet were trying to do and from discussing their attempt on its merits. They were trying to understand the importance of freedom as a human value and were concerned with something more than merely how English speakers use the word 'freedom' in ordinary conversation. But they were by no means unaware of the facts reported in lexicographical definitions and in a deeper sense than Cranston appears to have envisaged, their enterprise involves a linguistic aspect. They were really asking: in what sense, if any, ought we to think and speak about freedom in moral, social and political contexts? In their answer, they attempted to give some account of the nature of these contexts and to explain why it is significant and indeed important to think and speak about freedom in them. In doing this, they were not offering a stipulative definition to replace the lexicographical definition of 'freedom'. Accepting the lexicographical definition for what it is, they were trying to extend and deepen our understanding of what it is that we are thinking and talking about, whether or not we realize it, when we use the term in moral, social and political contexts. Whether they are right is another question, but there is nothing in the nature of language which makes what they attempted somehow illegitimate. On the contrary, it is something which the open-textured metaphorical character of language makes, if not necessary, at least very desirable.

B. *Sir Isaiah Berlin*

For a contemporary criticism of the positive theory on substantive rather than merely linguistic grounds and a vigorous re-affirmation of the negative theory, we turn to Sir Isaiah Berlin's monograph: *Two Concepts of Liberty*. These two concepts are the negative and positive theories. Berlin's version of the former is in essentials the same as Mill's. Expounding it, he writes: 'By being free in this sense, I mean not being interfered with by others. The wider the area of non-interference, the wider my freedom.' [1] His version of the positive theory has on the face of it obvious affinities with that of Green and Bosanquet. 'I wish above all to be conscious of myself as a thinking, willing, active being, bearing responsibility for his choices and able to explain them by reference to his own ideas and purposes. I feel free to the extent that I believe this to be true and enslaved to the degree that I am made to realize that it is not.' [2]

But this innocent appearance of the positive theory is deceptive. Bound up with it, there is a metaphysical doctrine of the self, which turns out to be essentially the same as that which Cranston imputed to theorists of 'rational freedom'. It is the doctrine that the self is made up of two sides, a natural or animal and a rational or spiritual part. The latter is the true or real self and ought to be in control of the animal side. Berlin does not maintain that advocates of the positive theory are logically committed to this doctrine but he thinks they have a strong tendency to be drawn to it. 'But the positive conception of freedom as a self-mastery,' he writes, 'with its suggestion of a man divided against himself, lends itself more easily to this splitting of personality into two: the transcendent dominant controller and the empirical bundle of desires and passions to be disciplined and brought to heel.' [3] According to Berlin, this metaphysical doctrine of the self leads all too easily to another; that when people are coerced for their own good, they are not really being coerced. If only the rational side of their personality could direct their conduct, they would do voluntarily what in fact they have to be forced to do. Therefore so far as their true selves are concerned, they are not being coerced but are free. Berlin does not deny that coercion of people for their own good may sometimes be justified but he objects vigorously to the contention that there is a sense in which such people can be called free, and still more to the idea that this is the most important sense of freedom. 'It is one thing,' he writes, 'to say that I may be coerced for my own good which I am too blind to see, and another that if it is my own good, I am not being coerced, for I willed it whether I know this or not, and am free even while my poor earthly and foolish mind bitterly rejects it and struggles against those who seek to impose it with the greatest desperation.' [4]

According to Berlin, the positive theory has a special appeal for rationalists who, he thinks, are and always have been prone to the temptation to coerce people for their own good. 'Thinkers of this type', he writes, 'argued that if moral and political problems were genuine as surely they were, they must, in principle, be fully soluble; that is to say, there must exist one and only one true solution to any problem. All truths could in principle be discovered by any rational thinker and demonstrated so clearly that all other rational men could not but accept them, indeed this was already to a large extent the case in the new natural sciences.' [5] Now according to Berlin, rationalists hold that: 'To understand why things must be as they must be is to will them to be so. Knowledge liberates, not by offering us more open possibilities amongst which we can make our choice, but by preserving us from the frustration of attempting the impossible.' [6] From this, it is a short step for rationalists to conclude that: 'Freedom is not freedom to do what is irrational or stupid or bad. To force empirical selves into the right pattern is not tyranny but liberation.' [7]

According to Berlin, rationalists assume that: 'There can in principle be only one correct way of life. The wise lead it spontaneously, that is why they are called wise. The unwise must be dragged towards it by all the social means in the power of the wise, for why should demonstrable error be suffered to survive and to breed?' [8] Behind this assumption there is a fundamental conviction, the belief that there can be a final solution to all the problems of human life. 'This ancient faith,' he writes, 'rests on the conviction that all the positive values in which men have believed must in the end be compatible and perhaps even entail one another.' [9]

Berlin challenges this ancient faith and the conviction on which it rests. 'It is a commonplace that neither political equality nor efficient organization is compatible with more than a modicum of individual liberty and certainly not with un-restricted *lassiez faire*; that justice and generosity, public and private loyalty, the demands of genius and the claims of society, can conflict violently with each other; and it is no great way from that to the generalization that not all good things are compatible, still less all the ideas of mankind.' [10] He goes on to argue that: 'The world that we encounter in ordinary experience is one in which we are faced with choices between ends equally ultimate, the realization of some of which must inevitably involve the sacrifice of others. Indeed it is because this is their situation that men place such immense value on the freedom to choose.' [11] In another passage he writes: 'But equally, it seems to me, that some sure formula can in principle be found whereby all the diverse ends of men can be harmoniously realized, is demon-strably false. If, as I believe, the ends of men are many and not all of them are in principle compatible with each other, then the possibility of conflict and of tragedy can never wholly be elimin-ated from human life, either personal or social. The necessity of choosing between absolute claims is then an inescapable charac-teristic of the human condition.' [12] It is because the negative theory emphasizes the value of individual freedom of choice, because it makes no assumptions about final solutions, and because it recognizes at least implicitly that human values can conflict, that Berlin espouses it and commends it to his readers.

What then according to the negative theory is a free society? Berlin answers that no society is free unless it is governed by two interrelated principles. 'First that no power but only rights can be regarded as absolute so that all men, whatever power governs them, have an absolute right to refuse to behave inhumanly; and second that there are frontiers not artificially drawn within which men should be inviolable, these frontiers being defined in terms of rules so long and widely accepted that their observance has entered into the very conception of what it is to be a normal human being and therefore also of what it is to act inhumanly and insanely, rules of which it would be absurd to say, e.g., that they could be abrogated by some formal procedure on the part of some court of sovereign body.' [12] He then adds: 'It is such rules as these that are broken when a man is declared guilty without trial or punished under a retroactive law, when children are ordered to denounce their parents, friends to betray one another, soldiers to use methods of barbarism, when men are tortured or mutilated, murdered, or minorities are massacred because they irritate a majority or a tyrant.' [13]

Berlin's case then comes to this. The positive theory of freedom strongly encourages, even if it does not logically entail, a false view of a fundamental side of human life. This is that all human values are compatible and are in principle capable of being harmoniously realized in one way of life. In fact the opposite is the truth. Human values can conflict and there is no one way of life in which they can all be realized together. The negative theory with its more modest claims, does not encourage any such error and with its emphasis on the absence of interference with the individual in the conduct of his life, points towards the true view. Does the version of the positive theory developed by Green and Bosanquet involve the error alleged by Berlin? Does it suggest that they think that all human values are compatible and are capable of being harmoniously realized in one way of life? The ethical doctrine of self-realization on which their theory of freedom is founded seems prima facie at least to point in this direction. It seems to suggest that there can be a single way of life in which each of us can become the best that we have it in us to be and in which all human gifts and capabilities can be harmoniously realized.

But if we accept Berlin's point that not all human values are compatible, can the matter be left there? He tells us that 'Men have to choose between ends equally ultimate'. Must this choice be merely capricious or can there be some sort of intelligible priority among the ends and the values they represent? Berlin's doctrine about the fundamental rules which would govern the life of a free society certainly suggests that he thinks that some values are more important than others. He seems to think that it is the negative theory rather than the positive theory which makes intelligible and justifies the importance which men place upon the freedom to choose. But consider how he has characterized the positive theory at the outset of his discussion. 'I wish above all to be conscious of myself as a thinking, willing, active being, bearing responsibility for his choices. . . .' This suggests that the claim to freedom of choice lies at the heart of the positive theory. He is more impressed however by the fact that the positive theory involves the ethical doctrine of self-realization and that this doctrine can be used to justify the claim that people who are coerced for their own good are being 'liberated' or 'forced to be free'. But the fact that a theory can be abused does not of itself show that it is false. People can abuse anything if they have a mind to. These considerations which arise out of issues raised by Berlin himself, suggest that further discussion is necessary before reaching any conclusion about the respective merits of the positive and negative theories. There is however one point upon which Berlin and Bosanquet are both agreed, namely, that in a free society the existence of a system of rights is fundamental. This may serve as our cue for turning now to the idea of rights.

Chapter 2
Some Theories of Rights

1. THE DOCTRINE OF NATURAL RIGHTS

A. *Thomas Hobbes*

The doctrine of Natural Rights has been historically important in practical politics and it is by no means dead today. But not all philosophers have accepted it and a number have criticized it on a variety of grounds. An inquiry into the general idea of rights can begin with an examination of the doctrine and of some of the arguments of its more important philosophical critics. The most influential statement of it by a philosopher was probably that given by John Locke in his 'Second Treatise on Civil Government', which was first published in 1690. But some forty years earlier, Thomas Hobbes expounded a very different version in the *Leviathan*, which may fairly be described as a 'minority view' less influential than that of Locke.

Hobbes' idea of natural rights is bound up with his conception of the 'state of nature'. This state is the condition of human life in the absence of organized political authority and government. It is the natural condition of man, in contrast to his artificial condition under government, and according to Hobbes, it is a state of war. 'Hereby it is manifest,' he writes, 'that during the time men live without a common power to keep them all in awe, they are in the condition which is called war, and such a war as is of every man against every man.' [1] That this melancholy condition is the natural state of man, is due to the constitution of human nature. The natural man, according to Hobbes, is an appetitive, passionate creature, bent upon the preservation of his life and the satisfaction of the desires which continually arise within him. He is also a rational creature, but his reason is subordinate to his passions and his appetites. Its role is to calculate the best way to preserve life and to satisfy desires. In a

37

situation where there are many such creatures and where the resources available for satisfying desires are limited, there will be perpetual conflict. Each, bent upon the preservation of his own life and the satisfaction of his own desires, will see all the rest as rivals to be thwarted and if possible defeated.

In a famous passage, Hobbes sums up the characteristic features of this natural state of war. 'In such condition there is no place for industry because the fruit thereof is uncertain and consequently no culture of the earth, no navigation nor use of the commodities that may be imported by sea, no commodious building, no instruments of moving and removing such things as require much force, no knowledge of the face of the earth, no account of time, no art, no letters, no society, and which is worst of all, continual fear and danger of violent death and the life of man solitary, poor, nasty, brutish and short.' [2] Hobbes' fundamental thesis is that only through government can this miserable state of affairs be ended. Men must have 'a common power to keep them all in awe'.

How then do natural rights fit into this picture? According to Hobbes: 'The right of nature which writers commonly call *Jus Naturale*, is the liberty each man hath to use his own power as he will himself for the preservation of his own nature, that is to say of his own life, and consequently of doing anything which in his own judgement and reason he shall conceive to be the aptest means thereunto.' [3] This liberty is a right of nature because each man has it in the state of nature. It is the only right anyone can have in the absence of government. But as Hobbes a little later points out, such a right is not worth much. 'And because the condition of man as hath been declared in the precedent chapter, is a condition of war of everyone against everyone, in which case everyone is governed by his own reason and there is nothing he can make use of that may not be a help unto him in preserving his life against his enemies, it followeth that in such a condition every man has a right to everything, even to one another's body, and therefore as long as this natural right of every man to everything endureth, there can be no security to any man how strong or wise so ever he be, of living out the time which nature ordinarily alloweth men to live.' [4]

The conclusion which Hobbes draws is that the 'natural right of every man to everything' must be given up as a necessary condition for establishing government and ending the anarchy of the state of nature. All must agree to obey unconditionally one supreme authority; or, what comes to the same thing, every man must behave as if he were a party to such an agreement. Only under such conditions can security be achieved and each man have a prospect of 'living out the time which nature ordinarily alloweth men to live'. Hobbes however adds a qualification to his doctrine of unconditional obedience to government. If the government orders a man to take his own life or others to kill him, he may resist. He retains this one natural right against the government. The reason for this qualification is that since men agree to obey government in order to preserve their lives, they cannot be expected to obey when government itself threatens them.

Hobbes is careful to distinguish between a right of nature and a law of nature. 'A law of nature, *lex naturalis*,' he writes, 'is a precept or general rule found out by reason by which a man is forbidden to do that which is destructive of his life or taketh away the means of preserving the same, and to omit that by which he thinketh it may best be preserved.' [5] He then continues: 'For though they that speak of this subject use to confound *Jus* and *Lex*, right and law, yet they ought to be distinguished because right consisteth in liberty to do or to forbear, whereas law determineth and bindeth to one of them, so that law and right differ as much as obligation and liberty which in one and the same matter are inconsistent.' [6] This is to say that to have a right is to be free to decide on any given occasion whether or not to do or to claim whatever it is that the right entitles you to do or to claim. There is an element of discretion in a right which is absent from an obligation. To be under an obligation is not to be free to decide whether or not you will discharge it. If there were no discretion in a right, no freedom to waive it if and when you thought fit, then rights and obligations would be indistinguishable.

The point is an important one, as we shall see in due course, but it is by no means clear that Hobbes can make it without inconsistency. He has said that a right of nature is: 'the liberty each man hath to use his own power as he will himself for the preservation of his own nature, that is to say of his own life, and consequently of doing anything which in his own judgement and reason he shall conceive to be the aptest means thereunto'. But he has also said that a law of nature is: 'a precept or general rule found out by reason by which a man is forbidden to do that which is destructive of his life or taketh away the means of preserving the same, and to omit that by which he thinketh it may best be preserved.' Now if there is a law of nature which lays down that a man must do what is necessary to preserve his life and must not do what destroys it, can he have any liberty in the matter? If a man's reason tells him that a certain action is necessary to preserve his life, then he must do it. He is not free to choose whether or not he will do it. Hobbes has said that: 'right consisteth in liberty to do or to forbear whereas law determineth and bindeth to one of them'. It follows on this view that there cannot be both a law and a right to the same thing. The existence of the one precludes that of the other.

Does Hobbes' account of liberty make any difference to this conclusion? 'By "liberty",' he writes, 'is understood according to the proper signification of the word, the absence of external impediments, which impediments may oft take away part of a man's power to do what he would but cannot hinder him from using the power left him according to his judgement and reason shall dictate to him.' [7] It follows, according to this negative view of freedom, that you have liberty to use your power to protect your life to the extent that there are no external impediments in the way. But such liberty is not a right if 'right' means 'liberty to do or to forbear'. For it to be a right, there must be no external impediment in the way of your not using your power to preserve your life as well as none in the way of your using it. This does make a difference. According to Hobbes, there is a law of nature which lays down that you must use your power to preserve your life. But this law of nature is 'a rule of reason'. On Hobbes' view of liberty, you are free to disobey it because there can be no external impediment in the way. It would not be rational to disobey it but there are no external impediments to irrationality. It follows that the existence of a law of nature which lays down that you ought to preserve your life does not exclude the existence of a natural right to preserve your life.

There is no inconsistency in saying that you ought to preserve your life and that there is no external impediment in the way of your either doing so or not doing so.

But this consistency has been purchased at the cost of undermining any rational foundation for the notion of 'a right of nature'. Since it is a rule of reason that you ought to use your power to preserve your life, it does not matter whether there are external impediments in the way of your not using it. The liberty to forbear, an integral part of the notion of a right, is otiose. In so far as you are rational, the law of nature deprives you of all discretion in the matter. But if this had been pointed out to him, Hobbes presumably would not have been worried by it. The notion of a right of nature can be dispensed with, without serious prejudice to his theory of the grounds and rationale of political authority and government. But the notion of a law of nature is of central importance in his argument and cannot be dispensed with. Why then did Hobbes bother to introduce the notion of a right of nature at all? The answer is that it already existed in the work of previous thinkers and he set out to render it innocuous. It is a cardinal point in his argument that if political authority and government are to be established, each man must give up his right of nature. That each man ought to give it up is a conclusion entailed by the law of nature which ordains that each man ought to preserve his own life, since only through the establishment of political authority and government can the anarchy of the state of nature and the risk to life which it involves be ended. Hobbes then can hardly be said to have done much for the doctrine of Natural Rights. But our discussion of him has brought to light the important distinction between a right and an obligation, namely that the former involves an element of discretion which the latter does not.

B. *John Locke*

Like Hobbes, Locke thinks of the state of nature as being the condition of human beings in the absence of government. But unlike Hobbes, he does not think that it is inherently a state of war. 'Men living together according to reason,' he writes, 'without a common superior on earth with authority to judge between them are properly in a state of nature.' [1] The state of war is a corruption of the state of nature. It arises when reason gives way to force. 'But force,' Locke continues, 'or a declared design of force, upon the person of another, where there is no common superior on earth to appeal to for relief, is the state of war.' [2] According to Locke, in the state of nature men are in 'a state of perfect freedom to order their actions and dispose of their possessions and persons as they think fit within the bounds of the law of nature, without asking leave or depending upon the will of any other man'. [3] He adds that it is 'a state also of equality, wherein all the power and jurisdiction is reciprocal, no one having more than another'. [4]

But this natural freedom is not freedom to do as you like. It is freedom 'within the bounds of the law of nature'. According to Locke, 'The state of nature has a law of nature to govern it,' and this law teaches 'all mankind who will but consult it, that being all equal and independent, no one ought to harm another in his life, health, liberty or possessions.' [5] The law of nature is, for Locke, the supreme moral law and all men ought to observe it. It can be known by reason, and because they have reason all men can know what it is and that they ought to observe it. 'For though it would be beside my present purpose,' Locke writes, 'to enter here into the particulars of the law of nature or its measures of punishment, yet it is certain there is such a law, and that too as intelligible and plain to a rational creature by a study of that law as the positive laws of commonwealths.' [6]

Where then do natural rights come into the picture? Locke speaks of man being born 'with a title to perfect freedom and an uncontrolled enjoyment of all the rights and privileges of the law of nature'. [7] But what precisely are these rights and privileges? From what has been said already, it seems to follow that every man is entitled by the law of nature, i.e., has a natural right to his life, to freedom of action, and to use his property as he thinks fit, provided that he does not interfere with any other man's enjoyment of the same conditions. But there is a complication about the right to life. On Locke's view, it does not include the right to suicide. Life is given to men by God to be enjoyed and eventually terminated not at their discretion but his. Moreover there is under the law of nature a duty to preserve human life as such. Locke says that every man: 'as he is bound to preserve himself and not to quit his station wilfully, by the like reason when his own preservation comes not in competition, ought he as much as he can to preserve the rest of mankind'. [8]

What he seems to have in mind is something like this. All men ought to observe the law of nature. Under that law they are entitled, i.e., have a natural right, to do anything which it does not forbid and to refrain from doing anything which it does not enjoin. Where the law of nature is silent, every man has a natural right to act according to his own discretion and a natural right against every other man not to be interfered with in so acting. But where it has spoken, there is no discretion and all must obey. Hence there is no natural right to life as such but there is a duty to preserve it and a natural right to plan and develop it according to your own judgement without interference by anyone else.

That Locke had something like this in mind is borne out by what he has to say about the right in the state of nature to punish offenders against the law of nature. 'And that all men may be restrained from invading others' rights and from doing hurt to one another and the law of nature be observed, which willeth the peace and preservation of all mankind, the execution of the law of nature is in that state put into every man's hands, whereby everyone has a right to punish the transgressors of that law to such a degree as may hinder its violation.' [9] This is to say that in the case of offenders against the law of nature, the prohibition of interference lapses. Every man who obeys the law of nature is entitled according to that law, i.e., has a natural right, to interfere with offenders against it to the extent necessary to inflict punishment. This is a right and not a duty. Every man may interfere with an offender, but he does not have to do so. He has a duty to preserve his own life and should not sacrifice it merely to inflict punishment against an offender. He must therefore have discretion in any given case to decide whether or not it is safe to interfere. So far as the offender is concerned, by breaking the law of nature he has forfeited his natural right not to be interfered with. 'In transgressing the law of nature,' Locke writes, 'the offender declares himself to live by another rule than that of reason and common equity, which is the measure God hath set to the actions of men for their mutual security.' [10] He cannot therefore claim the rights of the law of nature, since by his action he has announced that he does not recognize it. This is to say that a man's enjoyment of natural rights is conditional upon his recognizing and respecting the natural rights of everyone else.

There is one natural right which Locke discusses at some length. This is the right to property. He says that 'Every man has a property in his own person which nobody has any right to but himself'. [11] From this it follows, according to Locke, that in the state of nature every man has a natural property in whatever is produced by the labour of his body and the work of his hands. 'Whatsoever then he removes out of the state that nature hath provided and left it in, he hath mixed his labour with it and joined to it something that is his own and thereby makes it his property, it being removed by him from that common state nature placed it in, it hath by this labour something annexed to it that excludes the common right of other men.' [12] But what is this 'common right of other men' which labour excludes? Locke's point is that in the state of nature, the earth together with all it contains is equally available to all men. No one has by nature any special title or privileged status in relation to it. But once labour is expended upon the earth, what is produced by the labour is by right the property of the labourer. 'For this labour,' Locke writes, 'being the unquestionable property of the labourer, no man but he can have a right to what that is once joined to, at least where there is enough and as good left in common for others.' [13] This last point is important. Unless there is 'enough and as good left in common for others', the right to own what is acquired by labour cannot be equally enjoyed by all men. For there to be a natural right to property based on labour, there must be no shortage of land or natural resources. Locke seems to think that this condition held at least during the early history of mankind, when all lived in a state of nature without political organization and government.

But before developing this point, he introduces an important qualification to the natural right to property. He says that this qualification was recognized in the infancy of mankind when all lived in the state of nature. The man who gathered wild fruits or killed wild deer, had a prima facie right to property in them. 'But if they perished in his possession without their due use, if the fruits rotted or the venison putrified before he could spend it, he offended against the common law of nature and was liable to be punished. He invaded his neighbour's share and he had no right farther than his use called for any of them that they might serve to afford him conveniences of life.' (14) But why should there be this prohibition against waste? According to Locke, the natural right to property acquired by labour presupposes no shortage of land or natural resources. Why then should it matter if a man wastes what he has acquired by his own labour if there is 'enough and as good' for everyone else? He is not depriving others of what they might make use of. In a situation of shortage matters are of course different. Here to waste is to deprive others of what they could use. But in such a situation there can be no natural right to what is acquired by labour because all cannot equally enjoy it. Every man can at most have a natural right to compete peacefully with every other man to acquire by his own labour what he can make use of and to enjoy it without molestation. Presumably the losers in this competition, who failed to get enough to maintain themselves, would have a prima facie claim upon the bounty of the success-ful, since under the law of nature all have a duty to preserve human life as such.

Locke however is unaware of any loose ends in his account of the natural right to property. He goes on to argue that this right was the basis of property relations between men: 'until they incorporated, settled themselves together and built cities, and then by consent they came in time to set out the bounds of their distinct territories and agree upon limits between them and their neighbours, and by laws within themselves settled the properties of those of the same society.' (15) Where-ever and whenever, that is to say, the state of nature has been superseded by organized political society, the natural right to property has been superseded by artificial property rights drawn up and agreed to by those concerned and embodied in civil laws. This historical transformation of the natural right to private property was in accordance with the law of nature. It was a legitimate exercise of the natural right to freedom provided that all concerned consented to it. But unless there was already a natural right to property, there would be nothing to transform and no basis for agreement. The natural right to property remains the only moral basis for property relations, unless and until it has been modified by political arrangements which when they were first made, were entered into voluntarily by all concerned. This seems to have been Locke's idea of the significance of the natural right to property.

A necessary condition for the formation of political society is that the natural right of every man to punish offenders against the law of nature should be transferred to one authority, the government. According to Locke: 'Those who are united into one body and have a common established law and judicature to appeal to, with authority to decide disputes between them and punish offenders, are in civil society one with another.'[11] The main reason for forming such a society is that it affords conditions more favourable to life in accordance with the law of nature than are to be had in the state of nature. The members will be safer and will be able to enjoy in greater security their natural right to freedom of action within the limits of the law of nature. They will have the necessary institutional machinery for transforming their property relations from a natural to an 'artificial' legal basis, which will enable each to enjoy the free disposal of his possessions in greater security. The government of a civil society is entitled on its side to demand the obedience of the members so long as its activities are confined to making and enforcing laws which implement the law of nature, and to carrying out policies which are in the spirit of that law. If it uses its authority to do anything which violates the law of nature, its moral title to obedience is gone.

It follows that in Locke's account of the rationale and purpose of government, it is the idea of the law of nature which is fundamental. The doctrine of natural rights is derived from this idea and has no significance apart from it. The central thought in that doctrine is that under the law of nature every man is entitled to do anything not specifically forbidden by that law and to refrain from doing anything not specifically enjoined by it. The natural right to property is an application of this natural right to freedom in the light of the special provision of the law of nature, that the earth and its resources are equally available to all men. But as we have seen, Locke's account of the natural right to property is unclear owing to his failure to think out the implications of the prohibition against waste. In the eighteenth century however it was a simplified and inaccurate version of Locke's doctrine which was politically influential. He was interpreted as saying simply that under the law of nature and subject to obedience to it, every man had the right to life, to liberty and to property. These were the fundamental conditions to which all men as men were entitled, and it was the proper task of government to establish and maintain them. It was a version of the doctrine along these lines which seems to have inspired both the American Declaration of Independence and the French Declaration of the Rights of Man. But just when it was proving most influential politically, the doctrine of natural rights began to attract philosophical criticism.

2. SOME CRITICS OF NATURAL RIGHTS

A. *Jeremy Bentham*

In the course of an exposition and exposure of what he calls 'anarchical fallacies', Bentham says that 'Natural rights are simple nonsense; natural imprescriptible rights of man are rhetorical nonsense; nonsense upon stilts!' [1] He had already rejected the law of nature as the standard of morality in his *Introduction to the Principles of Morals and Legislation*, first published in 1789. 'A great multitude of people are continually talking about the law of nature,' he writes, 'and then they go on giving you their sentiments about what is right and what is wrong, and these sentiments, you are to understand, are so many chapters and sections of the law of nature.' [2] The law of nature is a case of what Bentham calls 'the arbitrary principle' or 'the principle of sympathy and antipathy.' To appeal to it in matters of morality is covertly to appeal to your own moral prejudices. No doubt many who appeal to it do not realize that this is all they are doing. They do not realize it because they do not understand the meaning of 'nature' and the 'natural' in relation to human action.

Bentham undertakes to put them right. In the famous opening passage of *Morals and Legislation* he writes: 'Nature has placed mankind under the governance of two sovereign masters; pain and pleasure. It is for them alone to point out what we ought to do, as well as to determine what we shall do. On the one hand, the standard of right and wrong, on the other, the chain of causes and effects, are fastened to their throne.' [3] On the face of it, there is a difficulty in this statement. If 'what we shall do' is determined by the two sovereign masters, how can there be any question about what we ought not to do? If all action is psychologically determined, can there be any room for morality? But this is just Bentham's point. Such room as there may be for morality must be found within this deterministic framework. Human beings are subject to two overriding psychological drives: desire for pleasure and aversion from pain. All action is the attempt to satisfy these drives, but the attempt may be well or ill executed. We therefore ought to do efficiently what we cannot help trying to do in any case. It is at this instrumental level that questions of 'ought' and 'ought not', of 'right' and 'wrong' properly arise, and it is here, if anywhere, that we must look for morality.

In the account of morality which Bentham then proceeds to give, the fundamental notion is that of utility. 'By "Utility",' he writes, 'is meant that property in any object whereby it tends to produce benefit, advantage, pleasure, good or happiness, all this in the present case comes to the same thing: or, what again comes to the same thing, to prevent the happening of mischief, pain, evil or unhappiness, to the party whose interest is considered. If that party be the community in general, then the happiness of the community; if a particular individual, then the happiness of that individual.' [4] According to Bentham, the standard of morality is simply the standard of utility to the community, that is, social utility. An action is morally right if on balance it contributes to the happiness of the members of the community, morally wrong if on balance it contributes to their unhappiness, or detracts from their happiness. This is how he arrives at his famous 'Principle of Utility', the principle of 'the greatest happiness of the greatest number'. In estimating the happiness of the community, one must look to the greatest happiness of the greatest number, and it is this principle which should guide the legislator in his work.

The legislator's work is of the utmost importance. Left to themselves, in the absence of law and government, human beings will collide with each other in their individual attempts to get pleasure and avoid pain. Not utility to the community but utility to himself, will be the standard guiding each man in his decisions and choices. What is of utility to the individual may be of disutility to the community. The two standards are different and come into conflict at many points. But although they are naturally opposed, something may be done to bring them together artificially by means of the institution of law. Law is not something natural but an artifice or contrivance of human intelligence and will. It consists of man-made rules and whatever may have been the purpose of such rules historically, there is one and only one purpose which they ought to have. This is to promote the greatest happiness of the greatest number. The legislator ought to make rules prohibiting as many as possible of those actions shown by experience to be contrary to the happiness of the community, and enjoining as many as possible of those shown by experience to be necessary. Penalties must be attached to breaches of these rules which will be just severe enough but no more to deter anyone from breaking them. The pain of the penalty must be just sufficient to outweigh the pleasure to be got from breaking a given rule, and by this means what is of utility to the individual will be artificially brought into line with what is of social utility. Bentham however does not claim that law can effect a complete reconciliation between the two standards. Law is necessarily limited to what can be brought within the scope of enforcible general rules. Over and beyond the law therefore, an enlightened and instructed public opinion is desirable which can act as a sanction where legal penalties are inapplicable.

For Bentham, the notion of a right is of primarily legal significance. 'Power and right, and the whole tribe of fictitious entities of this stamp,' he writes, 'are all of them, in the sense which belongs to them in a book of jurisprudence, the results of some manifestation or other of the legislator's will with respect to such and such an act.' [5] This clearly does not rule out other senses apart from that of jurisprudence, e.g., that of a moral right. But it is also clear that given Bentham's view of what law is and of its proper purpose, the juridical sense is primary, the other senses being ancillary to and indeed parasitic upon it. He goes on: 'To know then how to expound a right, turn your eyes to the act which, in the circumstances in question, would be a violation of that right. The law creates the right by prohibiting the act.' [6] This is to say that a legal right is the correlative of a legal obligation. What you have a right to is the carrying out of the obligation imposed by the law. On this view, a moral right might be construed as the right to an action or forbearance on the part of someone else, the action or forbearance being recognized by public opinion as a moral obligation. But for Bentham the important question is whether the legal obligations imposed by a given system of law and the moral obligations sanctioned by a given public opinion, are those which ought to be imposed and recognized. The latter are those justified by the principle of the greatest happiness of the greatest number, and it is this standard of social utility which is the proper basis for the criticism of existing law and morals.

It is now easy to see why Bentham rejects natural law and natural rights. Law is an artificial human contrivance, and the idea of a law of nature is literally a contradiction in terms. The aspect of nature which is of fundamental importance for human social life is the clash between personal and social utility. But is Bentham's own position tenable? Can it withstand criticism? Is it really true that all human action is motivated by nothing but desire for pleasure and aversion from pain? Can so simple a model of human action, which represents it as merely the attempt to satisfy the two overriding drives, really do justice to its complexity and diversity? Is the notion of morality really exhausted by that of social utility and is the latter notion itself intelligible in terms of the principle of the greatest happiness of the greatest number? Can the pleasures and pains of different people really be summed up quantitatively as this principle seems to require? These questions represent just some of the difficulties in Bentham's position to which later philosophers have drawn attention. But to one of them, D. G.

Ritchie, the notion of social utility appeared to be fruitful for the understanding of rights, although as we shall now see, he was far from accepting Bentham's view of that notion.

B. *D. G. Ritchie*

D. G. Ritchie's *Natural Rights* was first published in 1892. The first four chapters are devoted to a historical review and commentary. In the fifth, he turns to criticism and to the development of a positive view of his own. He begins by quoting a definition of 'right' in its legal sense and concludes: 'More briefly though with somewhat less precision, we might say that a legal right is the claim of an individual upon others recognized by the state.' [1] The point here is that the claim is one which the individual is legally entitled to make, or to have made on his behalf, and that if and when it is made, the state will uphold it. He then goes on to the question of moral rights. 'On the analogy of the definition of legal right, moral right might be defined as a capacity residing in one man of controlling the acts of another with the assent and assistance, or at least without the opposition of public opinion; or as the claim of an individual upon others recognized by society irrespective of its recognition by the state. The only sanction of a moral right as such is the approbation and disapprobation of private persons.' [2] This last point is important because it brings out the fact that when there is disagreement about moral rights, as there very well may be, 'there is no law court to which appeal can be made to pronounce abiding decisions'. [3]

Ritchie argues that it is with the aim of resolving disagreements about moral rights that appeals to the law of nature and natural rights have been made by critics of existing legal and moral rights. This is to appeal to an ideal standard, a standard of 'what ought to be'. 'Natural rights,' he says, 'are not identical with moral rights, because in many cases people have claimed that they have a natural right to do things that were not recognized either by the law of the land or by the prevalent public opinion or by the conscience of the average individual. Natural rights when alleged by the would-be reformer mean those rights which in his opinion would be recognized by the public opinion of such a society as he admires, and would either be supported or at least not interfered with by its laws, if it had any laws. They are the rights which he thinks ought to be recognized, i.e., they are the rights sanctioned by his ideal society, whatsoever that may be.'[4] He sums up by saying: 'What rights ought every society at the very least to guarantee its members? These, if we can agree about them, will be our natural rights.'[5]

But can we agree upon them? Not if we appeal to the law of nature, for human beings have notoriously failed to agree about that. 'The law of nature,' says Ritchie, 'if it really represented the consent of the human race, would serve to settle controversies. On the whole, it has helped to promote them.'[6] The law of nature, that is to say, is rejected by Ritchie on empirical grounds. Experience has shown it to be a broken reed in the settlement of controversies. Whether or not there really is such a law, it is irrelevant to human problems. But what then are we to do? What is to be our standard? 'Is it not simply human society?' Ritchie asks. 'If there are certain mutual claims which cannot be ignored without detriment to the well-being of, in the last resort to the very being of, a community, these claims may in an intelligible sense be called fundamental or natural rights. They represent the minimum of security and advantage which a community must guarantee to its members, at the risk of going to pieces if it does not, with some degree of efficiency, maintain them.'[7] This according to Ritchie is to appeal to utilitarian considerations and to make social utility the touchstone of natural or fundamental rights. But will this get over the difficulty? Ritchie recognizes that 'It may be and has been objected that people are no more agreed as to what is useful than they are as to what is right or just according to the law of nature.'[8] He answers: 'It's true the useful, taken by itself, is quite as ambiguous as the just. But the useful does not profess to be something incapable of further analysis. It is confessedly a relative term, useful for something. Useful for what? It is here that the Utilitarian theory stands most in need of revision and correction.'[9]

This Utilitarian theory is Classical Utilitarianism, the Utilitarianism of Bentham and, to a somewhat lesser extent, of Mill. Ritchie rejects its doctrine that pleasure is the sole good in human life. He thinks that the Idealist ethical doctrine of self-realization is probably the best account of the end or purpose of human life which has so far been developed. But such a doctrine, if it is to be adequate, must allow for change and development in human capacities. It must not assume that any one form of self-realization is ultimate or final, and it must not make the mistake of Classical Utiliarianism, the mistake of thinking that human nature is something fixed and finished, the same in all places and at all times. 'But how if the end of human life, individual and social, does not admit of a definite conception?' he writes. 'It is only with the progress of time that we discover the natural gifts and capacities of an individual and a society. If we say that in the end of the state should be included the development of the people's natural gifts, the very word 'development' would suggest growth and progress. A fundamental defect of the old Utilitarianism was the assumption of the identity of human nature in spite of difference of time and place and stage of growth.' [10]

Ritchie argues that in order to take account of development and growth, the bearing of the theory of evolution through natural selection upon human social life must be considered. The conclusion he draws is that Classical Utilitarianism must be transformed into 'Evolutionist' Utilitarianism. 'The conception of evolution, or more precisely the theory of natural selection,' he writes, 'has at once corrected the errors and vindicated the truth of Utilitarian ethics and politics. That is good for any particular society which furthers its success in the struggle for existence with nature and with other societies; that is evil which hinders such success. Those societies have succeeded best which have been most coherent and most vigorous and so courage and fidelity to those of the same society have been "selected" as good qualities; they are the primitive virtues.' [11] But human social evolution differs in a most important respect from merely natural evolution. It is no longer simply a blind unconscious process. Through self-conscious thought and critical reflection, human beings can come progressively to understand themselves and their situation better. By these means, their appreciation of the scope and opportunities of social living can be progressively enlarged, and with it, their recognition of those human qualities and capacities which are of the greatest social utility. Ritchie goes on: 'With the growth of reflection and a wider outlook, these good qualities and others can be recognized in new and wider spheres: and a society whose welfare determines what is right may come to enlarge its borders and change its character.' [12] But Ritchie does not think that the theory of evolution provides an adequate basis for understanding the ultimate nature of things. In metaphysics he was no naturalist but inclined towards a form of Idealism along the lines of that developed by Green in England and Royce in America. But if metaphysical considerations are neglected, and the perspective is confined to social ethics, he thinks that Evolutionist Utilitarianism is an adequate working theory.

What then are the implications of Evolutionist Utilitarianism for the theory of rights? Classical Utilitarianism thinks of a society as simply an aggregate of human beings, each having a fixed pre-social nature. Thinkers who advocate natural rights based on the law of nature share this substantialist view of human nature, although they differ from Classical Utilitarianism about its make-up. They think of a society as an association of morally conscious individuals formed for the purpose of securing the natural rights which they already possess under the law of nature. 'The transition from Individualist to Evolutionist Utilitarianism,' Ritchie writes, 'a transition which is being accepted by the great majority of writers on scientific ethics from whatever point of view they set out, makes what one may call a Copernican change in our way of considering the question of rights. The eighteenth-century thinkers looked on society as made by individuals joining together in order to secure their pre-existing natural rights. We, unless we remain uninfluenced by the more scientific conceptions now possible to us, we see that natural rights, those rights which ought to be recognized, must be judged entirely from the point of view of society.' [13]

These 'more scientific conceptions' are gained by thinking of human society in evolutionary terms, due allowance however being made for the important difference between social and merely natural evolution. They enable us to see that the individual taken apart from his social context is a fiction. He is born into an already existing society and becomes the individual that he is through participating in its concrete life. He can have rights only as a member of his society and the rights which he ought to have are those which will best enable him to participate in and contribute to its life. Ritchie puts this by saying: 'A person with rights and duties is the product of a society and the rights of the individual must therefore be judged from the point of view of the society as a whole, and not the society from the point of view of the individual.' [14]

Social utility in the sense of what is useful for the maintenance and development of the life of a society is to be the standard by reference to which claims to rights are to be decided. Ritchie proceeds to meet an objection. 'If it is argued that such an appeal is at least as ambiguous as a mere reference to natural rights, I answer "No!" For in appealing to social utility we are appealing to something which can be tested not merely by the intuitions of an individual mind but by experience.' [15] The experience in question is historical experience. It is to be gained through a comparative study of political and social history. 'History is the laboratory of politics,' Ritchie continues. 'Past experience is indeed a poor substitute for crucial experiments but we are neglecting our only guide if we do not use it. This means no slavish copying of antique models but trying to discover from consequences, which followed under past conditions, what consequences are likely to follow under similar and dissimilar conditions now.' [16]

According to Ritchie, what is true of rights is true of social institutions generally. They must be appraised and evaluated not on abstract universal grounds but with reference to social utility in the light of the particular conditions prevailing in a particular society at a particular time. One cannot say of any institution that it is absolutely wrong any more than one can say that it is right for all people everywhere. It may be right for a given society at a certain stage in its development, but wrong for another society which has passed beyond that stage, and wrong also for the first society after it has developed further. As an illustration Ritchie takes the institution of slavery. To adherents of natural rights based on the law of nature, slavery is absolutely wrong because it violates the natural right to freedom. But the Evolutionist Utilitarian takes a different view. 'To the scientific student of human history,' Ritchie writes, 'it seems almost certain that slavery was a necessary step in the progress of humanity. It mitigated the horrors of primitive warfare and thus gave some scope for the growth, however feeble, of kindlier sentiments towards the alien and the weak. It gave to the free population sufficient leisure for the pursuit of science and art, and above all for the development of political liberty; and in this way slavery may be said to have produced the idea of self-government. By contrast with the slave, the free man discovered the worth of freedom. Thus slavery made possible the growth of the very ideas which in the course of time came to make slavery appear wrong.'[17] Then guarding himself against possible misinterpretations, he goes on: 'But an historical justification of an institution is no justification for the continuance or revival of an institution when it is no longer socially beneficial, or when the purpose it once served can be otherwise provided for.'[18]

Ritchie's whole discussion may be summed up as a reasoned recommendation to the following effect. For the traditional doctrine of natural rights we should substitute the idea of morally justified social rights, where moral justification is on the basis of social utility, and where social utility is conceived not in terms of Classical but in terms of Evolutionist Utilitarianism. If we make this substitution, we can preserve what is of value in the traditional doctrine while avoiding its errors. What is of value is the idea of certain basic rights which ought to be secured to all members of a society. The chief error is the idea that these rights must be everywhere and always the same, irrespective of differences in social development. Behind this are two further errors: that of a fixed pre-social human nature, and an unhistorical, too narrowly individualistic view of society. Evolutionist Utilitarianism avoids these errors and the idea of morally justified social rights enables differences in social development to be taken into account.

That there is force in Ritchie's criticisms of the traditional doctrine can hardly be denied, and Evolutionist Utilitarianism is certainly free from some of the difficulties of Utilitarianism in its classical form. But is it a satisfactory position? Granted that the idea of morally justified social rights is an improvement upon natural rights, will the notion of social utility really bear the weight Ritchie puts upon it? Can history really be the 'laboratory of politics'? Is the notion of stages of social development tenable? What is the nature of the transition from one to another? While Ritchie does not leave his readers wholly in the dark about his answers to these and other similar questions, what he has to say is fragmentary, taking the form of passing comments and asides. But we shall be encountering the same questions ourselves in later chapters.

c. *Margaret Macdonald*

Margaret Macdonald's essay 'Natural Rights' appears in a volume called *Philosophy, Politics and Society*, which was published in 1956. This is a collection of pieces by different authors on a variety of topics in political and social philosophy. Its aim is to show how British philosophers in the years after the Second World War were approaching problems in these fields. Margaret Macdonald's essay, while in the broad stream of what is sometimes called 'analytic philosophy' is nearer in spirit to the Logical Positivism of the 1930s than to the linguistic or conceptual analysis of the post-war years. Her approach to the doctrine of Natural Rights is critical but by no means unsympathetic. Her conclusions about it are not dissimilar to Ritchie's but she reaches them by a very different route.

She argues that in its traditional form the doctrine is untenable because it involves a confusion of logical types. 'There are an indefinite number of different types of proposition and other forms of human utterance,' she writes. 'I will for my present purpose notice three. 1. Tautologies or analytic propositions which state rules for the use of symbols or which follow from such rules within a linguistic or logical system. 2. Empirical or contingent propositions which state matters of fact and existence, propositions which describe what does or may occur in the world and not the symbolic techniques employed in such descriptions. 3. Assertions or expressions of value. With the help of this classification it may be possible to show that some of the difficulties of the doctrine of natural rights have been due to an attempt to interpret propositions about natural rights as a curious hybrid of types 1 and 2 of the above classification.' [1]

How does this confusion of logical types arise? According to Margaret Macdonald: 'Propositions about natural law and natural rights are not generalizations from experience nor deductions from observed facts subsequently confirmed by experience.' [2] How then are they known? According to Margaret Macdonald's account of the traditional doctrine: 'They are known as entailed by the intrinsic or essential nature of man.' [3] Now the intrinsic or essential nature of man is to have reason. Propositions about natural law and natural rights are then known because they are entailed by the proposition that the essential property of man is to have reason. But to this Margaret Macdonald objects that the possession of reason is simply an empirical fact about human beings. She agrees that: 'It is by having this specific and natural characteristic of being rational that men resemble each other and differ from the brutes.' [4] But there are no grounds for elevating this natural characteristic which differentiates the human species from other creatures into an essence or intrinsic property. There is no essence or intrinsic property of man. 'Men do not share a fixed nature. Nor therefore are there any ends which they must necessarily pursue in fulfilment of such a nature. There is no definition of man.' [5] The most she will allow is that: 'There is a more or less vague set of properties which characterize in various degrees and proportions those creatures which are called human.' [6]

But there is also another error in the traditional doctrine. It holds that it is by virtue of their having reason that men are able to know propositions about natural law and natural rights. As she puts it: 'The standard of natural law is set by reason and is known because men have reason.' [7] But propositions which can be known by reason belong to class 1 of the three types. These, it will be recalled, 'state rules for the use of symbols', or 'follow from such rules within a linguistic or logical system'. They are analytic propositions or tautologies and as such, neither state facts nor assert values. Margaret

Macdonald concludes that: 'Because it is confused on these distinctions, the theory of natural law and natural rights constantly confuses reason with right and both with matter of fact and existence. The fact that men do reason is thought somehow to be a natural empirical confirmation of what is logically deduced by reason as a standard by which to judge the imperfections of what exists.' [8]

Her criticisms may be summarized as follows. The law of nature and natural rights as standards by which existing states of affairs may be criticized and evaluated are said to be known by reason because entailed by the essential property of man, viz., his possession of reason. But that men can reason is simply an empirical fact about them and no empirical fact can entail standards of value. Nor can such standards be known by reason because what reason can know is confined to analytic propositions or tautologies. Hence propositions about natural law and natural rights are not entailed by men's ability to reason, nor can they be known by reason. Locke certainly holds that the law of nature can be known by reason. Whether he also holds that it is entailed by the fact that men can reason is not clear. However, other advocates of the traditional doctrine may well have done so. Margaret Macdonald probably has in mind scholastic theories of natural law.

What then becomes of the doctrine of natural rights? Is it simply to be dismissed as a tissue of confusions signifying nothing? Margaret Macdonald thinks not. 'The exponents of the natural rights of man . . . were trying to express what they deemed to be the fundamental conditions of human social life and government.' [9] Statements about such conditions are by no means without significance but their logical type must not be misunderstood. 'Assertions about natural rights then' . . . 'are assertions about what ought to be as the result of human choice. They fall within class 3 of the division stated . . . as being ethical assertions or expressions of value, and these assertions or expressions include all those which result from human choice and preference in art and personal relations, e.g., as well as in morals and politics.' [10]

The reference to human choice in this passage is significant for it indicates an important feature of her view of the character of ethical and value assertions. She goes on to lay down what she takes to be the fundamental character of this class of utterances. 'But I cannot hope in a necessarily brief discussion to do justice to the enormous variety of value utterances, so I will plunge and say that value utterances are more like the records of decisions than propositions. To assert that freedom is better than slavery, or that all men are of equal worth, is not to state a fact but to choose a side. It announces: "This is where I stand".' [11] It does not however follow that the decisions which value utterances record and the choices which they express are arbitrary. They can be supported but not in the way in which a conclusion is supported by evidence in a theoretical inquiry. The sort of support which can be given is like the defence which a lawyer makes of his client or a literary critic of his judgement that one poet is better than another. Summing up, Margaret Macdonald writes: 'There are no certainties in the field of values, for there are no true or false beliefs about values but only better or worse decisions and choices, and to encourage the better decisions we need to employ devices which are artistic rather than scientific, for our aim is not intellectual assent but practical effects. These are not of course absolutely separate, for intellectual assent to a proposition or theory is followed by using it. But values, I think, concern only behaviour. They are not known but accepted and acted upon.' [12]

Now this statement prompts a question. By what standards and upon what principles can human choices and decisions in the field of values be judged better or worse? If such standards and principles are themselves chosen and decided upon, can these choices and decisions in their turn be judged better or worse? If so, upon what grounds? Either some standards and principles are not chosen and decided upon, in which case it is not clear that questions of truth and falsity are excluded from the field of values; or there is an arbitrary element at the root of all values because choices and decisions about fundamental human standards and principles are merely random. They are neither better nor worse but are simply made. But in fairness to Margaret Macdonald, if this point is left obscure, it must be remembered that she is only indicating a point of view and not advancing a full and finished theory.

There is also a point in her criticism of natural rights which calls for comment. She says that it is simply an empirical fact that men have reason and she does not seriously inquire into the nature of this capacity. Had she done so, she might have realized that in the exercise of reason, men necessarily commit themselves to certain standards. They do not choose them but find that as rational agents they must think and act in terms of them. In theoretical inquiry and argument they are committed to consistency; in practical action, to expediency and efficiency. Whether they are also committed to other standards, and if so what these are, can be answered only after a consideration of what it is to act rationally. This is something which we shall undertake in the next chapter and I shall not prejudge the outcome now. But Margaret Macdonald does prejudge it, or rather she fails to see that there is an issue to be settled. She fails to see this because she assumes that men's ability to reason is just one more empirical fact about them, no different in kind from the fact that they have two hands and two feet. She therefore does not think that any special inquiry is called for into what it is to have reason or to act rationally. But this assumption is dictated by her initial threefold classification of human utterances and the fact that it leads her to overlook an important matter suggests doubts about its adequacy. What all this shows is not that the doctrines of natural rights is true but that Margaret Macdonald's criticism is less than conclusive.

3. CONTEMPORARY PHILOSOPHERS ON RIGHTS

A. *H. L. A. Hart*

According to Locke, all men have a natural right to freedom within the limits of the law of nature. This is the central thought in his doctrine of natural rights. But neither Ritchie nor Margaret Macdonald seem to have paid much attention to it. What concerned them was rather the popular version of Locke's doctrine. However, H. L. A. Hart in an article entitled 'Are there any natural rights?' which was published in the *Philosophical Review* in 1955, seems to have had Locke's central thought very much in mind. 'I shall advance the thesis,' he writes, 'that if there are any moral rights at all, it follows that there is at least one natural right, the equal right of all men to be free.'[1] He goes on to explain what this natural right to freedom is a right too. 'In saying that there is this right, I mean that in the absence of certain special conditions which are consistent with the right's being an equal right, any adult human being capable of choice, firstly, has the right to forbearance on the part of all others from the use of coercion or restraint against him save to hinder coercion or restraint; and secondly, is at liberty to do, i.e. is under no obligation to abstain from, any action which is not one of coercing or restraining, or is designed to injure other persons.'[2] He then explains why he calls this right a natural right. There are two reasons, which according to Hart were always emphasized in classical versions of the doctrine of natural rights. 'Firstly, this right is one which all men have if they are capable of choice. They have it *qua* men, and not only if they are members of some society or stand in some particular relation to each other. Secondly, this right is not created or conferred by men's voluntary action. Other moral rights are.'[3]

Hart's understanding of the notion of a moral right is clearly of crucial importance to his main thesis. He says that: 'The concept of a right belongs to that branch of morality which is specifically concerned to determine when one person's freedom may be limited by another's.'[4] Later in the article he writes: 'It is, I hope, clear that unless it is recognized that interference with another's freedom requires a moral justification, the notion of a right could have no place in morals, for to assert a right is to assert that there is such a justification.'[5] In support of this, he appeals to linguistic use. 'The characteristic function in moral discourse of those sentences in which the meaning of the expression "a right" is to be found: "I have a right to . . .", "You have no right to . . .", "What right have you to . . .?" is to bring to bear on interferences with another's freedom, or on claims to interfere, a type of moral evaluation or criticism, specifically appropriate to interference with freedom and characteristically different from the moral criticism of actions made by the use of expressions like "right", or "wrong", "good" and "bad".'[6]

But although the concept of a right is a moral one, it is not a necessary feature of any and every morality. There can be and have been systems of morality which do not employ it; an instance, according to Hart, is the Decalogue. Where morality is thought of simply as obedience to a code of rules, there is no room for it. According to Hart, the rules of such a code are like penal statutes. They are limited to prescribing conduct. If the concept of a right is to have a place in morality, the notion of the moral must go beyond mere obedience to a code. Where it is confined to such obedience, interference with another's freedom may be prescribed as a duty under certain circumstances. It cannot be a right. This is because a moral duty, unlike a moral right, leaves no discretion to the agent. If it is his duty, then he must do it. If it is his right, then he is morally entitled but not obliged to do it. According to Hart: 'To have a right entails having a moral justification for limiting another's freedom and for determining how he shall act.'[7] But to be morally justified in doing something is not to be morally obliged to do it. There can be moral rights only within a system of morality in which the notion of moral justification as well as that of moral duty has a place.

But what is to count as a moral justification for interfering with another's freedom and determining how he shall act? According to Hart, the answer is to be found 'from an examination of the circumstances in which rights are asserted with the typical expression "I have a right to . . .".'[8] He goes on: 'It is, I think, the case that this form of words is used in two main types of situation. A. When the claimant has some special justification for interference with another's freedom which other persons do not have. "I have a right to be paid what you promised for my services". B. When the claimant is concerned to resist or object to some interference by another person as having no justification. "I have a right to say what I think".'[9] According to Hart, cases of type A are a justification of special rights, those of type B of general rights.

Special rights arise out of transactions and relationships into which particular people have voluntarily entered. Hart says that 'The simple case of promises illustrates points characteristic of all special rights. Firstly: the right and obligation arise not because the promised action has itself any particular moral quality but just because of the voluntary transaction between the parties. Secondly: the identity of the parties concerned is vital. Only this person, the promisee, has the moral justification for determining how the promisor shall act. It is his right. Only in relation to him is the promisor's freedom of choice diminished, so that if he chooses to release the promisor, no one else can complain.' [10] In addition to promising, special rights arise from consenting, authorizing and submitting to mutual restrictions. Explaining 'submitting to mutual restrictions', Hart writes: 'When a number of persons conduct any joint enterprise according to rules and thus limit their liberty, those who have submitted to these restrictions when required, have a right to a similar submission from those who have benefited from their submission.' [11] In other words, if I have obeyed a rule necessary for the carrying on of an enterprise in which you and I are both voluntarily participating, I am morally justified in interfering with your freedom to make you obey. I have this special right over you because we stand in the voluntary relationship of colleagues and because I have already submitted to the mutual restriction. This, as I understand it, is Hart's point.

So much for special rights; what about general rights? Hart writes: 'In contrast to special rights, which constitute a justification peculiar to the holder of the right for interfering with another's freedom, are general rights which are asserted defensively when some unjustified interference is anticipated or threatened, in order to point out that the interference is unjustified. "I have the right to say what I think"; "I have the right to worship as I please".' [12] Hart points out that general rights resemble special rights in that 'to have them is to have a moral justification for determining how another shall act, i.e. that he shall not interfere'. [13] Nor does it matter what the anticipated or threatened interference is, provided that it is not itself morally justified, i.e. is not a special right. But there are three respects in which general rights differ from special rights. 'General rights do not arise out of any special relationship or transaction between man. Secondly, they are not rights which are peculiar to those who have them but are rights which all men capable of choice have, in the absence of those special conditions which give rise to special rights. Thirdly: general rights have as correlatives, obligations not to interfere to which everyone else is subject and not merely the parties to some special relation or transaction, though of course they will often be asserted when some particular persons threaten to interfere, as a moral objection to that interference.' [14]

Now Hart's main thesis is that 'If there are any moral rights at all, it follows that there is at least one natural right, the equal right of all men to be free.' The case of general rights seems, on the face of it, to support this thesis, for if I have the moral right to resist any interference with my freedom which is not morally justified, it follows that I have the right to be free within the limits of morality. Hart says that to 'assert a general right is to claim in relation to some particular action, the equal right of all men to be free, in the absence of any of those special conditions which constitute a special right to limit another's freedom'. [15] And he adds: 'The assertion of general rights directly invokes the principle that all men equally have the right to be free.' [16]

What about special rights? Hart thinks that they indirectly invoke the same principle. This can be seen by considering what is implied by the types of moral justification which constitute special rights. These types of moral justification, it will be recalled, arise out of certain types of voluntary transaction and relationship between men; promising, consenting, authorizing, and submitting to mutual restrictions. Why do we think that these types of voluntary transaction and relationship are types of moral justification for interfering with another's freedom? According to Hart, it can only be because we think that all men have the equal right to be free. 'For we are in fact saying,' he writes, 'in the case of promises, authorizing and consenting, that this claim to interfere with another's freedom is justified because he has in exercise of his equal right to be free, freely chosen to create this claim, and in the case of mutual restrictions, we are in fact saying that this claim to interfere with another's freedom is justified because it is fair; and it is fair because only so will there be an equal distribution of restrictions and so of freedom among this group of men. So in the case of special

C   65

rights as well as of general rights, recognition of them implies the recognition of the equal right of all men to be free.' [17]

So much for Hart's defence of his thesis; it suggests two comments. The first concerns his doctrine of special rights: namely that the moral justification which constitutes them arises out of certain types of voluntary transaction and relationship between particular persons. But what about the moral right of a father to receive special consideration from his grown-up son? As we shall see, another contemporary philosopher, A. I. Melden, regards this as an important moral right. It is not clear that this right arises out of a voluntary relationship. Granted that if the father has this right, he must to some extent at least, have played his part as a parent, what about the son's position? The obligation correlative to the right rests upon him by virtue of the special relation in which he stands towards his father, a relation which he does not freely create but rather finds, on becoming grown up, that he is already in, not one into which he has entered voluntarily. However this need not undermine Hart's thesis. The existence of general rights, and of at least some special rights which indirectly invoke the principle of a right to freedom is sufficient, for the right to freedom is admitted to be subordinate to morality. The thesis needs to be amended to state that: 'If there are any moral rights arising out of certain types of voluntary transactions and relationships, then it follows that there is a natural right to freedom.' Hart does not have to claim that all moral rights must arise in this way.

The second comment concerns his recognition that there can be and in fact have been systems of morality which do not employ the concept of a right. In the face of this recognition, can it be maintained that the right to freedom is a natural right? Has Hart done more than show that in systems of morality which include moral rights, there is a residual general right to freedom? In order to go farther and show that this is a natural right must he not show that only those systems which include moral rights are genuine systems of morality and that those which do not are inherently defective? If the right to freedom is one which all men have as men, and if it is not created nor conferred by men's voluntary action, then Hart must show that moral rights are a necessary feature of morality as such, and that any system which excludes them is something less than morality properly so called. Unless he can do this, his defence of his thesis must be judged to have failed. In spite of this, his article is of great interest because of its discussion of the concept of a moral right, and of the question of justifying interference with another's freedom.

B. *A. I. Melden*

Hart draws a distinction between the type of moral criticism and evaluation involved in asserting a right ('I have a right to . . .' 'You have a right to . . .') and that which is involved in judgements of right and wrong, good and bad. This distinction is the central theme of a monograph by A. I. Melden entitled *Rights and Right Conduct*, which was published in 1959. It has attracted the attention of some British philosophers, not a few of whom think highly of it. Melden begins by stating his purposes. 'My ultimate objective in this discussion,' he writes, 'is to invite attention to relatively neglected issues in moral philosophy and by thus opening up the subject of moral philosophy, help to remove some of the staleness of the subject that derives in no small measure from the narrow compass within which arguments and counter-arguments have been confined. But my immediate objective is to explore some of the so-called foundations of certain familiar moral rights and the manner in which these operate in the moral justification of conduct.' [1] However in the event, Melden's own argument turns out to be confined within a rather narrower compass than the foregoing suggests. He concentrates attention upon 'the special moral right which, as we all recognize, depends in some way upon an individual's status as a parent and the respect of which his son has the correlative obligation to his parent to favour him in his conduct'. [2] He specifically warns against hasty generalizations from this case. 'Whether and to what extent, what I shall have to say about the special sort of right to be discussed may be applied generally to rights and liberties, I shall not attempt to decide.' [3]

Melden's main task as he sees it is to elucidate two relations.

'One is the relation between being a parent and having the right which parents have; the other, between the right of the agent and the rightness of the actions called for. Clearly no elucidation of the concept of a right of this kind will be complete unless both relations are adequately and correctly specified.' [4] Melden thinks that the first of these relations poses the more difficult problem since it seems to involve a transition from fact to value. But he proposes to begin with the second relation and in fact devotes about three-quarters of the monograph to discussing it. 'By showing how a right operates in the justification of conduct,' he writes, 'I hope to be able to throw light on the manner in which the right is derived from the given matter of fact, in our present example the parental status of the individual.' [5]

Melden points out that the right of a parent involves a correlative moral obligation upon the son. The action which the right calls for is, from the standpoint of the son, an obligation-meeting action. But it is not on that account necessarily a morally obligatory action. Being obligation-meeting and being morally obligatory are not identical. An action may have the former characteristic without having the latter. The distinction is important because it reveals one way in which a right does not operate in the justification of conduct. It does not justify the action which it calls for as one which is morally obligatory in any and every situation. In some situations the action which is morally obligatory for a son may be one which is incompatible with giving special consideration to his father. Melden points out that 'Moral rights and their correlative obligations do compete for satisfaction. To favour one's parent in this or that situation may entail a needless sacrifice of the development of one's own talents or render it impossible to meet an enormously important obligation that one has incurred to other persons.' [6] He also points out that having a right does not mean that one has a moral duty always to exercise it. There are occasions when a parent may be morally justified in waiving his right over his son. 'If it is not self-contradictory,' he writes, 'to say that one is morally justified in waiving one's right, moral right, then we can state what would count as a case of this sort. And surely there are cases when a parent would be morally justified in waiving his right, on insisting that in the specific circumstances then on hand his son must not meet his obligation to him if by doing so he puts himself in moral jeopardy with others or sacrifices the development of his own talents.' [7]

How then does a right operate in the justification of conduct? According to Melden, this question can be answered in the case of the moral right of a parent by examining the role in moral discourse of statements of the correlative moral obligation. 'What then is the role of the utterance: "one ought to give special consideration to one's parents"?' he asks, and answers: 'Apart from instructional purposes, the function of this utterance is to remind ourselves and others of a matter of moral relevance to some desiderated action, the fact that it is one's parents whose interests are affected and that as such, these interests are moral considerations that count for or against the conduct in question.' [8] The right of a parent, that is to say, is a morally relevant consideration which a son ought to take into account in determining his conduct. But what makes it morally relevant? The answer is: the contribution which the action called for by the right makes to the life of the moral community. 'In short; to give special consideration to one's parents,' Melden writes, 'is to take account in one's action of their moral role and of ours in respect to the common life of the family and the community within which the life of the family proceeds. It is to give persons so situated with respect to ourselves, the special favours and attention by which we acknowledge their moral roles with respect to our own and thus serve the common moral life in which in diverse ways all of the persons concerned participate.' [9]

But because the right of a parent is always a morally relevant consideration for his son, it does not follow that the action called for by the right is always the morally right action for the son to perform. The distinction between obligation-meeting and obligatoriness is here significant and in the concrete situation it is the obligatory action which is the morally right one. 'For the question of the rightness of an action described as giving special consideration to one's parents,' Melden writes, 'is the question whether or not it serves and thus preserves the moral structure of the community.'[10] He then goes on: 'In general, actions described in this way are also describable as doing what is morally required, although sometimes not; and no general formula is possible which would render unnecessary the employment of good judgement in determining whether, when the first description is applicable, the latter is also in order.'[11] This implies that what is normally required of every agent is that he should serve and preserve the moral life of the community. Everywhere and always this is the morally right thing to do. Melden agrees. 'It is self-evident, analytic,' he writes, 'that it is right that one maintain the moral community of which one is a member. To be right is the very same thing as to be the kind of action that does serve, however that may be, the moral community. There is no further meaning over and above this one that is the rightness and needs to be connected with it.'[12]

So much for the second of the two relations which Melden sets out to elucidate; what about the first, that between being a parent and having the rights which parents have? This relation, it will be recalled, appears to involve a transition from fact to value, namely from the status of being a parent to the having of a right. But according to Melden, we are concerned here with a human, not a merely physical, fact. 'In matters of human fact,' he writes, 'the term "matter of fact" is a relative term and so is the term "description"; and there are all sorts of "matters of fact" and "descriptions" too, and what will be called a "matter of fact" will depend upon what is at issue.'[13] A human being may be described as an organism. He may also be described as a moral and social agent. Which description is applicable will depend upon what we are interested in. But there is a sense in which the second description is fuller than the first, for it tacitly includes it while drawing attention to something else over and above biological features. 'In this full-fledged sense,' Melden writes, 'to speak of A as the father of B is not to remark on a matter of genealogical fact but rather on a matter of social and moral fact, the status of A with respect to B in the complex circumstances of family life.'[14] Now if the status of being a parent is a moral one, there is no problem about the transition from fact to value. There is an element of value already present in the fact.

Melden goes on to argue that a parent's right is not something separate from his parental status, something derived from it. It is actually a part of that status. 'If we are to say then,' he writes, 'that it is in virtue of A's parental status that A has the right he has, we must not suppose that we are thereby calling attention to something other than the right he has from which in turn the right is derived. On the contrary, to say this is to identify the right as the moral role that A plays with respect to B.'[15] The moral role of being a parent of course includes much more than the right to receive special consideration from one's children. It includes responsibilities towards them. But Melden's point is the simple one that it does include the right and that to justify the right is to point this out. In order to justify your claim to receive special consideration from your son, that is to say, you have to show that you are his father not only biologically but morally, that this is the moral relation in which you stand to him. 'For it is only when A, the immediate forbear of B,' Melden writes, 'stands in the appropriate moral relation to B, that A has the requisite moral status, i.e. that A has the parental right in question and B the filial obligation to A which he can meet only by giving A special consideration. Justifying the claim that A has a special right to the treatment B has accorded him, consists in explaining the person A by specifying his moral status with respect to B.'[16]

Melden concludes his monograph with some remarks designed to forestall possible objections. One of these is the charge of moral conservatism. 'Is not all of this a blow for conservatism, the *status quo*, the perpetuation of our common social institutions and ordinary moral prejudices?'[17] he asks. He rebuts the charge by arguing that nothing he has said precludes the possibility of change in social institutions and in morality. There are times when changes in these quarters are desirable and an appreciation of what Melden calls 'the point of morality' will, he thinks, help to facilitate them. 'But morality has a point as well as a content,' he writes, 'the achievement for those who participate in the moral life of the diverse forms of happiness open to moral agents. Given this point of our morality, critical scrutiny and reappraisals of moral institutions and relations are not only possible but during times of social

change consequent upon increased knowledge and technological developments, they are altogether necessary.'[18] However, he excuses himself from discoursing further on the nature
and type of moral criticism, adding only that his view of
happiness does not involve the muddles of traditional Utilitarianism about that concept.

But in the light of his doctrine about the point of morality,
he feels it necessary to touch on another matter. 'For those
whose morality has been conceived of as a matter having to
do with the commands of God,' he writes, 'the remarks made
in this section do present an altered moral picture, and no
doubt they do present altered conceptions of duty, right,
obligation, etc.'[19] But this is no objection to his doctrine.
He maintains that the conception of morality as obedience to
divine commands belongs to an older cultural climate and that
his own view is the one which reflects present-day moral
attitudes, at least so far as the Western world is concerned.
No doubt there are those for whom the older cultural climate
still lingers on, and who still think in terms of the older theistic
morality, but theirs is not the predominant view. What is
important, according to Melden, is to realize that concepts
including moral ones undergo alteration and modification as a
result of altered opinions and acquired knowledge. 'Right'
once meant 'obedience to God's commands'. Today for most
people in the Western world its meaning is not only different
but wider. Summing up the present function of 'right' in moral
discourse, Melden writes: 'It is a term that is given unity in
diverse ways and which is applied by reference to an overriding concern of moral agents with conduct in so far as it serves
and preserves the moral life, in which all of us participate in
ways that are both common and diverse, and in which varied
ways human beings can achieve some measure of their appropriate forms of happiness.'[20]

In view of Melden's repudiation of moral conservatism, it is
pertinent to ask: how has this change in the meaning of 'right'
come about? Is it the outcome of rational criticism or is it
merely fortuitous? Has new knowledge had anything to do with
it and if so, what? More generally; are there good reasons for
regarding the transition from a theistic morality of obedience

to a liberal morality of happiness as moral progress? Is the morality of happiness a better form of morality or is it merely what happens to be accepted in the Western world today? If it is only the latter, then Melden seems to be involved in a form of moral relativism; namely, that morality is relative to the attitudes and beliefs of particular societies in particular places at particular times. Such a relativism might well have conservative moral implications, but if there are good reasons for holding it, then moral conservatism need not be regarded as an accusation to be repudiated with indignation. But are there good reasons for holding it? Melden's remarks in the concluding section of his monograph give no clear indication as to his position on this point.

Nor is the liberal morality of happiness as stated by him free from ambiguity. Its point is said to be the achievement by those who participate in the moral life, of the forms of happiness appropriate to moral agents. But what differentiates the appropriate forms from the inappropriate? Are there good reasons for preferring the former and for trying to be a moral agent, assuming that we know already what it is to be one? These are considerations which arise out of Melden's concluding remarks. What about his discussion of the moral right of a parent? Three points of importance emerge from it. First: the distinction between obligation-meeting and obligatory actions; second: his account of the way in which the right of a parent operates in a son's determination of his conduct, namely, as a morally relevant consideration: third, his contention that the right of a parent is part of the moral role of being a parent. But in all of these the notion of the 'moral' is crucial and just how important they are cannot be decided until the ambiguities in Melden's liberal morality of happiness have been cleared up.

4. RETROSPECT: SOME OUTSTANDING ISSUES

Has this discussion of rights any bearing upon the issue between the negative and positive theories of freedom? There is Hobbes' point: that to have a right is to be free to do or to forbear from doing whatever it is that you have a right to. There is also the natural right to freedom as it is conceived by Locke and by Hart. Both these seem on the face of it to support the negative theory. The natural right to freedom is the right to be free from constraint in the shape of coercion or interference by other people within the limits of morality, whether morality is conceived in terms of the law of nature or in some other way. The freedom involved in every right is freedom from compulsion to exercise it. To have the right to freedom is thus to be entitled but not obliged to resist unjustified coercion or interference. It is up to you to decide whether or not you will resist on any given occasion and no one should try to make you resist. But the exponents of the positive theory will be unmoved by all this. They will point out that the freedom involved in every right is the freedom to choose and to decide, and will point out that if a man is to choose and decide rationally and responsibly and not merely capriciously, he must be positively free. To the extent that a man lacks positive internal freedom and is at the mercy of his inclinations, desires and emotions, his choices and decisions will lack rational justification and will be merely capricious. In short, the exponents of the positive theory will argue that it is only from the standpoint of their theory that the value and significance of rights can be understood. The issue between the two theories therefore remains where it was.

In Locke's doctrine of natural rights, the idea that there is a law of nature which is the supreme moral law is of fundamental importance. But this idea is rejected by each of the three critics. Bentham argues that it results from a mistaken conception of nature and the 'natural'. Ritchie points out that men have notoriously failed to agree about what it is that the law of nature prescribes. Margaret Macdonald argues that a moral law such as the law of nature is not the sort of thing which can be known by reason, and that the idea of its being entailed by the fact that men are rational reflects a confusion of logical types. But a supporter of natural law may object that these arguments are not conclusive. Bentham's doctrines about nature, about human action, and about morality raise at least as many problems as they solve. That men have disagreed about the content of the law of nature does not show that there is no such law. It only shows that knowledge of its content is hard to come by. Margaret Macdonald's case rests upon her doctrine of the three types of significant statement. But this doctrine is itself questionable. It leads her to overlook significant features of human rational activity which have implications for her own account of values. It also makes her prejudge the question of whether the human capacity for rational activity entails the idea of a moral law of nature. But if the arguments of the critics are not conclusive, they at least put the onus of proof on the supporter of the law of nature. It is up to him to show how such a law can be known and to explain why, if it can be known, there has been so much disagreement about it.

But is the law of nature really essential to the central thought in Locke's doctrine of natural rights? Hart thinks not. If there is a natural right to freedom within the limits of morality, there must be moral rights and morality must include the notion of rights, but it need not be the morality of the law of nature. But while Hart shows that within such a morality there must be a residual right to freedom, it is not clear that in any significant sense this is a natural right. He recognizes that there can be and have been moralities which exclude the notion of rights, and this admission of a diversity of moralities seems to rule out any strictly natural rights. Moreover his idea of special moral rights as arising out of certain types of voluntary transactions and relations is open to question. It is not clear that it covers the moral right of a parent over his son. Melden's contention that this right is part of the moral role of being a parent seems nearer the truth although giving rise to further questions about the nature of such moral roles and of morality in general.

Returning to the critics: Bentham rejects natural rights wholesale along with the law of nature. For him, the notion of a right is primarily a legal one, although he leaves room for a derivative notion of moral rights. The important question is: what rights ought the law to secure? And the answer is: those which are justified by the principle of utility, i.e., the principle of the greatest happiness of the greatest number. Ritchie, however, thinks that the idea of natural rights is significant as the idea of the fundamental conditions which in a good society will be secured to all the members. It is the idea of morally justified social rights. He agrees with Bentham to the extent of holding that social utility should be the standard with reference to which social rights are to be morally justified but completely rejects Bentham's hedonistic conception of social utility. He replaces it by an 'evolutionist' conception in which ideas of social development and of the social basis of individual human personality are of central importance. Like Melden, he lays emphasis upon the changes which have occurred historically in operative moral ideas, but also goes further, affirming the fact of moral progress. But while it is clear that he thinks that critical reflection is an important agency in this progress, its precise *modus operandi* remains obscure. Margaret Macdonald agrees with Ritchie that the idea of natural rights is significant as the idea of the basic conditions which ought to be secured in a good society. Assertions about them are value assertions. But she disagrees with both Bentham and Ritchie about the nature of moral and social values, maintaining that they result from human decisions and choices. She also maintains that these decisions and choices are not arbitrary, although it is not clear that she is able to support this contention.

There are three overlapping problems about which there is no clear agreement among the philosophers whom we have been discussing. The first concerns the right to freedom. Are there good reasons for thinking that in some sense it is the foundation of all other rights? The second concerns the nature and significance of moral rights. What justifies them? Do they in some sense presuppose the right to freedom? The third has to do with the idea of basic or morally justified social rights, the rights which ought to be secured in a good society. With reference to what standards, if any, can claims to such rights be justified? How far are they affected by differences in social conditions? Bound up with these problems is the wider question of the nature of morality and of human values generally. This question is also involved in the issue between the negative and positive theories of freedom. We shall have to deal with it if we are to understand the significance and value of freedom and rights as operative ideas in human life. But if there is one definite conclusion which has emerged so far, it is that there is no simple straightforward answer. We shall approach it indirectly by first taking up a topic which has already cropped up more than once.

This is the general theme of human reason and rational activity. It figures prominently in the issue between the negative and positive theories. From one point of view, the positive theory is a theory of rational activity. Berlin regards it as the outcome of certain deep-seated errors made by people whom he calls 'rationalists'. According to him, the trouble with the positive theory is that it embodies a false view of reason and of the nature of human values. Margaret Macdonald criticizes the traditional doctrine of natural rights on the ground that it misunderstands the significance of the human capacity for rational activity. According to her, this capacity is just one more empirical fact about human beings and no consequences for human values follow from it. But is she right? What is it to act rationally and what are we to understand by rationality in human conduct? The answers to these questions may throw some light on the wider question about morality and human values, and may put us in a better position to return to freedom and rights, and the problems connected with them.

Freedom, Rights and Rationality

Chapter 3

Rational Activity

1. UTILITY: RATIONALITY AS EXPEDIENCY AND AND EFFICIENCY

Rational activity is activity in which the agent has reasons for what he does. The better his reasons, the more rational his action. But what sorts of reason are there; what makes one better than another? By what standards can the rationality achieved on any given occasion be judged? The multifarious reasons which people may have for action may be grouped provisionally under three main heads. The first is utility. When an action is done not for its own sake but because it is useful for something else, i.e. for the sake of the consequences of doing it, it is done for a utilitarian reason. The second is intrinsic value. When an action is done not for the sake of its consequences but because in some way it is worth doing for its own sake. The third is morality. When an action is done because the agent regards it as his duty or as something which he morally ought to do, it is done for a moral reason. But these three types are not mutually exclusive. An action which is a duty may be worth doing for its own sake apart from being a duty. It may also be useful. But what makes it useful is different from what makes it intrinsically worthwhile, and both are different from what makes it a duty.

Utilitarian action is commonly thought of in terms of ends and means. To do an action for the sake of its utility is to do it as a means to an end. But it is important to distinguish between two senses of the term 'end'. In the first, it means the anticipated result of deliberate action. A hole while it is being dug, a house while it is being built, a piece of furniture while it is being made: each is an end in this first sense. So is any state of affairs and any process which can be envisaged in advance and brought into being by deliberate action. In the second, it does not mean an anticipated result. Rather it means a future human activity, or a future human experience involving conscious attention, which deliberate action either makes possible or facilitates. Consider the following cases: enrolling in a university to study for a degree, going to a theatre to see a play, training for an athletic event; studying for the degree, seeing the play, competing in the event, are ends in the second sense. Enrolling, going to the theatre, and training, are the respective means.

To do an action as a means to an end in the first sense is to do it in the belief that its performance is a sufficient condition for attaining the end. The end is the effect, the action done as a means the cause. But to do an action as a means to an end in the second sense is to do it in the belief that its performance is not a sufficient but a necessary condition for attaining the end. Here causal language is inappropriate. This is because deliberate action can never be more than preparatory for a future human activity, or for a future human experience involving conscious attention. It cannot guarantee the doing of the activity or the having of the experience. Having enrolled in a university, a student may devote all his time to extra-curricula activities and fail to do any studying at all. Having arrived at the theatre, a man may fall asleep before the curtain rises and wake up only at the end of the last act. Rigorous training does not insure success on the day. It does not even guarantee the athlete's presence on the starting line. For ends in the second sense to be attained, something more than preparatory action is required: the agent's decision to engage in the activity when the moment comes, the subject's conscious attention throughout the time necessary.

But action done as a means to an end in the second sense is always also a means to an end in the first sense. This is because of its preparatory character. It prepares for the future activity or experience by bringing about conditions which either make it possible or facilitate it. These conditions are ends of action in the first sense. The athlete's training is a means to producing maximum physical fitness and this is a favourable condition for a good performance on the day. The playgoer goes to the theatre in order to be physically present when the curtain rises which is a necessary condition for seeing the play. The student completes enrolment formalities in order to satisfy necessary conditions laid down by the authorities for anyone who is to study for a degree. Because an action done as a means to an end in the second sense is always also a means to an end in the first sense, we shall henceforth speak of ends in the second sense as 'ulterior purposes', using the term 'end' only in its first sense. Thus to do an action as a means to an ulterior purpose is to do it in order to prepare for a future human activity or experience by bringing about conditions which are either necessary for it or favourable to it. To do an action as a means to an end is to do it for the sake of its anticipated result.

What has just been said suggests a corollary. Ends are relative to ulterior purposes. The only reason for doing an action as a means to an end is for the sake of a future human activity or experience which attaining the end makes possible. What other reason could there be for merely utilitarian action? But it may be objected that there are some ends which are wanted simply for their own sake. 'A thing of beauty is a joy for ever.' People sometimes try to acquire things of beauty simply for their own sake. But this is not really so. It is the experience of contemplating the thing of beauty which is wanted for its own sake. What is 'a joy for ever' is the aesthetic experience of the beautiful thing. It is because ownership of the beautiful thing greatly facilitates this aesthetic experience that its acquisition is adopted as an end of utilitarian action. More generally: to try to bring about a state of affairs or to produce something which contributed nothing whatever to any human activity or experience would be pointless.

But this conclusion that ends are relative to ulterior purposes, will have to be modified as we shall see in the next section. For the present, however, we may accept it as a provisional conclusion and go on to ask: what about these ulterior purposes themselves? Among the activities and experiences which they comprise must be some which are worthwhile for their own sake or some which the agent believes to be morally incumbent upon him. If they were all nothing but the means to further ends, the utilitarian action would be unintelligible. It would be merely doing something in preparation for something else which was in its turn merely a preparation for something else, and so on *ad infinitum*. This is not to deny that an action can be done as a means to an ulterior purpose which is itself to do something as a means to a further end: going to London airport to catch the plane to New York. It is only to insist that somewhere along the line there must be an ulterior purpose which is to do or to experience something which is not merely a means to an end, whether the doing or experiencing is that of the agent or of others. In other words, utilitarian reasons for action are relative to and ultimately only intelligible in terms of reasons which come under the heads of intrinsic value and morality. An action is useful if, and only if, directly or indirectly it contributes to the doing or experiencing of something else which is worthwhile for its own sake or is a moral duty. But these reasons are not mutually exclusive. Action which is a means to an end, e.g., gardening, may to some people be worthwhile for its own sake. Doing something useful may also itself be a moral duty: taking one's share of camping chores on an expedition.

Utilitarian action then is possible only for an agent who has an ulterior purpose which is not itself utilitarian. But given that he has such a purpose, an agent may well have a reason for utilitarian action. It is rational for him to try to bring about those ends the attainment of which is necessary for or favourable to its execution. What these ends are, and what actions are the best means to them, are matters which he must decide in the light of his ulterior purpose and of the circumstances of his situation. He may decide well or ill. What he does is open to criticism on the score of its expediency for his ulterior purpose. Are his particular ends really those most favourable to its execution? Are the means really the best he could have chosen for attaining them? Expediency then is a relevant standard of rationality in utilitarian action. Such action is rational to the extent that it is expedient for the agent's ulterior purpose. Margaret Macdonald to the contrary notwithstanding, expediency is not a standard which the agent can choose. If it is rational for him to embark on utilitarian action, then he is committed to it.

But an agent who on a given occasion has in mind a number of ulterior purposes rather than merely one, is faced with another problem. He has to decide not only what to do as a means to each of his various purposes but also how best to allocate his available resources among them. Some of these, e.g., money, materials, energy and especially time, will always be limited. The more of them he devotes to one purpose, the less he has left for the rest. He has an economic problem to consider once he has more than a single ulterior purpose. Now the action which is the most expedient as a means to a particular purpose if not necessarily the most efficient in its use of limited resources. A student who wants to compete in a certain event in an athletics meeting may find that the best training programme for that event leaves him little time and less energy for his studies. An agent with a number of ulterior purposes must be prepared if necessary to sacrifice some degree of expediency for the sake of efficiency. He must try to prepare adequately for the execution of them all, not ideally for one and inadequately for the rest.

What he does as a means to a particular ulterior purpose is open to criticism on the score of its efficiency rather than merely its expediency. Is it the best means having regard not only to what is necessary and desirable for that purpose but also for his other purposes? An efficient action will always be an expedient one but not necessarily the most expedient for the execution of the ulterior purpose in question. Efficiency is the standard of rationality in utilitarian action to which an agent with a number of different ulterior purposes is committed. While it is rational for him to try to do what is expedient, it is more rational for him to try to do what is efficient. As a standard of rationality, efficiency includes but also goes beyond expediency because it takes account of the economic problem while expediency does not. In trying to be efficient, just what degree of expediency should be sacrificed for the sake of economy must depend partly upon what is required for adequate preparation for all the agent's ulterior purposes, and partly upon the relative importance which he attaches to the execution of each. But what relative importance should he attach to each of them? Is it merely a matter of his own preferences, or are there other considerations to take into account? We have already seen that ulterior purposes must include human activities or experiences which are either worthwhile for their own sake or else are in some sense the agent's moral duty, i.e. for reasons of intrinsic value or morality.

An agent is responsible for his ulterior purposes. They are his decisions no less than what he does as a means to them. An important consideration is the question of possibility. To formulate an ulterior purpose which you believe to be impossible of execution is irrational. Utilitarian considerations are also relevant. They may lead to a revision of possible ulterior purposes. If all the tickets are sold, then you cannot attend the performance. If a Mediterranean holiday proves too expensive, a fortnight at Brighton will have to do instead. But these are considerations which bear only on the range of choice open to an agent in deciding upon his ulterior purposes. The question of what choices to make will be discussed in the next section as will the second type of reason for action, intrinsic value. But we have learned something about rational activity in the form of utilitarian action. It presupposes ulterior purposes in preparation for which it is undertaken. But given such purposes, questions of utility are genuine questions and expediency and efficiency are genuine standards of rationality with reference to which utilitarian action can be criticized. We may express this by saying that utility is the simplest and lowest level of rational activity. Above it are others which we have still to explore, at which decisions about ulterior purposes are taken.

2. PERSONAL WELL-BEING: RATIONALITY AS PRUDENCE AND WISDOM

A man's life is a self-conscious unity in the sense that however various and diverse his activities and experiences, he lives through and is present in them all. He is conscious of each of them as an activity or experience of the particular desiring, feeling, thinking subject who is himself. It is also an on-going unity in the sense that what is done in the present may affect what can be done or experienced in the future. This is sufficiently obvious at the level of utility where all present action is for the sake of the future. But it is also true of activities and

experiences which are worthwhile for their own sake. Although
not entered into for the sake of their consequences, they do have
consequences some of which may affect the agent's future. In
making decisions about ulterior purposes, he has good reason
to take into account not only the intrinsic value but also the
foreseeable consequences of the activities and experiences open
to him. Failure to do so may mean unnecessary hardship or
suffering, even death. More generally because his life is a self-
conscious on-going unity a man has good reason in all his
conduct to make his personal well-being a leading consideration.
Whether it should be the overriding consideration is a further
question to which we shall return later. It is at least an important one which, if he is to go on living, it would be irrational
to neglect.

But what does personal well-being consist in? Safety and
security have something to do with it. A man who pays no
heed to his safety is likely to come to a premature end and
with the cessation of his being, all prospect of well-being is
gone. Security is rather more complex. It includes the preservation of health, wealth, status and reputation, and in general
all in his life which a man finds valuable, whether intrinsically
or on account of its utility. It follows that a man has good reason
in the name of safety and security to act prudently in all that he
does. Prudence is a standard of rationality to which anyone in
pursuit of personal well-being is logically committed. It applies
both to intrinsically worthwhile activities and experiences and
to action at the level of utility where it takes precedence over
efficiency and expediency. No matter how efficient or expedient
an action may be, if it is dangerous or threatens security it is,
from the standpoint of prudence, irrational.

But personal well-being is something more than merely
safety and security. While total disregard of safety is irrational,
a policy of 'safety first' is not the path of reason. A man whose
chief aim is to minimize risk is cutting himself off from all
activities with an element of danger. Such a policy may prolong
his life, but mere survival in the absence of anything worth
surviving for is itself worthless. Security is an essentially
conservative notion. It emphasizes the preservation of what
one already has but says nothing about its development or

improvement. But assuming that a man has something worth preserving, why should he rest content with it? While there will inevitably be much in his situation about which he can do nothing and which he must necessarily accept, what sort of life he has rests at least in part with himself. He has good reason to try to make it as good a life as he can and he may well find that calculated risks are worth incurring. After all he cannot live for ever. Over and above safety and security, it is the quality of a man's life which is the decisive factor in his personal well-being.

But what is worth preserving is also worth acquiring. The idea of security therefore throws light on what enhances and enriches the quality of life. The general proposition was that a man has good reason to preserve all in his life which he finds valuable whether intrinsically or on account of its utility. But utilitarian value is relative to intrinsic value. Wealth for instance is worth having not for its own sake but because of the intrinsically valuable activities and experiences which it makes possible. By the same token poverty is bad not in itself but because of what it prevents. It is what a man finds intrinsically valuable in his life which enhances and enriches its quality, but utilitarian and intrinsic value may overlap.

Health is clearly of utilitarian value. A man in good health can do and enjoy much which is denied to one whose health is bad. Bad health may mean discomfort and pain, and these are positive evils. They are bad not only because of what they prevent but in themselves. While he is enduring them, the quality of a man's life is directly impaired. Good health is intrinsically valuable even if it is usually taken for granted and appreciated only when it is lost. A man's physical well-being is a constituent of his personal well-being. Status and reputation are undoubtedly useful. A man who possesses them enjoys opportunities denied to one who does not. Whether they are worth having for their own sake is a rather more subtle question. Great concern or anxiety about them may impoverish rather than enrich a man's life. But he may take pride in a status and reputation which he believes fairly reflect his merits. On the other hand, if he is denied the status or reputation to which he thinks he is entitled, his resentment may cloud his whole life. All this shows that there are some things which may be both useful and at the same time contribute either positively or negatively directly to the quality of life.

But a man's life is more than his health or his status and reputation. As a self-conscious on-going unity it is made up of his day-to-day activities and experiences and for the most part it is to them that he must look for whatever of intrinsic value he is to find in it. If an activity or an experience is to be worthwhile for its own sake, it must arouse the agent's interest and engage his faculties. He will find it intrinsically valuable to the extent that it offers scope for the exercise and development of his physical or his intellectual powers, his capacity for affection and love, his practical ingenuity or his creative talent, or any combination of these. But people notoriously differ in the degree to which they are endowed with these various capacities, and activities and experiences differ in the degree to which they afford them outlet. Moreover no one knows in advance just what he may be capable of in any of these spheres. He can discover the scope and limits of his powers, the nature and direction of his potentialities, only by trial and error in the course of actual life. A man's problem therefore in trying to improve the quality of his life, is to discover just what activities and experiences most appeal to him and give him most scope for the exercise of his individual combination of gifts and talents, and to arrange matters so as to enable him to devote time and energy to their regular practice and cultivation. But in tackling this problem, he does not have to start from scratch. He is born into and grows up in an already existing society whose culture and way of life embody the accumulated experience of previous generations. This is there for him to assimilate and use in trying to make the best life he can for himself and he has good reason to take advantage of it.

So something more than prudence is required of a man who is trying to maintain and develop his personal well-being. He must endeavour to act wisely. Wisdom is a standard of rationality to which in the nature of the case he is committed and with reference to which his decisions about ulterior purposes may appropriately be criticized. How far do these decisions, and also the relative importance which he attaches to each of his purposes, reflect a mature understanding of himself and his situation, and more generally, of the opportunities which the world offers for intrinsically worthwhile activities and experiences? How far do they show him to be aware of the possibilities, open to someone situated as he is, with his cast of mind and character, his personal make-up and temperament, for enhancing and enriching the quality of his life? These are the issues which he must ponder and assess if he is to determine his conduct wisely.

Wisdom is a higher standard of rationality than prudence. It includes but goes beyond it just as efficiency includes but goes beyond expediency. It allows, as mere prudence does not, for the positive contribution which an element of risk and danger may make to life. It tries to make the best of life rather than merely acquiescing in its condition regardless of what that may be. But prudence remains a genuine standard of rationality. While it may be the path of wisdom to incur calculated risks, it is never wise to be rash. A wise course of action will always be a prudent one although not necessarily the most prudent one possible in the situation. Just what degree of prudence should be sacrificed and what risks it is rational to run are matters of wisdom. Like prudence, wisdom is applicable to the level of utility and takes precedence over efficiency and expediency. No matter how efficient or expedient a given action may be, if it is inherently dull, wearisome or painful, then it may be wise to abandon it. The positive gain to the agent's life may not be worth the price which has to be paid for it.

This means that a man who is capable of making the maintenance and development of his personal well-being a leading consideration in the determination of his conduct has reached a level of rational activity higher than that of utility. He can act wisely and prudently as well as efficiently and expediently and is thus in a position to decide upon his ulterior purposes rationally rather than capriciously. I said that utilitarian action is relative to ulterior purposes. This is true for an agent who is only capable of rational activity at the level of utility and for whom decisions about ulterior purposes will therefore be capricious. But it needs amending in the case of one who is capable of the higher level of personal well-being. Having a practical understanding of the fact that his life is a self-conscious on-going unity, he will see that he has good reason to make general provisions for his future. In his case utilitarian action is rational not only for the sake of specific ulterior purposes but also in order to establish and maintain the conditions which are necessary for him to have and to execute any ulterior purposes at all. The satisfaction of his bodily needs through the provision of food, clothing and accommodation, the preservation and care of his health, the acquisition and maintenance of private property in the form of household effects and other articles of daily use: all of these are ends of utilitarian action which an agent at the level of personal well-being has good reason to pursue not for the sake of any particular ulterior purpose but for the sake of his life as a whole. Rational activity at the lower level of utility forms an integral part of rational activity at the higher level of personal well-being while being modified by its new context. Its scope is widened by the need to make general provision for the maintenance of daily life while its content is also affected by considerations of wisdom and prudence. This is because the level of personal well-being is concerned with the conduct of life as a whole.

3. IS IT RATIONAL TO BE MORAL?

No one is born a fully fledged rational agent. The capacity for rational activity at the level of utility and still more at the level of personal well-being has to be developed gradually. But everyone is born into an already existing society and as he grows up, learns to participate in its life. The individual human being first encounters morality as an integral part of the social life which is already going on around him. He meets it in the shape of established ways of acting and rules of conduct which he is expected to follow. He learns that he must be truthful, must keep his word, must be considerate to others and be prepared to help them. As he grows older, he learns the prevailing ideas about sex, marriage and family life. and comes to know the rules and conventions which govern this side of life. He gradually becomes acquainted with the various institutions of his society and with the rules and conventions connected with them. The result is that by the time he becomes capable of pursuing his own personal well-being with some degree of prudence and wisdom, he is already caught up in the life of his society. He is already a member of it and has become a moral agent in the sense that he is capable at least to some extent of the personal discipline necessary to meet recognized obligations and standards of conduct. He knows what is expected of him in his society and is more or less able and willing to meet these demands. Unless he has acquired at least this much self-discipline, he will scarcely be in a position to become a rational agent at the level of personal well-being at all.

But once he has reached this level, what should his attitude to morality be? Granted that he is already a moral agent in this limited sense, why should he go on being one? Has he good reason from the standpoint of personal well-being to continue? A wise conception of personal well-being will include care and concern for those whom he likes or are useful to him. But this is not the same thing as morality. It rests in part on the caprice of the agent's feelings, and in part on utility. It includes no recognition of responsibilities towards others which ought to be discharged regardless of how one feels about them or of whether they are useful.

It may be thought that on prudential grounds it is rational to be moral. Failure to observe established moral rules and conventions may be harmful to security and perhaps dangerous. But this prudential attitude towards established morality is not itself a moral one. It amounts only to the advice: don't be immoral unless you can get away with it. Moreover the argument is double-edged. The prospects of getting away with it are sometimes pretty good. Respecting the claims of morality may sometimes be tiresome, painful, or dangerous. It may therefore sometimes be rational on the score of wisdom, prudence or expediency to ignore them and to take shrewd steps to get away with it. But it may be objected that such a course is never really wise. The rational agent at the level of personal well-being was admitted to be a moral agent, if only in a limited sense. Will he not suffer pangs of conscience since he will have been habituated to think and feel in terms of the established morality of his society? Will he not suffer more from these pangs than from anything which may happen through doing his duty? This objection misses the point. The question is whether at the level of personal well-being, he has any reason to be troubled by conscience any more? If there is no good reason for being moral other than the fact that in the past he has been conditioned to it, his wisest course will be to put all that behind him and adopt the prudential attitude. The pangs of conscience will lose potency once he realizes that there is no good reason for him to be moral apart from considerations of his own well-being, no reason for being moral as distinct from being wise and prudent.

But there is a weightier argument. The established moral rules and conventions of a society are an integral part of its way of life. The matrix of human relationships, of inter-dependent and co-operative activities, which make up that way of life can be maintained only if the great majority of people most of the time acknowledge the claims of these moral rules and conventions and conform to them. The rational agent at the level of personal well-being is involved in this matrix of relationships and activities. If it breaks down, his personal well-being will be harmed. If everyone disregards the claims of morality whenever it suits them, it will break down and as a result both he and everyone else will suffer. It therefore follows that he ought to acknowledge the claims of morality since by doing so, he will be helping to maintain the way of life of his society and this way of life is a necessary condition for his own continued personal well-being.

But to this, there is a rejoinder. The argument is still one of prudence. The rational agent is advised to respect the claims of morality because it is in his interest to do so. But prudential considerations may sometimes point the other way. Acting morally may sometimes mean hardship, suffering or even death. Moreover, granted that it is in the rational agent's interest because contributory to his well-being that the way of life of his society should continue, and therefore in his interest that the claims of morality should be respected by the great majority of the members most of the time, why should this affect him? It is in his interest that other people should be moral but this does not mean that it is in his interest to be moral himself. From the standpoint of his personal well-being, a rational agent has no reason to view the claims of morality in anything but a prudential light. He has no reason to be a moral agent properly so called. Rational activity at the level of personal well-being is not moral activity. Within its perspective moral reasons for action have no place.

Let us look more closely at just what is being said in the rejoinder. It is in the interest of my personal well-being that everyone else should be moral but that I should not. They are to put the claims of morality before their personal well-being while I am to do precisely the opposite. This is reminiscent of the doctrine put by Plato into the mouth of Callicles in the 'Gorgias' and of Thrasymachus in 'The Republic'. It is to claim for myself a position of special privilege which is denied to other people. There is one law for them and another for me. But what justifies me in arrogating to myself this specially favoured position? Are there any reasons which could possibly support it? Callicles and Thrasymachus notoriously failed to produce any and surely there are none. The claim is arbitrary in the sense that I am demanding for myself what I refuse to allow to other people without being able to give any reasons why I should be so favoured.

The argument of the rejoinder therefore fails. It overlooks something of fundamental importance, namely that in the absence of relevant grounds for treating people differently, they should all be treated alike. It is rational for all to be treated alike unless or until good reason can be shown for differential treatment. Now so far as the claims of morality are concerned, all rational agents are in the same position. There are no relevant grounds which will justify one being treated differently from the rest. Morality is necessary if the way of life of a society is to be maintained. Every rational agent is a member of a society and it is in the interest of his personal well-being that its way of life should be maintained. It is therefore in the interest of the personal well-being of every rational agent that all members of his society should respect the claims of morality. But if all members of his society are to respect the claims of morality, he must do so too.[1]

[1] Cf. R. M. Hare on 'Universality' in *Freedom and Reason*, Oxford, Clarendon Press, 1963; also Marcus Singer, *Generalisation in Ethics*, London, Eyre and Spottiswoode, 1963.

It follows that after all it is rational to be moral. Because he is already a member of a particular society and is already caught up in its way of life, a rational agent has good reason, in determining his conduct, to take into account not only the maintenance and development of his personal well-being but also the claims of morality. If and when these come into conflict, he has good reason to give priority to the claims of morality. While it is rational for him to make his personal well-being a leading consideration in determining his conduct, it is not rational for him to make it the overriding one. That position belongs to morality by virtue of his inescapable commitment to social living. The trouble with personal well-being as a level of rational activity is that its perspective is too narrow. It fails adequately to take into account the implications of the commitment to social living. But this defect is made good at a higher level of rational activity which we may call the level of social morality. It is only at this level that the significance of moral reasons for action as distinct from those of intrinsic value and utility can be appreciated. But just what is involved in acting rationally at the level of social morality? What does respecting the claims of morality and giving priority over personal well-being really mean?

4. SOCIAL MORALITY: RATIONALITY AS JUSTICE AND SOCIAL RESPONSIBILITY

The rational agent at the level of social morality must act in the spirit rather than merely the letter of his society's established morality. This means having some understanding of the ideas, beliefs, and values, which are the foundation for its rules and precepts, and acting in the light of that understanding. It also means acting justly. No doubt acting justly is an obligation which is prescribed in some form or other by the established morality of every human society. But if action is to be in the spirit rather than the letter, it is important to understand the meaning of justice, and what it is to act justly.

The rational basis of justice is the principle that like cases should be treated alike.[1] Now human beings are all alike in

[1] M. Ginsberg, *Justice in Society*, Heinemann, 1965.

a simple but fundamental respect: they are all human. This means that so far as human beings are concerned, it is differential treatment, and more especially unequal treatment, which has to be justified. Justice does not mean universal equality of treatment. But it does mean equal treatment in the absence of relevant grounds for unequal treatment. To act justly is to treat the claims and interests of everyone with whom you have any dealings as equal in value to your own unless there are relevant grounds for regarding them as unequal and hence for differential treatment.

Now this is to say that acting justly is a way of acting rationally. More precisely: acting rationally in your dealings with other people means acting justly. But acting justly is also acting morally. If it is rational in principle to be moral, then in particular, it is rational to act justly in all appropriate situations. Justice is a standard of rationality to which the rational agent at the level of social morality is logically committed. It is a standard by which all his conduct in his dealings with other people can be rationally criticized. It also gives him direction and guidance in trying to act in the spirit rather than the letter of his society's established morality, especially when particular rules and precepts are in conflict, or require interpretation.

This indicates the frame of mind necessary for rational activity at the level of social morality. The rational agent must be able and willing to adopt the standpoint of what Adam Smith in *The Theory of the Moral Sentiments* called an 'impartial spectator' towards his own interests and claims. He must not favour them simply because they are his. Nor should he undervalue them. Altruism is no part of justice. In situations where equal legitimate interests and claims conflict, he must take the initiative in seeking a mutually acceptable compromise. In every situation he must be prepared to consider candidly what are put forward as relevant grounds for preferential treatment and act accordingly. All this is, of course, easy to say but notoriously harder to do.

But what are to count as relevant grounds for unequal treatment? This is clearly the key question. The answer lies in a simple but inescapable fact of human life. 'No man is an island.'

Every man is born into and grows up to be a member of an already existing human society: a tribe, a kingdom, a nation. Within this wider society he associates with other people in a variety of ways: in the domestic life of the family, at work, and in leisure pursuits and activities. He is a member not only of the group which is his society but also of various groups within it. Joint activity on any scale constitutes a group. The point of central importance is that as members, people have good reason to treat one another in ways which are consistent with the nature and purpose of the common enterprise which the group exists to carry on. As a participating member of the group, each is entitled to insist that the others should do what is necessary to enable him to share in the common enterprise on terms consistent with its nature and purpose, provided that he acts reciprocally towards them. He is therefore justified in claiming preferential treatment if that is necessary to enable him to play his proper part.

Relevant grounds for unequal treatment lie in what is necessary to enable the members of a group to share in its joint activity on proper terms. But this does not mean that there can be justice only between the fellow members of the same group. There is good reason to act justly towards all with whom you have any dealings, strangers and foreigners no less than neighbours and fellow countrymen. It does mean that inequality of treatment is just only when it is required by a common enterprise in which the people concerned are all involved. Acting justly will largely be a matter of acting justly towards the members of his family, his neighbours, his fellow workers, customers or clients, his fellow members in voluntary associations like clubs, trade unions and churches, and over and beyond this, towards his fellow citizens at large.

But, and this is important, those involved must be in substantial agreement about the nature and purpose of these activities. This agreement is necessary as a common basis for deciding what constitutes relevant grounds for treating some people differently from others. Where it is absent this common basis will be lacking and there will be irresoluble conflicts about what is just action. All this points a presupposition of rational activity at the level of social morality; namely, an already existing society with widespread agreement among its members about the fundamental character of its way of life. It therefore clearly behoves the rational agent who is to act in the spirit rather than the letter of justice, to seek out and make the most of the possibilities of reaching agreement in every situation.

But justice is not the only standard of rationality at the level of social morality. No joint activity or enterprise can prosper unless those involved help to promote and advance it. As a participating member of the group, each has good reason to consider the needs and problems of the group as a whole in the current situation and to decide for himself how best he can contribute to meeting them. It may well be that his best contribution will simply be to follow the lead of others more able and experienced than himself. But this does not relieve him of the responsibility of thinking about the matter and of exercising his own initiative if and when he judges he can best serve the common enterprise by doing so. In other words, the rational agent must act responsibly in all the various spheres of activity in which he is involved, e.g. in his family life, in his neighbourhood, at work, in his voluntary associations, and as a citizen in the public life of his society. No doubt acting responsibly will be a recognized duty in the established morality of his society. But as a rational agent he must act in its spirit rather than its letter, something which once more is notoriously easier to say than to do.

There is a sense in which what is responsible can never be unjust. Each member of a group is entitled to insist that the others should do what is necessary to enable him to play his proper part. But his proper part, whatever else it may be, must always first and foremost be to act as a responsible member of the group. He can never be entitled to insist on doing or having done anything which weakens or undermines the common enterprise. By the same token he has no grounds for objecting to anything done by another member which genuinely serves the group as a whole, even if it means that his own share in the common enterprise must be different from what he had hoped. In such cases, he must reconsider his own position in the group and what is just to him as a member. This is to say that in any joint activity or enterprise, responsibility takes priority over justice. Relevant grounds for preferential treatment may arise out of what is necessary to render a particular form of service to the group as a whole; e.g. higher rations for armed forces in wartime; exempting the family bread-winner from at least some of the more wearisome daily household chores.

But while responsibility and justice overlap, they remain distinct. A person can act justly as a member of a group without acting responsibly. He can take pains in all his dealings with the other members to treat them in ways which are consistent with the nature and purpose of their common enterprise, while not troubling himself about the needs and problems confronting the group as a whole in the current situation. He may be content to leave such matters to others whose lead he will follow without question or criticism. But the rational agent at the level of social morality has good reason to act responsibly and not merely justly. The perspective of responsibility includes but goes beyond that of mere justice. It takes account not only of the nature and purpose of the common enterprise but also of the problems of the group as a whole in the current situation. Since there will always be a current situation with its special problems and difficulties, it follows that while it is rational to be just, it is more rational to be responsible and to interpret justice from the wider perspective of responsibility. It is the higher of the two standards of rationality at the level of social morality, and the rational agent's conduct may appropriately be criticized with reference to it.

But a man is always a member of a number of groups and their respective interests may on occasion conflict; e.g. those of his family or his club with those of his neighbourhood; those of his firm or his trade union with those of his nation. He may find himself placed in an awkward situation where acting responsibly in one sphere seems to involve acting irresponsibly in another. When this happens, it is rational to give priority to the responsibilities of the wider, more inclusive community. His family and his club are part of his neighbourhood; his firm and his union are part of his nation. To push the interests of the part at the expense of the whole is clearly unjustified. The interests of the smaller group must be reconsidered to take account of responsibilities of membership of the wider group. The same principle applies to conflicts between groups whose membership is mutually exclusive, e.g. between different families, different sects, between management and labour, agriculture and industry, town and country. The rational agent must view the conflict in the perspective of a relevant wider community to which both the rival groups belong, e.g. the neighbourhood, the church as a whole, the nation.

It is social responsibility rather than merely responsibility which is the higher standard of rationality at the level of social morality. The rational agent's primary responsibility is always to the wider and more inclusive community and he must decide for himself on any given occasion where in fact this primary responsibility lies. For the most part, the widest and most inclusive community likely to be relevant will be the already existing territorial human society in which he is making his life. Today, in the mid-twentieth century, this will be the nation. At different times in the past, it may have been the tribe, the clan, the kingdom, the city or the empire. The wider community can be supra-national when the nation itself is involved in joint activities and enterprises with other nations, e.g. the European 'Common Market', NATO, or, on a wider scale, the United Nations. In the sphere of politics, the rational agent's primary responsibility may on occasion be to one of these international groups.

Since it is rational to be moral even if necessary at the expense of personal well-being, it follows that social responsibility and justice take precedence over standards of rationality at the two lower levels of rational activity. No matter how efficient or expedient a given course of action may be, if it is socially irresponsible or unjust, the rational agent at the level of social morality must not undertake it. The same applies to action which from the point of view of wisdom or prudence has everything to recommend it. We have seen already that there is a sense in which utility undergoes expansion at the level of personal well-being. It undergoes an analogous expansion at the level of social morality. The needs and requirements which confront any group as a whole, necessitate many kinds of utilitarian action which it will be the responsibility of the members to undertake. Moreover, many groups are avowedly utilitarian in nature and purpose: e.g. a firm, a trade union, an employers' association. They are formed to carry on utilitarian activities and their members take part in them because, directly or indirectly, it is useful to them to do so. Such groups, however, require at least some degree of trust and willingness to co-operate among the members. Prospects will be the better, the more the members are able and willing to act justly towards each other and responsibly for the sake of the common enterprise. Rational activity at the level of social morality, enlarges and facilitates the opportunities for co-operative utilitarian action.

There is also a sense in which it presupposes some capacity for rational activity at the level of personal well-being. Acting justly means treating the interests and claims of other people as equal in value to your own. But you must already have interests and claims of your own, which implies that you are capable of directing your life with some degree of prudence and wisdom. Moreover, just as it enhances the prospects of fruitful co-operation in utilitarian action, so rational activity at the level of social morality also facilitates co-operation in the pursuit of intrinsic values. Associations devoted to the exploration and cultivation of intrinsically worthwhile activities and experiences will prosper to the extent that their members are able to act justly and responsibly. The individual may also find that bearing office in some group directly enriches the quality of his life. Personal well-being, no less than utility, undergoes expansion at the level of social morality.

5. THE LIMITATIONS OF SOCIAL MORALITY

Rational activity at the level of social morality presupposes an already existing society with widespread agreement among its members about the fundamental character of its life. This needs both elaboration and qualification. It does not mean that such agreement is necessary for any society to exist at all. If that was so, there could be no such thing as a 'Minorities' problem. But it does mean that where it is absent, a society will consist of two or more groups, one of which will be in a position of

101

dominance. The dominant group need not be a majority of the total population, as, e.g. in contemporary South Africa. What is necessary is that it should be able to make its view of the society's way of life prevail, being able to force those who do not agree with it to nonetheless accept it. It means that there must be widespread agreement among the members of the dominant group not only about the fundamental character of their own life but also about that of the society which they are dominating. Even in a deeply divided society, rational activity at the level of social morality will be possible and indeed necessary for the members of the dominant group. It will be possible within the dominant group because the conditions which it presupposes are also those which are necessary for the group to be dominant. It will be necessary because if they are to make their view prevail in the wider society, the members must be willing and able to act responsibly and justly as members of the group.

In so acting, the members of the dominant group will think that they are acting responsibly and justly as members of the wider society. But this will be denied by the members of the subject group. They will disagree about the nature and purpose of the wider society, in particular rejecting the place allotted to them in the scheme of things by the dominant group. These differences will be reflected in the body of moral rules, conventions and ways of acting recognized in each group. Each will have its own established morality in which its own fundamental ideas and values are embodied. No doubt acting responsibly and justly will be a recognized moral way of acting in the subject no less than in the dominant group. But because they cannot agree about the terms on which they are to share in the life of the wider society, there will be no agreed common basis for deciding what is to count as relevant grounds for differential treatment. Nor will they be able to agree about the nature and urgency of the problems and difficulties confronting the society in the current situation. In other words, because the wider society is an artificial thing held together by force rather than by common ideas and sentiments, it cannot provide a framework for rational activity at the level of social morality. This will necessarily be confined within the limits of each group.

That societies which are deeply and painfully divided along racial, religious or cultural lines have existed and do exist needs no stressing. In such societies the lot of the dominant group is by no means an altogether happy one. The lives of its members will be warped and distorted in a variety of ways by the suspicion, the fear, and often the hatred which they will feel towards the subject group. But the plight of the latter is worse. Its members are compelled to accept the position allotted to them by the dominant group and can maintain their own way of life, if at all, only under serious difficulties. These may sometimes become so crippling that the attempt breaks down altogether. When this happens, the subject group will lose its corporate character. It will tend increasingly to become merely a class of alienated and demoralized individuals without security in the present or hope for the future. They will more and more become incapable of rational activity not only at the level of social morality but also at the level of personal well-being. They will have little reason to act wisely and prudently, let alone responsibly and justly.

A class of virtual social outcasts may also be generated in a society which is not divided along racial, cultural or religious lines. Technological and economic changes may result in the effective exclusion of a whole section of the population from participation in the way of life of a society. There need be no overt conflict between rival views of the fundamental character of its life. Rather what happens is that, in new circumstances, some people find that they can no longer carry on their lives in time-honoured ways. Many of the British industrial working class seem to have been in this position in the nineteenth century. Old ideas about the society's life are no longer adequate in the new situation. The failure to meet this challenge and re-think old ideas indicates some degree of failure in social responsibility on the part of the leaders of the society. All this reveals the inherent practical limitations of rational activity at the level of social morality. In a divided society, or in one in which old ideas are becoming increasingly irrelevant to current problems, what is socially responsible and just in the eyes of one group will appear as mere calculated selfishness to another.

It may be objected that, in spite of these limitations, people can and should still treat each other justly as human beings. If they cannot agree upon relevant grounds for differential treatment, they ought to regard each other's interests and claims as being of equal value and, in the spirit of justice, seek to compromise in the face of conflict. But, unfortunately, matters are not so simple. In a divided society the dominant group will not think of the subject group as fellow human beings like themselves, but rather as people who, while admittedly human, are inferior.

The refusal by the subject group to accept what the dominant group consider to be relevant grounds for differential treatment will be attributed by the latter to the ignorance and perversity of the former. The idea of compromise will be ruled out as a betrayal of all that they stand for. Much the same situation will prevail in a society where long accepted ideas are becoming obsolete. Those who are not adversely affected by the new circumstances will dismiss those who are as weak, lazy and immoral. To admit that the latter might have a case, would be to undermine the whole body of ideas and values in terms of which their own lives are directed. In other words: what prevents people from agreeing upon relevant grounds for differential treatment will also prevent them from treating each other justly as human beings. They can treat each other's interests and claims as equal in value and compromise to avoid conflict, only if the differences between them are not too serious and deep-seated.

Similar considerations are applicable to the case of strangers and foreigners. Unless a man has learned to act justly towards those with whom he is sharing a common life, he will not be able to do so towards outsiders. This is because a man's daily life is lived as a member of a variety of groups ranging from the family to the nation. It is in these contexts, if anywhere, that he must first learn to act justly. Casual encounters with foreigners and strangers are in the nature of the case exceptional. The very designations 'stranger' and 'foreigner' imply the existence of a group to which the persons so designated do not belong. If the normal conditions of a man's life are such as to make it difficult for him to become a rational agent at the level of social morality, he will not be able to act as one in exceptional cases. Acting justly towards human beings as such is logically prior to acting towards one's fellow group members in the sense that it is the rational ground of the latter. But in fact, one first lives and has dealings with human beings who are fellow group members. Only after one has learned to live and act as a member of a group is it possible to have dealings with human beings as such and cope with the exceptional case of casually encountered strangers and foreigners.

In the last section, the principle of primary responsibility to the wider, more inclusive community was said to be applicable to conflicts between mutually exclusive groups. But what about conflicts between nations? The fact that both sides profess to recognize a wider international order has all too frequently failed to prevent them from resorting to war. This is because the wider order to which both sides pay lip-service is not a genuine international community. Neither is prepared to sub-ordinate national interest to international responsibility, and that is why there is war. There can be a genuine international community only when the nations of the world can agree about its nature and purpose, and therefore about the terms upon which they are all to participate in it and the procedures which are to regulate their dealings with each other. It is just because such agreement has not so far been forthcoming that the United Nations remains a diplomatic forum rather than becoming an international community. In recent years nations have managed to co-operate fruitfully together in military and economic fields. But it has been possible only where the nations concerned have been able to find some common ground in matters affecting them all, and to put at least some degree of trust in each other.

So far we have been concerned with the inherent practical limitations of rational activity at the level of social morality. It is possible only to the extent that people are in agreement about the fundamental character of their common life and where what they are agreed about is applicable in the current situation. But this emphasis on agreement points to a deeper problem. Granted that it must be applicable, does it matter what the agreement is about? Are there any rational grounds for saying that it would be morally better if people could agree on one way of life rather than another? More generally: upon what rational grounds, if any, can the way of life of one society be judged morally better or worse rather than that of another? In a divided society, are there any rationally defensible moral grounds for supporting one rival group rather than another? In a society where long accepted ideas are becoming inapplicable, upon what rational moral grounds is the necessary re-thinking and revision to proceed? To put the same problem in another way: as a rational agent, I have good reason to act morally. Not to do so would be arbitrary. But granted that I ought to be socially responsible and just, what reasons are there apart from prudential ones why I should be so in terms of the particular ideas and values accepted in my society? What after all is so special about the way of life of my society? I may be told: 'If you don't like it here, go away and live elsewhere!' But is it only a matter of liking? Can nothing be said for the life of my society on moral grounds: that in some sense it is good, or holds out the prospect of becoming good?

At the level of social morality, rational agents can criticize their own and each other's conduct on the score of its social responsibility and justice. But what they cannot do is criticize and evaluate the fundamental character of their common life. Agreement about that is presupposed and it must be accepted as something already settled and not to be reopened. It follows that at the level of social morality, the questions asked in the last paragraph cannot be answered. Strictly speaking, they ought not even to be asked, for they imply that the fundamental character of the life of a society can be called in question instead of being accepted uncritically. It follows also that the perspective of social morality as a level of rational activity implies what may appropriately be called 'moral relativism'. It implies that moral judgements can have a rational basis only within the framework of the agreed way of life of a particular society. One society can be judged morally better or worse than another only within the framework of the way of life of a third society which is taken as a standard.

But, it may be objected, surely the proper conclusion to draw from all this is: so much the worse for social morality as a level of rational activity. That certain questions cannot be answered or even asked in terms of its perspective shows only that its perspective is limited, not that they are illegitimate. All that has been shown is that as a level of rational activity, social morality rests upon a non-rational foundation: the merely contingent fact of agreement. What follows is not that moral relativism is the last word on morality but that social morality points beyond itself to a higher level of rational activity, at which the defect of its non-rational foundation is overcome and the spectre of moral relativism is exorcized. The fact that very few people are really moral relativists when it comes to actual living is surely of some significance. What is required is to carry the theory of rational activity further. To stop short at the level of social morality is to break off the inquiry prematurely.

These are weighty objections and the idea of developing the theory of rational activity further is tempting. At the same time, the difficulties in the way of doing so should not be underestimated. The fact that most people are not moral relativists does not show that moral relativism is false. It shows only that if moral relativism is true, most people are mistaken about the nature of morality. Nor does it follow that because most people are in some sense moral absolutists or universalists, they can give a rational justification for their beliefs. Their inability to do so would in fact be grist to the relativist's mill in the sense that it would lend support to the contention that moral judgements can have a rational basis only within a framework of agreement. However, I think that something may be done to develop the theory of rational activity further and I propose to attempt it in a later chapter.[1] But let us provisionally accept social morality as the highest level of rational activity in the full knowledge of its imperfections. This will enable certain problems connected with freedom and rights to be more effectively highlighted. Moreover, the fact that social morality as a level of rational activity has imperfections should not lead us to undervalue it. It is always rational to be socially responsible and just, even if something more is required for the highest achievement of rationality.

[1] See Chapter 7.

6. KINDS AND DEGREES OF RATIONALITY

At each level of rational activity there are corresponding standards of rationality. Whether an action is rational in terms of a given standard necessarily depends upon the situation in which it is done. No action is expedient in itself. It is expedient in so far as, in a particular situation, it is a good means to a given end. What is true of expediency is also true of each of the other standards. How far a given action is wise depends upon how far it is likely to contribute to the maintenance and development of the agent's personal well-being and this in turn depends upon who he is and how he is situated. Whether an action is just depends upon whether in the particular situation there are relevant grounds for differential treatment and whether any differential treatment which it involves is in accordance with these grounds. The agent's problem in trying to act rationally in terms of a given standard, is to do that action which in the particular situation meets the requirements of the standard better than any other. His action is rational to the extent that it is more efficient, more prudent, more just, than any alternative, given the scarcity of resources at his disposal, the inevitable risks confronting him and the particular constellation of interests and claims involved. There is a sense in which the rationality of an action in terms of a given standard is always a matter of degree. Granted that the agent is trying to act in terms of the standard, the question in principle always remains open: in the particular situation, does the action meet the requirements of the standard better than any alternative?

But what about the given standard itself? We have seen that at the level of utility, it is more rational to do what is efficient rather than merely what is expedient; at the level of personal well-being, more rational to be wise than merely prudent; at the level of social morality, more rational to be socially responsible than merely just. But in each case, the lower standard is included in the higher, although it is modified by considerations arising out of the larger perspective of the latter. An efficient action is also an expedient one but expedient in the light of considerations relevant to the economic problem of scarce resources. A wise action is also a prudent one, but prudent in the light of considerations, relevant to the enhancement and enrichment of the agent's life. A socially responsible action is also just, but just against the background of the problems and difficulties currently facing the society. It follows that it is not enough for an action to be rational simply in terms of a given standard. It is necessary to ask also: is that standard the relevant one? Where it is expediency, do considerations of efficiency make any difference? Where it is prudent, does the same action still appear rational when considered from the point of view of its wisdom? If it is justice, is the action also socially responsible? A verdict as to the rationality of an action reached in terms of the lower standard at each level is always open to revision in terms of the higher standard at the same level. Some other action may turn out to be more rational because efficient and not merely expedient, wise and not merely prudent, socially responsible and not merely just.

Nor is this all. We have seen that the standards of the higher levels take precedence over those of the lower. No matter how efficient or expedient a given action may be, if it is imprudent or unwise, unjust or socially irresponsible, then it will not be rational to do it. On the other hand, a given action may be highly efficient but imprudent and unwise because dangerous, and yet just and socially responsible: e.g. a military operation in wartime. In such a case, the standards of social responsibility and justice will overrule those of the lower level of personal well-being and the action will be rational. *Mutatis mutandis*, an action which is wise and prudent will not be rational if it is unjust or socially irresponsible.

To return to the relation between the two standards of rationality at each level of rational activity. In each case, the difference between them is at once a difference both of kind and of degree. Efficiency is both a different and a better standard of rationality than expediency. Wisdom is not only a different but also a better standard of rationality than prudence. The same is true of social responsibility in relation to justice. The notion of a difference of kind which is also one of degree may seem strange because we are accustomed to think of differences as being either of kind or of degree but not both. This familiar way of thinking is drawn from the procedure of classification in terms of genus and mutually exclusive species. But this does not mean that a difference of kind cannot also be a difference of degree.[1] It means only that where it is, the relation involved cannot be that between genus and mutually exclusive species. Now clearly it is not involved in the case of the two standards of rationality at each level of rational activity. If it were, then what was efficient could never be expedient, what was wise could never be prudent, and what was socially responsible could never be just. In fact what is efficient is always also expedient but expedient with a difference, and equally with the other two pairs. Efficiency is a better standard of rationality than mere expediency alone because it embodies a better understanding of utility. Wisdom is a better standard of rationality than mere prudence because it embodies a better understanding of personal well-being. Social responsibility is a better standard of rationality than mere justice because it embodies a better understanding of social morality.

But the notion of a difference of kind which is also one of degree is applicable not only to the relation between the standards at each level but also to the relation between the levels themselves. Each level embodies a different conception of what rational activity is but this difference is not only a difference of kind, it is also one of degree. To think of rational activity in terms of personal well-being rather than merely in terms of utility, is to think of it not only in a different but in a better way. To think of it in terms of social morality rather than merely in terms of personal well-being is again to think of it not only in a different but in a better way. But why is personal well-being a better conception of rational activity than utility? The answer is: because it rests upon a fuller and more adequate view of human life and the world in which it is lived than does utility. The perspective of utility is confined to what can be made use of to bring about the conditions necessary for the agent's ulterior purposes. These purposes themselves fall outside the scope of thought and decision, apart from

[1] Cf. R. G. Collingwood, *Essay on Philosophical Method*, Clarendon Press, 1933.

questions of possibility. The perspective of personal well-being recognizes that the agent's life is a self-conscious on-going unity and his ulterior purposes now come within the ambit of thought and decision as does the whole direction of his life. In the same way, social morality is a better conception of rational activity than personal well-being because it in its turn embodies a better understanding of life and the world. The perspective of personal well-being is confined to the life and well-being of the agent and to what contributes to it. Neither the social character of human life nor the nature and significance of morality are understood for what they are. But within the perspective of social morality, these are taken into account partially if not completely.

This suggests that the notion of a difference of kind which is also one of degree is applicable not only to the relation between the two standards of rationality at each level but also to that between the standards of different levels. We should then have a scale of standards of rationality, beginning with expediency and culminating in social responsibility. Just as efficiency is not only a different but a better standard of rationality than expediency, so prudence is better than efficiency, wisdom than prudence, justice than wisdom and social responsibility than justice. Now it is certainly more rational to be prudent rather than merely efficient and to be just rather than merely wise. But nevertheless the scale is misleading because it glosses over the distinction between each level of rational activity. An action cannot be efficient without being in some degree expedient. But in order to be prudent, it does not have to be efficient at all, since it does not have to be a means to an end. It may be some phase of an intrinsically worthwhile activity which is carried out with as little risk as possible. Again, an action cannot be wise unless it is in some degree prudent. Recklessness is no part of wisdom. But in order to be just, an action does not have to be wise. It need not contribute to the maintenance and development of the agent's personal well-being. It may even do the reverse, involving him in hardship or sacrifice. Prudence is more rational than efficiency not because it reflects a more adequate understanding of utility but because it embodies a better conception of rational activity than utility, a conception which while it includes utility includes more besides. The same is true of justice in relation to wisdom. The idea of a single scale of standards of rationality obscures these important distinctions.

In order to act rationally at the level of utility, it is not necessary to be able to act rationally at either of the higher levels. What is necessary is that the agent should be able to envisage and bring about the conditions requisite for the execution of his ulterior purposes. But these purposes themselves can be formulated without reference to personal well-being, still less social morality. The agent can arrive at them through the suggestion, advice, or example of other people, or else just capriciously. But in order to act rationally at the level of personal well-being, it is necessary to be able to act rationally at the level of utility. A man utterly incapable of envisaging and bringing about the conditions necessary for the maintenance of his life, would be unable to set about enhancing and enriching its quality wisely and prudently. By the same token, in order to act rationally at the level of social morality, it is necessary to be able to act rationally at the level of personal well-being. A man utterly incapable of determining his conduct wisely and prudently would be unable to form any clear idea of his own interests. Consequently he would be unable to act either justly or unjustly in his dealings with other people. In other words: some capacity for acting rationally at the level of utility is a necessary condition for any rational activity whatever at the level of personal well-being, and some ability to act rationally at the level of personal well-being is a necessary condition for even the most minimal rational activity at the level of social morality, as distinct from the uncritical observance of the prescriptions of established morality.

There is a sense in which the idea of personal well-being may be said to be immanent in rational activity at the level of utility. In order to act efficiently, a man must establish priorities among his several ulterior purposes. Unless he does so, he has no basis for the rational allocation of his scarce resources. What should these priorities be? With reference to what should they be established? Reflection on these questions may suggest to him that he has good reason to make the maintenance and development of his personal well-being a leading consideration in the determination of his conduct. In a similar way, the idea of social morality may be said to be immanent in rational activity at the level of personal well-being. The rational agent at this level is already a moral agent in the sense of knowing how to conform to the prescriptions of the established morality of his society. There will be occasions on which the demands of these prescriptions will conflict with his pursuit of personal well-being. Reflection on the meaning of these conflicts may lead him to see that he has good reason to be moral and to act in the spirit rather than the letter of established morality. Reflection upon the nature and purpose of the various joint activities in which he is involved and with which his personal well-being is bound up, may also lead him to the same conclusion. But neither at the level of utility nor at the level of personal well-being is there anything which inevitably compels a man to advance to the higher level.

A man is rational to the extent that his conduct is rational. But we have seen that conduct may be rational in different degrees and also in different ways, and that the different ways are themselves rational in different degrees. A man is rational to the extent that his conduct is efficient and expedient. But to the extent that it is wise and prudent and not merely efficient and expedient, he is more rational. He is more rational again in so far as he is socially responsible and just rather than merely wise and prudent. It follows that even if one man is wiser and more prudent than another in pursuing his personal well-being, he is still the less rational of the two if the other is more socially responsible and just. Nor does a high degree of efficiency and expediency make up for a lack of wisdom and prudence. It is the wiser man, not the more efficient, who is the more rational. It is the degree of achievement at the higher level which counts in the over-all assessment of a man's rationality. The wise and prudent man will in any case necessarily be capable of some degree of efficiency and expediency and the socially responsible and just man will not be lacking in wisdom and prudence.

What has been said about the rationality of the action of an individual agent is applicable to action undertaken on behalf of a group. In appropriate contexts it is likewise applicable to the corporate action of a group as a whole. Action taken in order to bring about the conditions necessary for a common enterprise to be carried on may be less or more efficient and expedient. The common enterprise itself may be developed with greater or less wisdom and prudence, given its nature and purpose and the opportunities and limitations of the current situation. Again what is done by the group as a whole or on its behalf, may be less or more socially responsible and just having regard to the responsibilities of a wider community and the interests and claims of other groups and individuals. This does not mean, of course, that a group, e.g. a family, a club, a firm, or a nation, has a life and activities of its own over and above those of its members. The action, thought and feeling of a group is always the action, thought and feeling of its individual members. But it is their action, thought and feeling in their capacity as members arising out of the common purposes which they share.

Only a rational agent can be irrational. To be irrational is knowingly to choose the less rational course. It is, e.g. knowingly to adopt the less efficient course; to act with conscious and deliberate recklessness; to do deliberately what you know to be socially irresponsible or unjust. I am irrational, that is to say, whenever I do what I know I have good reason not to do, or fail to do what I know I have good reason to do. To ask: 'Why should I be rational?' is to ask a meaningless question. It amounts to asking: 'What good reason have I to do what I have good reason to do?' Nor can I intelligibly recommend irrationality as a policy of action. To do so would be tantamount to urging that there are good reasons for acting with no good reasons. But all of us some of the time and some of us perhaps much of the time are irrational. What is denied is that all of us are irrational all the time, and what is asserted is that there is such a thing as rational activity of which many of us are capable in various and fluctuating degrees.

This chapter has been concerned not merely with what rational activity is but with what it can be and up to a point necessarily must be. What rational activity can and must be has not been laid down in advance. It has been progressively elicited and elucidated. Starting from the fact that there is such a thing as rational activity which is normative in the sense of being purposive and self-critical, our task has been to explore its character and structure. We have been trying to reach a systematic theoretical understanding of what in a unsystematic practical way we understand already. But we have by no means yet finished. The non-rational foundation of the level of social morality and the problem of moral relativism which it poses have been deferred for discussion in a later chapter. Nor have we so far considered the nature of rule-following activity.

Chapter 4

Rules and Principles

1. RULES AND ORDERS

Rules and orders are not the same but are clearly connected. The typical form of a positive order is an instruction issued on a given occasion commanding the doing of a specific action: 'Shut the door!' 'Stand to attention!' 'Take the letters to the post!' When the action ordered has been carried out, that is the end of the matter. If the action is to be done again on a future occasion, a fresh order must be given. A positive rule, like a positive order, is an instruction to do something. But unlike an order, it is an instruction to do something not merely on a given occasion but on all occasions of a certain kind. When the action prescribed has been carried out once, that is uot the end of the matter. It must be repeated on every occasion of the specified kind unless or until the rule has been repealed.

This suggests that a positive rule is a generalized positive order. 'Always shut the door when you leave a room!' 'Always stand to attention in the presence of an officer!' 'Take the letters to the post every day at lunch-time!' That this is so is borne out by the way in which a rule is enforced. An order must be given on an occasion of the specified kind, commanding the doing of the action prescribed by the rule for all occasions of that kind. But as the above examples show, it is not enough merely to generalize an order. 'Always do . . .!' must be supplemented by a statement of when the prescribed action is to be done. This may take the form of a definite time reference. 'Every day, do . . .!' On the other hand, the time reference may be indefinite. 'Whenever you are in a situation of a certain kind, always do . . .!' Some qualification about time and place is necessary. A merely generalized order would not be a rule. It would only be the command to do something and to keep on doing it *ad infinitum*.

But rules and orders can be negative as well as positive.

They can prohibit and forbid as well as prescribe and command. 'Never kill!' 'Never steal!' 'Never commit adultery!' 'Do not enter that room!' 'Do not talk!' But negative rules, unlike positive rules, need not involve qualifications about time and place. They can prohibit absolutely and unconditionally. 'Never at any time or in any situation, do . . .!' This is possible simply because they are negative. A rule which prescribed that a specific action was to be done at all times, everywhere, would be pointless. No one would be able to follow it. But a rule which prohibits the doing of a specific action at all times and in all places is not pointless. It can be followed since all that is necessary is to refrain from the prohibited action. But negative rules do not have to be absolute and unconditional. They may, and in fact usually do, prohibit the doing of something not everywhere and always but at certain times and in certain kinds of situation. 'Never overtake on a blind corner!' 'Never swim until at least one hour after a meal!' 'Never smoke during Lent!' At times or in situations other than those specified, the prohibited action may be done.

So far we have been concerned only with first-order or primary rules: i.e. rules which directly prescribe or prohibit particular actions. But there are also second-order or secondary rules to be considered.[1] These do not directly prescribe or prohibit particular actions. They are rules about the making and following of rules and the giving and obeying of orders. They confer the authority to make rules and give orders, and specify those who are subject to it. They are positive rules but what they prescribe is that the rules made by a designated authority should be followed and that the orders which it gives should be obeyed. Secondary rules are therefore observed by obeying the orders and following the primary rules of the authorities which they designate. A soldier who obeys the order of his commander is following the secondary rule which prescribes that soldiers are to obey whatever orders are given to them by their officers. The citizen who observes the particular traffic regulations of a given city is following the secondary rule which prescribes that whatever rules the city council sees fit to make to control the traffic are to be followed by all users of the city's roads.

[1] Cf. H. A. L. Hart, *The Concept of Law*, Clarendon Press, 1961.

Secondary rules normally not only confer authority but specify the purposes for which it is to be used. Even in the case of the soldier's obedience to whatever orders his superiors give, it is normally tacitly understood that these orders are to be concerned with military matters. But this need not be so. There is nothing in the form of a secondary rule which makes it necessary that the authority conferred should be limited to specified purposes. Positive secondary rules unlike positive primary rules can be absolute and unconditional. The secondary rule of the Jesuit Order which prescribes absolute and unconditional obedience to the Vicar-General is a case in point. So is the secondary rule binding on all Communist Party members which prescribes absolute and unconditional obedience to the instructions and decrees of Moscow. According to certain theologians, there is a secondary rule which is binding on all mankind and which prescribes absolute and unconditional obedience to the will of God. The content of the divine will is presumed to have been historically revealed in certain sacred texts which include divine primary rules. I have said that secondary rules are positive. This is true since they confer authority and prescribe obedience to it. But what may be called negative quasi-secondary rules are also possible, e.g. a rule of a resistance group in an occupied country prohibiting obedience to the occupying power. Such a rule does not directly prohibit a particular action and is not therefore a primary rule. Nor does it confer authority to make rules and give orders. But it is quasi-secondary as well as negative, since it prohibits obedience to whatever is ordered or enacted by a designated body of persons.

Some rules may come into being at a given moment of time: e.g. when deliberately enacted by a rule-making authority, or when agreed upon by a meeting called for the purpose such as a constituent assembly. But there are many others which are not deliberately enacted and which come into being not at a given moment but gradually over a period. The rules of a language, although they may be formalized by grammarians are not created by them. Other instances are the rules of courtesy and good manners, the rules of the established morality of a society and those general social rules usually called 'the customs of the country'. Rules such as these which originate gradually over time may be called 'conventional' rules to distinguish them from those which come into being through deliberate enactment or explicit formal agreement. They lack the formal sanctions which may be attached to deliberately enacted rules. But since they depend for their continued existence upon continued recognition, they will have at least the informal sanction of public opinion. Rules which originate conventionally may be deliberately enacted into formal codes. Thus moral rules such as the prohibition of murder, theft and rape, to take only obvious examples, have in most countries today been formally enacted into criminal law.

Conventional rules are more fundamental than deliberately enacted rules. The authority of the rule-maker must be respected if a deliberately enacted rule is not to be a dead letter. If this authority is conferred by a deliberately enacted secondary rule, then the authority of the maker of the secondary rule must in its turn be respected. In other words, all secondary rules cannot possibly be deliberately enacted. Some at least must be conventional in origin if there are to be any deliberately enacted rules, whether primary or secondary at all. To put the same point in another way: it is possible deliberately to confer authority only where some authority which has not been deliberately conferred already exists and is respected. A society can exist with only conventional rules, but not with only deliberately enacted rules. The latter are a relatively sophisticated social achievement and presuppose a body of conventional rules as a necessary basis for their development.

It was earlier suggested that rules are generalized orders. This seems to imply that the ability to obey orders must be developed before the ability to follow rules. You must first learn to obey: 'Do X now!' before you follow: 'Always do X on occasions of this kind!' But except under duress, there can be obedience to orders only where a commander's authority to give them is respected. Now to respect an authority is to follow a rule: namely the secondary rule which confers authority upon a designated person or body of persons and prescribes obedience to what they say. It follows that even if primary rules can be regarded as generalized orders, secondary rules cannot be. They are already involved in the giving and obeying of orders. Obeying orders, that is to say, is itself a form of secondary rule following. It is a form which begins to develop early in childhood. To respect parental authority is already albeit implicitly to follow a secondary rule.

Now a child's respect for the authority of his parents must come initially from himself. While they may be able to foster this respect, his parents cannot inculcate it *ab initio* by formal teaching. There can be formal teaching only where the authority of the teacher is already respected. Moreover if a child is to understand what his parents say to him, he must already be able to use language at least in a rudimentary way, and he must therefore already know how to follow certain conventional primary rules. Once more this is something which initially he must learn to do for himself. All this shows that the activity of following both primary and secondary rules has its roots in certain natural human capacities which begin to show themselves at a very early stage in life. Among these are the inter-related capacities to select, recognize, compare and discriminate the objects encountered in early experience. It follows that by no means all primary rules can be regarded as generalized orders, that characterization must be restricted to those articulate primary rules both conventional and deliberately enacted, the following of which can be taught, and which presuppose some capacity for following rules already.

From now on instead of speaking of the 'activity of following rules and obeying orders', I shall speak simply of 'regularian activity'.[1] So far we have been concerned with what regularian activity is and how it is possible, but not with its value and significance for human life. Granted that regularian activity is a necessary feature of human life, in what contexts and for what reasons should rules be made and orders given? What are the scope and limits of regularian activity and when are there good reasons for disobedience? We must consider these questions against the background of the discussion of rational activity in the last chapter.

2. REGULARIAN ACTIVITY AND RATIONAL ACTIVITY

In regularian activity the agent must know what he is doing

[1] Cf. R. G. Collingwood, *The New Leviathan*, Clarendon Press, 1942.

but he need not know why he is doing it. He must know what the rule prescribes or prohibits in order to follow it. He does not have to know the reason for the rule. But in rational activity the agent must know not only what he is doing but why he is doing it. He acts rationally to the extent that he has good reasons for what he does. What the regularian agent does is either right or wrong. He either follows the rule correctly or he does not. But the rational agent's problem is to do what is efficient, wise or responsible, in a given situation. His decision may be relatively good or bad. What he does is better or worse rather than simply right or wrong. The regularian agent's task is the simpler. In a given situation he has only to do what is prescribed for situations of that kind by the appropriate rule and to avoid doing anything which is prohibited. He is concerned with the situation only as being one of a certain kind, not with what is unique or peculiar about it. But the rational agent is concerned with whatever in the situation has a bearing upon his particular ends, his personal well-being, his social commitments. He must take account of whatever is relevant in the situation and must therefore consider what is unique or peculiar about it as well as what it has in common with other situations. More is thus demanded of the rational agent than of the merely regularian agent. Rational activity is a more developed form of human action than merely regularian activity.

But before anyone can become a rational agent he must first become a regularian agent. He must be capable of the less developed before he can achieve the more developed form of activity. A young child lacks the knowledge and experience necessary for rational activity. He is not yet ready to formulate ulterior purposes and take steps to bring about the conditions necessary for their execution. Still less is he ready to take charge of the maintenance and development of his own personal well-being or face the responsibilities of social living. He has to look to others for instruction and guidance. This involves regularian activity in the shape of following secondary rules which confer authority upon parents, teachers and other adults, and which prescribe obedience to what they say. Until he has mastered this elementary regularian activity, he will not make much progress in acquiring the knowledge and experience necessary for rational activity.

But this is only the first step. The development of his ability to follow articulated primary rules marks a further advance. It is rules of this kind which can properly be regarded as generalized orders. As he learns to follow them, a child is in effect learning to generalize instructions and commands. Instead of having to be told each time what to do, he can decide for himself by following the appropriate primary rule. These decisions are not yet those of a rational agent. They are decisions only about what kind of a situation he is in and what rule is appropriate. But his ability to make them is a sign that he is no longer utterly dependent upon others and is in some degree capable of determining his own conduct. Regularian activity in the shape of following articulated primary rules is a step on the way to the fuller self-determination represented by rational activity. A child's capacity for rational activity gradually matures within the framework of his already developed capacity for regularian activity. It begins at the level of utility with his first attempts to formulate ulterior purposes to himself and to set about bringing into being the conditions necessary for their execution.

This account would be misleading if it was taken to mean that regularian activity is only a stepping-stone on the way to rational activity, and can be progressively discarded as the ability to act rationally develops. While it is a stepping-stone, it is also something more. It is itself involved in rational activity and has an indispensable contribution to make to it, even though rational activity is something more than merely regularian activity. At the level of social morality, the rational agent must act in the spirit rather than the letter of established moral rules. While rational activity at this level is clearly more than merely following moral rules, such rule-following is not thereby excluded. We must now try to see what the relation between regularian and rational activity is.

It is always significant to ask about any rule: what is its justification? Why should we have it? This is not the same thing as asking: why should it be followed on this particular occasion? There may be good reasons for having a certain rule and at the same time good reasons for breaking it on a particular occasion owing to special circumstances. The first question may be asked about conventional no less than deliberately enacted rules. What is at issue is not origins but current justification. There are two ways of justifying rules.[1] One is pragmatically: i.e. with reference to the consequences which may be expected to result from its being followed. The other is on substantive grounds: i.e. on the grounds that the actions concerned are of such a nature that they ought to be prescribed or prohibited. We may therefore distinguish between pragmatic rules and substantive rules, according to which kind of justification can be given for them.[2] It is a distinction which will help to understand the contribution which regularian activity can make to rational activity. We shall consider first, primary rules in terms of this distinction at all three levels of rational activity, before going on to the rather more complex case of secondary rules.

Pragmatic primary rules in the shape of rules of technique and skill are clearly relevant at the level of utility. In appropriate cases, it will normally be expedient to follow them since they afford reliable ways of attaining given ends. To do so will also be efficient so far as the agent's time and energy are concerned. Pragmatic rules are also relevant at the level of personal well-being in the shape of rules of health and safety. It will normally be prudent to follow them. More generally: pragmatic primary rules enable past experience to be 'funded' and made available for present rational activity. Consequently it will normally be both wise and efficient to take advantage of them wherever they exist. But such rules are also of great importance in social contexts. Without routine procedures and uniformity of action in recurrent situations, the stability and predictability necessary for social co-operation will be lacking. Primary pragmatic rules enable such routines and uniformities to be established. They are justified in the name of social efficiency and expediency. But such rules will be socially useful only if they are followed by everyone. It will

---

[1] Cf. John Rawles, 'Two Concepts of Rules,' *Philosophical Review*, 1955.
[2] But these two kinds of justification are not mutually exclusive, a rule may be justified on either or both of them.

therefore normally be both just and socially responsible for the individual rational agent to follow them. It will be just because what applies to all, necessarily applies to each, and it will be responsible because it contributes to the better achievement of social purposes. Traffic rules and public health regulations are obvious instances.

Moral rules provide the clearest instances of substantive primary rules. The justification for them lies in what they prescribe and prohibit. That one ought to treat other people in certain ways and not in others is part of the teaching of every established morality. To murder, to steal, to lie, for example, is to treat other people in ways in which they ought not to be treated. To keep one's promises and deal honestly with them at all times is to treat them as they ought to be treated. Rules prohibiting the former actions and prescribing the latter, whether conventional or deliberately enacted, are therefore justified on substantive rather than merely pragmatic grounds. Such rules are clearly relevant at the level of social morality. To follow them will normally be a necessary although not a sufficient condition of acting justly. While acting justly is some-thing more than merely keeping promises and not stealing or murdering, it is normally not less. The rules of games may be described as quasi-substantive primary rules. They are justified as part of any game. To play it necessarily involves following them. They are relevant at the level of personal well-being. If it is wise to play on a given occasion, it is wise to follow the rules, to say nothing of being just to the other players.

Many secondary rules have a pragmatic justification. In many social contexts it is frequently expedient that there should be people in a position to make primary rules. But if this is to come about, all those concerned must be able and willing to follow secondary rules which confer the necessary authority and prescribe respect for it. These secondary rules are justified by the consequences which may be expected to result from their being followed: namely, that certain people will be in a position to make primary rules which will be themselves justified on either pragmatic or substantive grounds. It is not because of who they are that those on whom authority is conferred are to be respected and obeyed. It is because of what they should be able to do with their authority. Pragmatic secondary rules are clearly relevant at the level of social morality. It will normally be socially responsible to follow rules which prescribe obedience to the rules and orders, e.g. of town councils, public health authorities, gas boards and railway companies. At the levels of personal well-being and utility, they will be relevant in the shape of rules conferring authority upon experts. In appropriate contexts it will normally be wise and prudent and also efficient and expedient to do what the doctor says or to follow the directives of the engineer.

But secondary rules may be justified on substantive rather than merely pragmatic grounds. Where this is so, respect for authority will be prescribed on the grounds that those on whom it is conferred possess certain characteristics in virtue of which they inherently deserve it. Respect for their authority, that is to say, is prescribed not because of certain consequences which may be expected to result but because of who they are. The authority of priests over the laity, of absolute monarchs over their subjects, and of parents over their children, has in many societies traditionally been justified on such grounds. In modern Western democracies, respect for the authority of the government is typically justified on the ground of who its members are: namely the constitutionally elected representatives of the people. In the United States, respect for the abstract authority of the Constitution is justified on the substantive ground that it embodies the genius and spirit of the American people. In all these cases, justification is couched in terms of deeply held beliefs and values which lie at the centre of the society's way of life and furnish the foundation for much of its established morality. Secondary rules which are in these ways substantively justified, will always be conventional in origin although they may come to be deliberately enacted for ceremonial reasons. They are clearly relevant at the level of social morality and it will normally be socially responsible to follow them.

Where justified rules exist, it will normally be rational to follow them. To ask for the justification of a rule is already to manifest some degree of rational self-consciousness. The fact that a rule has a pragmatic or substantive justification is a *prima facie* reason to follow it when you are in any situation to which it refers. But a rational agent must deal with the actual situation which confronts him. He must take into account what is unique or peculiar about it as well as what it has in common with others. Now rules cannot take account of what is unique or peculiar about a situation. They can deal only with kinds of situations. Their rubric runs: 'Always . . .', 'Whenever . . .', 'Never . . .' Not only is rational activity inherently something more than merely regularian activity, it may on occasions involve breaking a rule which is justified pragmatically or substantially. Special circumstances may make it more rational to do something else.

That this is so is not difficult to see in the case of pragmatic primary rules. At the level of utility, it is normally efficient and expedient to follow relevant rules of technique and skill. But where owing to special circumstances it is not, the rational agent need have no qualms about breaking them. At the level of personal well-being, if it is wise to run a calculated risk, it will be rational where necessary to violate rules of safety and health. The same is true at the level of social morality where such risks may be necessary for the sake of social responsibility and justice. It is normally responsible and just to follow primary rules which in social contexts have a pragmatic justification. But in an emergency where prompt and decisive action is necessary, it may be socially responsible to ignore such rules: e.g. by-laws or traffic regulations. Again the operation of a procedural rule may involve hardship in a particular case where some purely formal requirement has not been satisfied: when a form has not been filled in correctly, or a subsidiary qualification has not been obtained. In such cases it may well be just to make an exception to the rule.

But what about substantive primary rules? Can it ever be just or socially responsible to break a promise, to lie, to steal, or to kill? There can be no doubt about the answer: there are occasions when it may be. In spite of Kant's doctrine to the contrary, to lie to a would-be murderer about the whereabouts of his intended victim is a lesser evil than telling the truth. Not to lie in such a case is unjust to the victim. It is to sacrifice the victim together with all his interests and claims to your desire for your own formal moral rectitude. There are no relevant grounds upon which such preferential treatment for yourself can be justified. More generally: knowingly to choose the greater rather than the lesser evil will always be unjust to those who have to suffer it because it is to discriminate against their interests and claims without having relevant grounds for doing so. It will also be socially irresponsible where the choice is between social evils, i.e. between greater or lesser harm or damage to the conditions and prospects of social life. The trouble with any moral rule is that, just because it is a rule, it affords no scope for assessing and weighing different evils. If on a given occasion you are confident that to break a promise, to lie, to steal, or to kill, really is the lesser evil, it is rational because it is just, and in appropriate contexts socially responsible, for you to do so. But it will also be socially responsible for you to satisfy yourself to the best of your ability that your confidence is well grounded before acting.

The case of pragmatic secondary rules does not present a serious problem. Such rules are broken when a primary rule made under the authority which they confer is broken, or when an order given under the same authority is disobeyed. Their pragmatic justification lies in the consequences which may be expected to result from the authority which they confer being respected. It follows that where a subordinate has good reasons on the score of social responsibility or justice to disobey an order from a superior, he has *ipso facto* good reasons for breaking the secondary rule which confers authority on his superior and prescribes that he shall respect it. In other words a good reason for breaking a pragmatic secondary rule on a given occasion is and can only be constituted by the fact that on that occasion there is a good reason for breaking a primary rule or disobeying an order made under it. But whenever a secondary rule is broken, respect for the authority it confers is weakened. This must be taken into account over and above the fact that there is a good reason to disobey the order or primary rule. The rational agent must be satisfied that the weakening of respect for the authority concerned is not more irresponsible than complying with the order or rule it has made.

But matters are different in the case of substantive secondary rules. These rules reflect some of the fundamental beliefs and values of a society's way of life. Respect for the authority they confer is justified on the grounds that according to these beliefs and values, those on whom it is conferred deserve to have it. You are to respect the authority of the priest, of the king, of your father, not because of the consequences which should result but because of who he is. To disobey him is not only to weaken his authority, it is to strike at the beliefs and values on which his authority rests, and so to strike at the way of life of your society. In view of this, can it ever be socially responsible to break a substantive secondary rule? Can it ever be the lesser evil? On the face of it the answer is no, since it can never be the lesser evil and hence socially responsible to strike at your society's way of life. This is however only a provisional answer. More will have to be said about it at a later stage in this book. But now we must turn to something which has so far been neglected. What is a principle? How does it differ from a rule? What is the difference, if any, between acting on a principle and acting according to a rule? What is the relation between principles and standards of rationality, and between acting on principles and acting rationally?

3. PRINCIPLES AND THEIR ROLE IN ACTION

The notion of principles is a familiar one in both theoretical and practical contexts. The student of any academic subject encounters it at the outset: principles of mechanics, principles of economics, etc. They are the leading or 'principal' ideas of the subject being studied and it is by their means that he is able to grasp it in detail. They sum up what is fundamental in the body of ideas which make up that subject. Practical principles like theoretical principles are leading ideas but their significance is for action rather than for inquiry and knowledge. They are guides to action in some sphere or context of human activity: e.g. moral principles, political principles, legal principles, principles of strategy and of tactics, principles of engineering, of physical training and of architecture. Some specific instances may be helpful: e.g. moral principles: the lesser evil, and the

'Golden Rule', 'Do unto others as you would have them do unto you'. Political principles: freedom to oppose the government within the limits of the law and to associate for this purpose. Legal principles: equality before the law. Military strategy: the principle of the offensive.

These illustrations show that practical principles imply ideas about the general character of the field to which they are applicable as well as ideas about its nature and purposes and what is important in it. If one asks: 'Why choose the lesser evil?'; 'Why should there be freedom to oppose the government?'; 'Why should there be equality before the law?'; 'Why is the principle of the offensive a good one in military operations?'; significant answers can be given only in terms of moral ideas, of political theory, of legal doctrine and of the theory of strategy. If particular practical principles are to be explained and justified, it must be in terms of relevant theory. This is not of course to say that all practical activity involves or necessitates explicit principles which the agent consciously tries to implement, still less that before you can act practically you must first work out a systematic theory. But it is to say that wherever a deliberate attempt is made to act on principles, theory is implied and at least some understanding of it is necessary in order to implement the principles. It is to point out also that the deliberate formulation of principles necessarily involves systematic theorizing.

Regularian activity is either right or wrong. A rule is either correctly followed or it is not. But with principles, things are not so simple. A given principle may be relatively well or relatively badly implemented. An element of discretion is involved in acting on a principle which is not required in merely following a rule. Unlike a positive primary rule, a principle does not prescribe the action to be done in a situation of a certain kind. Rather it prescribes the policy to be followed in dealing with the current situation in a certain context or field of human activity. What course of action will best carry out this policy must be decided by the agent in the light of the particular circumstances prevailing on a given occasion. The principle of the lesser evil tells the moral agent what to look for but leaves it to him to decide which course in fact is the lesser evil. The political principle of constitutional opposition tells the citizen that he can criticize the government of the day but it does not tell him what to criticize it for. The principle of equality before the law tells those charged with the administration of justice what to aim at in their work. But it is left to them to decide what arrangements must be made to achieve this aim and what special steps may be necessary in particular cases.

Regularian activity may sometimes call for the exercise of discretion. It is a moral rule that promises are to be kept but what a man must do to follow it necessarily depends upon what promises he has made. Considerable ingenuity may sometimes be necessary if he is to do what he said he would. But he cannot be in any doubt about the action which is called for by the rule. His problem can only be how to put himself in a position to do it. A man who is trying to act on a principle has a tougher problem. He has to decide how to meet a given situation in a way most appropriate to the context to which it belongs. His principle will tell him what to look for and what to aim at. But it will not tell him what action is called for. That he must decide for himself in the light of the particular circumstances of the current situation. Unlike the regularian agent, he cannot simply treat it as a situation of a certain kind. He must take account of what is unique or peculiar about it.

This suggests that acting on principles is more like rational activity than regularian activity. Indeed it is clear that more than just resemblance is involved. Rational activity is itself a case of acting on principles. Each standard of rationality may be regarded as a principle of action. Thus expediency is the principle of doing whatever will best enable a given end to be attained: efficiency, the principle of allocating scarce resources among various ends according to the relative priority of each; prudence, the principle of safety first; wisdom, of the realistic enhancement and enrichment of the quality of personal life. Justice is the principle of treating the interests and claims of other people as being of equal value to your own except where there are relevant grounds for treating them differently. Social responsibility is the principle of making whatever contribution one can to promote and advance the various social enterprises in which one is involved. The relations between the standards at each level can also be formulated as principles of action: e.g. that expediency should be subordinated to efficiency; prudence to wisdom; and justice to social responsibility. So can the relations between the levels themselves; e.g. utility is for the sake of personal well-being and social morality; social morality must take precedence over personal well-being. All these principles sum up the leading ideas of the theory of rational activity and for their explanation and justification one must go to that theory. Rational activity then is not something different from acting on principles. It is acting on principles of the highest generality and greatest relevance.

But if standards of rationality are the most general principles of action, how are they related to the specific principles of particular fields and contexts? Rational activity is activity in which the agent has reasons for what he does and on any given occasion the better his reasons the more rational his action. What reasons are there for trying to implement the specific principles of a particular field or context? At first sight, the question seems foolish. If you are engaged in engineering or navigation, it is surely obvious that you should try to implement the relevant principles. But why should you engage in engineering or navigation in the first place? Are there good reasons for doing so? The answer depends partly upon your circumstances and situation and partly upon the nature and purpose of engineering and navigation as fields of human activity. They are primarily techniques, i.e. organized ways of achieving certain kinds of ends. If you happen to want ends of these kinds, then it may well be expedient and probably also efficient for you to engage in them and to try to implement their relevant principles. On the other hand, it may be more efficient for you to hire someone else suitably qualified to do the work for you. But other reasons are also possible. Engineering and navigation are not merely techniques. They are or can be professions. If you find them intrinsically interesting and possess some aptitude for them, it may well be wise to embark on one of them as a career. If you have done so and become a professional, it follows as a matter of justice to your clients as well as a wise contribution to your own personal well-being, that on any given occasion you ought to implement the relevant specific principles.

Take the case of military operations: in battle, there are obvious reasons for trying to act on tactical principles. But why are you fighting in this battle on this occasion? I am carrying out the orders of my commanding officer. But why are you carrying them out? Because on military service it is one's duty to obey one's commander. But why are you on military service? Because it is my profession; or again: because it is my duty as a citizen at the present time. The last two answers involve considerations of personal well-being and of social morality. Granted that it is wise from the standpoint of personal well-being to make soldiering a career, or socially responsible to enlist and serve in the army, the rest follows. What all this shows is that standards of rationality regarded as principles of action do not apply directly to particular fields and contexts. Rather they apply to the situations in which decisions have to be made about whether to engage in them. But they also take precedence over specific principles if there is a conflict: e.g. where implementing a given engineering principle endangers the lives of workmen, considerations of justice constitute an overriding reason for abandoning the attempt. But standards of rationality as principles of action cannot replace or supersede specific principles. The latter remain valid within their own fields. When they are set aside, it is because on a given occasion there are good reasons for sacrificing what can be achieved by implementing them, reasons which derive from outside the particular field or context in question.

But what about moral principles? Morality is not a limited field like engineering, navigation or military operations. It is co-extensive with conduct in the sense that moral considerations are never irrelevant. Moral principles such as 'the Golden Rule' or 'the lesser evil', are clearly not specific principles. On the contrary they are principles of the highest degree of generality. How then are they related to standards of rationality since the latter are also general principles of action? The answer is that they are abridgements or partial formulations of them. 'You ought to do unto others as you would have them do unto you' because this is to act justly towards them. You ought to choose the lesser evil because to do so is both socially responsible and just. General moral principles must be explained and justified in terms of the theory of morality and the theory of morality is itself an integral part of the general theory of rational activity. It follows, according to the development of that theory in the last chapter, that social responsibility and justice are ultimate moral principles. This conclusion however is only provisional until our discussion of rational activity has been completed.

But there are specific as well as general moral principles, for example, codes of ethics of various professions. Such principles concern the members of the profession in their dealings with the public. They involve the accepted ideas in the profession about its nature and purpose and the relevant values of the society in which the profession is being practised. In every established morality there will also be specific moral principles connected with particular virtues which the members of the society are expected to cultivate and practice. They ought, e.g. to be resolute and unflinching in the face of danger; to be kind and considerate to other people; to stand by and defend their friends when they are in trouble, regardless of personal inconvenience; to bear success with modesty and failure with equanimity. It is by implementing these principles that they will practise the virtues of courage, unselfishness, personal loyalty and fortitude. These virtues themselves are constituents of the established morality. They represent ideals to be pursued in the various aspects of life to which they severally refer.

Where there is a clash, standards of rationality as general principles of action take precedence over the specific principles of particular fields and contexts. In the same way, general moral principles, social responsibility and justice take precedence over specific moral principles if and when a conflict between them arises. For the sake of justice it may sometimes be necessary to forego kindness and consideration. The demands of social responsibility may make it necessary to ignore a friend's call for help: e.g. when he is wanted by the police. If your failure on a given occasion is due to someone else's malice or deceit, it may well be just for you to protest vigorously rather than merely acquiesce in the outcome with equanimity. On a particular occasion, social responsibility may make discretion the better part of valour and point to withdrawing from danger rather than facing it: e.g. where you have family commitments or an important official position. Specific moral principles, just because they are specific and not general, cannot be ultimate.

Summarizing the main conclusions of this section: principles, like rules, prescribe, but what they prescribe are policies rather than particular actions. Unlike the merely regularian agent, the man who acts on principles has to exercise discretion in the face of the current situation. He must take account of its peculiarities as well as its resemblances. Rational activity may be regarded as acting on principles of the highest order of generality. But acting on the specific principles of particular fields and contexts, or on specific moral principles, is something less than fully-fledged rational activity, since the rationality of engaging in the particular field or context remains open, as does the question of whether there is any conflict between its specific principles and standards of rationality. Acting on specific principles thus appears to be a form of action intermediate between regularian activity and rational activity properly so-called.

4. SOME FURTHER CONSIDERATIONS

The capacity to act rationally is gradually developed within the framework of regularian activity. An agent must be able to act with some degree of rationality in terms of the lower standard at each level before he can go on to the higher standard. He must have at least some notion of expediency before he can begin to be efficient. Before he can become wise he must already be prudent. He cannot begin to be socially responsible until he knows how to be just. Social responsibility and wisdom are relatively sophisticated standards. They presuppose at least some personal maturity and experience of the world. Efficiency involves establishing priorities among ulterior purposes and therefore presupposes some knowledge of intrinsically worth-while activities and experiences. But this is not true in the case of expediency, prudence and justice. Once some capacity for regularian activity has developed, rudimentary action in terms of these standards can begin early in life. A child who, in the course of play, formulates an ulterior purpose for himself and tries to bring about the condition necessary for its execution, is already attempting to act in terms of expediency. When he begins to decide for himself whether or not something is safe, he is beginning to be prudent. When he begins to be concerned about what is fair as between himself and his fellows, he is already beginning to pay heed to the idea of justice. These rudimentary efforts are not yet rational activity at the levels of utility, personal well-being and social morality properly so called. They are natural tendencies in the child which the established morality of his society will foster and encourage. They are the seeds out of which fully-fledged rational activity will later develop. As a child comes to act justly, prudently and expediently with increasing regularity and reliability, he progressively acquires the character of a rational agent.

This has a bearing on the conclusion that acting on principles is a form of action intermediate between regularian and rational activity. It would be false if it was taken to mean that before one can act rationally at all, one must first be able to act on specific principles. The attempt deliberately to implement the specific principles of a particular field or context of human activity calls for a certain amount of intellectual sophistication. It can be made only by an agent who already has some idea of what it is to act expediently and prudently. Something more than the rudimentary abilities of a child will be necessary before an agent can grasp and master the specific principles of say, taxidermy or horticulture. He must already to some extent at least be a rational agent at the level of utility if not at the level of personal well-being. This does not alter our conclusion that acting on specific principles is something less than rational activity properly so called. As a form of action, it is intermediate between regularian and rational activity, calling for more in the way of discretion and initiative from the agent than the former but less than the latter. But the order of development of these capacities is rather different.

What in fact happens is something along the following lines. The capacity for regularian activity makes its appearance in early childhood in the bosom of the family. Next comes the first signs of embryonic rational activity in the shape of the child's rudimentary efforts to act expediently, prudently and justly. Then as the child's experience widens and he encounters new rules in new contexts, his capacity for regularian activity is further developed. He learns to act on specific principles only after he has passed beyond his first rudimentary efforts to act rationally and has become capable of acting at the level of utility with some degree of expediency and perhaps efficiency. But after he has been initiated into particular fields and contexts of human activity and become able to implement their several specific principles, his capacity for rational activity goes on developing. As he grows up he gradually becomes capable of rational activity at the level of personal well-being and at the level of social morality, and becomes able to act rationally in terms of the higher standards at each of these levels. After he has become a rational agent at all three levels, he may further develop his ability to act on specific principles as the range and scope of his activities expands and he becomes proficient in new fields and contexts. Rational activity begins to develop within the framework of regularian activity, and the ability to act on specific principles develops within the framework of the still developing capacity for rational activity. The one grows out of the other, which continues to develop alongside it.

But this needs qualifying to take account of specific moral principles which are part of the established morality of every society. A child first encounters them and is encouraged by the praise and blame of adults to begin trying to implement them, at about the same time as he learns to follow the substantive primary rules of morality. While learning that he must not lie or steal and must keep his word, he also learns that he ought to be kind and considerate to other people, to be brave in the face of discomfort and pain and, perhaps a little later, helpful to those in difficulties. The ability to act on specific moral principles develops earlier than the ability to act on the specific principles of particular fields and contexts. The child must be capable of the elementary regularian activity involved in respecting the authority of his parents, et cetera. His capacity for rational activity need not have developed to the extent which is necessary in the case of the latter principles. He is likely at this stage to think of the 'moral' largely in terms of substantive secondary rules. He must not lie or steal and ought

136

to be brave and unselfish because his parents have told him so. Even his independent rudimentary apprehension of justice as fairness will largely be coloured by the parental approval which it calls forth. Not until later when he is on the way to becoming a fully-fledged rational agent will he be in a position to understand what is to be said for moral rules and specific moral principles on their own account.

But it is not only children who think of morality in terms of substantive secondary rules. What is called religious morality involves the same idea. Let us imagine a society whose way of life is centred round the practice of a certain religion. According to this religion, there is a god and all must obey him. His will has been revealed to certain persons in the past and takes the form of a set of instructions for the conduct of life. These consist of rules to be followed, virtues to be cultivated and specific moral principles to be implemented. Among the rules there are certain substantive secondary ones conferring authority upon priests to interpret the divine will in doubtful cases and where necessary to fill it out in detail, and prescribing obedience to them. For such a society, to be moral is to carry out to the best of one's ability the divine instructions. This means following the divine rules, cultivating the divine virtues, implementing the divine specific moral principles, and doing whatever may be commanded by the priests. To be immoral is to flout the divine instructions and to fail to respect the authority of the priests.

While this society is imaginary it has certain historical overtones. Its religion has something in common with Judaism and with some forms of Christianity. In such a society, morality is fundamentally regularian in character. It is a matter of following the substantive secondary rule which prescribes obedience to the will of God and of following other secondary rules which prescribe respect for the authority of divinely appointed officials, i.e. priests. This means that for the laity, moral conduct is a matter of living according to the divine instructions as they are interpreted by the priests. This is true for the priests themselves who must also live by their interpretations. But they have in addition the special duty of doing the interpreting and of acting as both moral and religious authorities over the laity, being the final abiters of both conduct and belief.

In such a society, a theocracy, there is scope for rational activity on the part of the members, the laity no less than the priesthood. That this is so at the levels of utility and personal well-being will scarcely be contested. No doubt their religious beliefs, especially on the subject of the hereafter and personal salvation, will influence their ideas about what is wise and prudent here below. But each of them clearly has good reason to do the best he can according to his rights, to enhance and enrich the quality of his life, and to act efficiently and expediently in doing what is necessary to maintain and develop it. But that there can be rational activity at the level of social morality is by no means so obvious. The regularian character of the morality of a theocracy appears, on the face of it, to rule it out.

But this is not so. The members of a theocracy are involved in the joint activity of trying to maintain and develop a way of life based on their common religion. As a participating member of the group each has good reason to treat the others justly. The religious beliefs in which the common life is centred and especially the divine instructions, furnish a basis for deciding what is to count as just treatment. By the same token, each has good reason to do whatever he can to promote and advance the common enterprise and to help the group meet and surmount the problems which currently face it. For the laity this may for the most part mean little more than co-operating loyally and intelligently with the policies and plans of the priests. But all have good reason to live and act as socially responsible members of the theocracy. Notwithstanding its fundamentally regularian character, there is scope within the framework of theocratic morality for rational activity at the level of social morality on the part of all the members.

In Section 2 of this chapter we saw that there are occasions on which it may be just or socially responsible to break a substantive primary rule. The substantive justification for the primary rules in the divine instructions is simply that they are included in these instructions. It is the divine will that the actions which they prescribe should be done and those which they prohibit should be left undone. But there will be occasions in a theocracy no less than in other societies when to break a substantive primary rule may be the lesser evil. To follow it may mean acting unjustly or irresponsibly. It may mean violating a specific moral principle contained in the divine instructions: e.g. telling the truth at the expense of being cruel or keeping a promise at the cost of failing to help a friend in dire distress. If the principle of the lesser evil is not expressly stated in the divine instructions, it is one which intelligent priests may reasonably be expected to recognize and authorize. The conclusion that there are occasions when it may be just or socially responsible to break substantive primary rules applies to a theocracy as to any other society.

We also saw in Section 2 that it can never be socially responsible to break a substantive secondary rule. This is well illustrated in the case of a theocracy. The foundation of theocratic morality is the substantive secondary rule which prescribes obedience to the divine will. For members of a theocracy it can never be the lesser evil to disobey the divine will. The same is true of the substantive secondary rules which confer authority upon priests and prescribe obedience to them by the laity. The priests are to be obeyed because of who they are: namely the deity's human proconsuls and the official interpreters of his instructions. It follows that within the regularian framework of theocratic morality the priests have more scope for rational activity at the level of social morality than the laity. In interpreting the divine instructions, the priests will have to consider individual situations. In the face of novelty and change they cannot apply old rubrics mechanically. They must exercise responsible leadership on behalf of the whole theocratic society in the face of the current exigencies in its life. But the laity have only to co-operate intelligently and loyally with the policy of the priests without troubling themselves about its formulation.

The substantive justification for the fundamental secondary rule of theocratic morality, that the divine will is to be obeyed, lies in the religious beliefs around which the life of a theocratic society is centred. If a lay member asks: 'Why should I obey the divine will?' he is reminded of these beliefs thus: 'We believe that there is a god, that his will has been made known, and that it is our duty to obey it.' If the questioner remains obdurate, all that can be done is to affirm the truth of these beliefs. They cannot be called in question without threatening the foundations of the way of life of the theocratic society. But what is true of theocratic morality is true of rational activity at the level of social morality in general. Rational agents at this level can criticize their own and each other's conduct on the score of its justice and social responsibility. What they cannot do is call in question the fundamental character of their common life. There is a principle of social conservatism implicit in rational activity at the level of social morality: namely that the fundamental character of the existing way of life is to be preserved. To the extent that there is doubt or ambiguity about its fundamental character, there will be doubt and ambiguity about what is just and socially responsible and then rational activity at the level of social morality will be the more difficult. But this brings us back to the problem of moral relativism.

Chapter 5

Freedom and Rights: an Interim View

1. THE NEGATIVE THEORY OF FREEDOM

According to the negative theory, freedom is the absence of constraint. For Mill, the problem was: upon what principle is the exercise of socially organized constraint justified? If constraint is not to be arbitrary, it must be socially organized and exercised on the basis of a principle. A state of affairs in which people interfered with and coerced one another capriciously would be a Hobbesian state of nature. But why does there have to be socially organized constraint at all? Is it really necessary? Mill's answer is contained in his principle of self-protection. The exercise of socially organized constraint is justified for the sake of preventing harm to others. Some people are prepared to harm others and a society is justified in taking steps to prevent them. From the standpoint of common sense, this settles the matter. But it is worthwhile pursuing the question further against the background of the last two chapters. What is the nature of constraint? What are its scope and limits?

There is a difference between constraint and restraint. To constrain someone is to make him do what he does not want to do. To restrain him is to prevent him doing what he wants to do. But we shall for brevity speak only of constraint, treating restraint as negative constraint. The essence of the matter in both cases is the exercise of coercion. Constraint can be used to enforce regularian activity. People can be made to follow rules and obey orders through fear of the consequences if they do not. It can also be used to enforce rational activity at the level of utility to enforce the implementing of relevant specific principles. A man may be ordered to bring about a certain end, threatened with dire consequences if he fails, but left to himself to decide how to do it. Blackmail is an obvious instance. But constraint cannot be used to enforce rational activity at the levels of personal well-being and social morality. A man cannot be forced to pursue his personal well-being wisely and prudently. Nor can he be forced to act responsibly and justly as a member if his society.

This is not all. A man faced by constraint can resist instead of submitting. But it may well be the path of prudence, if not of valour, to submit. Does this mean that constraint can be used to force a man to be prudent? On the face of it, no: since in submitting, a man is choosing the path of prudence instead of valour. He is deciding, albeit most reluctantly, to allow someone else to determine his conduct for him, instead of determining it for himself. His being subject to constraint, that is to say, consists in his reluctant compliance with the will of another. But this overlooks something. A man may try to resist but his resistance may be broken. He may be tortured and literally forced to adopt the path of prudence. This means that it may be possible to force a man to be prudent if those exercising constraint are sufficiently ruthless. It follows that constraint properly so called is always external. It is always exercised by a person or body of persons against another. It is only in a metaphorical sense that a man can be said to constrain himself by self-discipline. But it may sometimes be appropriate to speak of external constraint in order to emphasize that it is constraint in the literal not the metaphorical sense which is meant.

The distinction between deliberately enacted and conventional rules has a bearing on the limits of socially organized constraint. Deliberately enacted rules presuppose conventional rules. What is true of deliberately enacted rules is true also of socially organized constraint. Systematic methods of compulsion to secure obedience to rules can be developed only in a society where most people most of the time are already obeying without compulsion. In a Hobbesian state of nature, it would be impossible to organize systematic compulsion to put an end to anarchy and establish order. Those who are to do the organizing would already have to be in a social state not a state of war. They would have to be capable of co-operating together and therefore of following conventional rules without compulsion. This means that organized constraint cannot be the basis of social life. Social life must already be going on if socially organized constraint is to be possible. This is not to deny the possibility of tyranny or of enforced enslavement, But there must be people to establish the tyranny and to enforce the slavery. These people at least cannot be slaves or subject to tyranny; and those subjected to tyranny must be capable of maintaining a way of life of their own before they can be forced to modify or abandon it.

Some measure of constraint is necessary within the family. Children are not fully fledged rational agents. They must sometimes be made by their parents to do things which they do not want to do. But what about the wider society within which the family has its being? Why does there have to be socially organized constraint at all? The short answer is: human shortcomings. Without it, law breaking would be more frequent. In any society the law consists, or at least ought to consist, of rules which in social contexts have either a pragmatic or substantive justification. If a society is to hold together, most of its members most of the time must be able and willing to obey these rules without compulsion. But there will be some who will be strongly tempted to break them. Socially organized constraint in the shape of an efficient police force, judiciary and penal institutions, provides strong prudential considerations not to yield to the temptation and gives protection to the rest of society. Societies can exist and have existed without socially organized constraint but constraint is necessary if the members of a society are to be protected from those who are unwilling to meet the minimum obligations of social living. Those against whom it is exercised are only being made to do what they ought to be prepared to do without compulsion. Mill is substantially right. Socially organized constraint is justified for the sake of preventing harm, if by 'harm' is meant the avoidable inconvenience and injury resulting from the breach of rules which from the standpoint of social morality there is normally good reason to follow.

But some qualifications are necessary. It does not follow that every rule which in social contexts is pragmatically or substantively justified should automatically be brought within the scope of socially organized constraint. A completely unenforceable law is a bad law. It can be broken with impunity and this brings law as such into disrepute. On the other hand, the legal enforcement of any rule can never be one hundred per cent successful. The most that can be done is to make it highly probable that offenders will be caught. In many cases the limited efficacy of enforcement must be weighed against the social evil of the offence. Prostitution is a case in point. In deciding whether or not to bring any rule within the scope of socially organized constraint, the only rational test is the net advantage to the life of the society.

There are occasions on which it may be socially responsible or just to break a rule which is pragmatically or substantively justified. Rules can deal only with kinds of situation. They cannot allow for special circumstances or individual peculiarities. When a rule is made compulsory, inconvenience or suffering may result if provision is not made for exceptions to it. This may be done through a specific principle which indicates what is to count as a legitimate exception: for instance, killing in self-defence. But the specific principle must be capable of un-ambiguous interpretation and speedy implementation. A court must be able to decide beyond reasonable doubt and without undue delay that the particular circumstances in which an action was done really makes it a legitimate exception. But where such decisions are inherently difficult, or require much time and trouble, compulsory obedience to the rule may be the greater evil. Legal prohibition of 'living in sin' would be an instance. Here too, the only rational test is the principle of net advantage.

In justifying socially organized constraint, I said that those against whom it is exercised are only being made to do what they ought to be prepared to do anyway. But this assumes that all the members of a society, including those against whom organized constraint is exercised, are in agreement about the fundamental character of its way of life. Where this is lacking, for instance in a divided society or in one in which old ideas and values are becoming obsolete, some of those subjected to organized constraint will not agree that they are only being made to do what they ought to be prepared to do anyway. A religious minority will not agree that they ought to follow rules which have their substantive justification in the alien creed of the majority. In other words: the inherent limitations of rational activity at the level of social morality are limitations also upon the moral justification which can be given for the exercise of socially organized constraint.

What then is the idea of a free society which is logically implied by the negative theory of freedom? It is not the idea of a society without any system of organized constraint at all. That would mean that many of the members would be subjected to arbitrary constraint in the shape of avoidable inconvenience and injury. Rather it is the idea of a society with such a system, the exercise of which is controlled by two considerations. The first is that it is never used except to enforce obedience to orders and rules which in social contexts have either a pragmatic or substantive justification. The second is that it should be exercised to compel obedience to such rules and orders only when there is a net advantage to the life of the society in doing so. It follows as a necessary condition that only a society in which there is widespread agreement among the members can be a free society. This fact of agreement, together with the two considerations governing the exercise of socially organized constraint, make up the necessary and sufficient conditions for a society to be free according to the logic of the negative theory.

But there is an important corollary. The idea of a free society is not the idea of a society with a way of life of a special and distinctive kind. Provided that the members are in fundamental agreement, it does not matter what the way of life is, about which they are agreed. A highly stratified society whose way of life is based upon a hereditary caste system can in principle be a free society. So can a theocracy. So even can a slave-owning society, provided that the slaves accept their servile status without resentment. This may be surprising but it is a conclusion which the negative theory entails.

It is a conclusion which presumably is quite acceptable to Cranston. At all events there is nothing in his argument which gives him rational grounds for objecting to it. But it is one which Mill, albeit inconsistently, would have repudiated. For him, a free society is one in which all the adult members enjoy freedom of speech, and freedom for individuality. This rules out a caste society, a theocracy, and a slave-owning society, no matter how agreed their members may happen to be. This suggests that Mill needs something more than a merely negative theory of freedom if he is to justify his idea of a free society. Such a society on his view has a way of life of a special and distinctive kind. Whether the conclusion entailed by the negative theory is acceptable to Berlin is at least doubtful. His remarks about freedom of choice suggest that he regards it as something of intrinsic value. It is also clear that he thinks of the way of life of a free society as being characterized by certain specific moral rules. But this only shows that, like Mill, he needs something more than a merely negative theory of freedom to make good his case.

2. THE POSITIVE THEORY: PERSONAL AND MORAL FREEDOM

The positive theory is bound up with the ethical doctrine of self-realization. According to this doctrine, selfhood is something to be achieved rather than a merely empirical phenomenon. Moreover, it is something which can be achieved only through social co-operation, and rational moral conduct is conceived of as intelligent and responsible social co-operation devoted to its achievement. This is the point of departure for the positive theory. Freedom has an internal as well as an external side. On its internal side it is the condition of mind and character of the rational moral agent. Such an agent is emancipated from subjection to the natural impulses and inclinations which make up his merely empirical self and is free to become the best that he has it in him to be. But the significance of the external side of freedom is also recognized. What is important is not the absence of external constraint as such but its absence in the form of interference by anyone, with anyone else's rational moral conduct and hence with his self-realization. This external freedom can be secured by a system of rights maintained by law, and a society in which it is secured is a free society. So much for the essentials of the positive theory according to Green and Bosanquet: its central thought may be summed up in the proposition that rational moral conduct, self-realization, and freedom are co-extensive. They are different but complementary aspects of a single idea: that of a society devoted to the harmonious development by all its members of their various gifts and capacities.

There is a sense in which the concept of constraint lends support to the positive theory. This has nothing to do with being forced to be free. Rather it is a matter of what is implied by the concept of constraint. To subject someone to constraint is to make him do what you want and prevent him doing what he wants. He is not free because his conduct is being determined not by himself but by you. Now this is another way of saying that he is free when he determines his conduct for himself. To be free is to be self-determining. Absence of constraint by other people is a necessary condition for self-determination. But the ability to determine one's conduct for oneself is a positive human capacity. This is recognized by the positive theory with its distinction between the external and internal sides of freedom. Only someone capable of at least some degree of self-determination can be subjected to constraint. You can be compelled to do something against your will only if you already have a will, that is, are able to determine your conduct for yourself. You must first be free before you can be made unfree by constraint.

We saw in the last chapter that rational activity is a more developed form of action than merely regularian activity. The rational agent determines his conduct for himself in a way in which the regularian agent does not. But the development of the ability to follow explicitly articulated primary rules marks a step forward towards the fuller self-determination involved in rational activity. This development from secondary rule-following to primary rule-following, and from the latter to rational activity, may fairly be regarded as a development in personal freedom because it is a development in the agent's powers of self-determination. The child who has learned to follow explicitly articulated primary rules is no longer dependent upon adults for instructions and orders. The development of the capacity to act rationally, and along with it to act on specific principles, marks a further development in personal freedom. The rational agent is not dependent upon rules. He is not limited to treating a given situation as one of a certain kind which is covered by a particular rule. He can treat it on its merits as the individual situation which it is.

There is however a sense in which personal freedom has a negative aspect. The child who has learned to follow primary rules has freed himself from complete dependence upon adults. The man who has become a rational agent has freed himself from dependence upon rules. But this freedom from dependence upon other people and upon rules comes about through a development in the individual's powers of self-determination. What frees him is not the removal of an external constraint but the growth of a positive capacity within himself. In other words, the negative aspect of personal freedom is a by-product of its positive character as self-determination. This is not to deny that the absence of external constraint is a necessary condition for personal freedom. If a man is subject to constraint by other people, he cannot determine his conduct for himself. But a view which, like the negative theory, equates personal freedom with the absence of external constraint, sees only half the picture. The positive theory, with its distinction between the external and internal sides of freedom, is able to do better.

The distinction between the levels of utility and personal well-being has a bearing upon the idea of personal freedom. In order to act rationally at the former level, a man must be capable of deciding what ends are necessary for the execution of his ulterior purposes, as well as how best to bring them about. He is more free than the merely regularian agent because he does not have to depend upon advice and instructions from other people, nor upon established technical rules, although he can avail himself of both if he judges it efficient or expedient to do so. But at the level of utility, there is no rational basis for making decisions about ulterior purposes. The agent must either rely upon the precept and example of other people, or else just follow his own whims and inclinations. But at the level of personal well-being, this defect of the level of utility is overcome. The agent now has a touchstone with reference to which he can formulate ulterior purposes and make decisions about their execution. He is no longer dependent either upon other people, or upon his own whims and inclinations. To the extent that he directs his life wisely and prudently, he achieves a degree of self-determination and hence of personal freedom, which is not open to the merely utilitarian rational agent.

Green and Bosanquet however based their version of the positive theory upon their ethical doctrine of self-realization. Its central tenet is that selfhood is something to be achieved, rather than a merely empirical phenomenon. So far as it goes, this is unexceptionable. What a man becomes, rests at least in part with himself. He can make deliberate efforts towards self-cultivation and development, and with a little luck, may have some success. Nobody knows what he can do until he tries, and so long as a man retains his health and the normal range of human faculties, the possibility of his becoming more than he has so far become, remains open. In an obvious sense, self-realization falls within the scope of rational activity at the level of personal well-being. A man who directs his life wisely has good reason to do what he can to discover, exercise, and develop his native gifts and capacities.

Self-determination is itself a positive human capacity. It follows that if a man achieves the degree of self-determination of which he is capable, he is in one respect becoming what he has it in him to be. But it does not follow that he will be successful in developing specific gifts and capacities, although he may be well endowed and is trying to promote his personal well-being wisely and prudently. Lack of opportunity, pressure of circumstances, or sheer misfortune, may prevent him from developing his potentialities to anything like their full extent. A distinction must be drawn between the generic capacity for self-determination, and specific gifts and capacities which relate to particular spheres of human activity and experience. This distinction discloses two senses of 'self-realization'. It may mean either the realization of the generic capacity, or of specific gifts and capacities, and these are not identical.

A man may realize himself satisfactorily in the first sense without doing very well in the second. The converse is also possible. He may meet with a fair degree of success in the second sense while being largely baulked and frustrated in the first. A slave with natural gifts as a craftsman may succeed in developing them under the auspices of an enlightened master.

But his servile status may well prevent him from achieving anything like the degree of personal self-determination of which he is innately capable. A man may be richly endowed with certain specific gifts and capacities, while being well below average so far as the generic capacity is concerned. As a poet, or a composer, he may rank as a genius, and yet may be temperamentally incapable of directing his life wisely and managing his affairs prudently. If he is to do his best work and realize himself as an artist, other people must look after him and organize his life for him.

Green and Bosanquet however do not distinguish between the two senses of 'self-realization'. This weakens their version of the positive theory by introducing an element of ambiguity. According to the first sense, self-realization and personal freedom are different sides of the same thing. A man realizes himself by developing his generic capacity for self-determination and becoming as much of a free person as he has it in him to be. But according to the second sense, this is not so. A man may be able to realize himself with some degree of success, without being able to develop his generic capacity for self-determination to anything like its full extent. In view of this, it may be thought that little is to be gained by introducing the concept of self-realization into the theory of freedom. It is the concept of self-determination, not the concept of self-realization, which is important. But as we shall see, the concept of self-realization has something to contribute, provided that the distinction between the two senses is observed.

We have seen that rational activity involves a greater degree of self-determination than merely regularian activity, and that within rational activity, the same is true of the level of personal well-being in relation to the level of utility. This suggests that it is at the level of personal well-being that personal freedom is most fully achieved. But for Green and Bosanquet it is the rational moral agent, not the merely rational agent, who is internally free. This prompts the question: why stop at the level of personal well-being? Social morality is a higher level of rational activity than personal well-being, and may therefore be expected to involve a greater degree of self-determination. Rational activity as such involves a greater degree of self-determination than regularian activity, and this suggests that the higher the level of rational activity, the greater the degree of self-determination. This in turn suggests that it is the rational agent at the level of social morality, rather than at the level of personal well-being, who is most fully a free person.

But this must be examined more closely. Unlike the regularian moral agent, the rational agent at the level of social morality acts in the spirit rather than the letter of established moral rules. If and when he judges it to be necessary for the sake of social responsibility or justice to break any of them, he will do so. He therefore achieves a greater degree of self-determination and is more free than the regularian moral agent. But is he more free than the rational agent at the level of personal well-being? We saw in Chapter 3 that a man must first become a regularian moral agent before he can become a rational agent at the level of personal well-being. But what about after he has reached this level? Does he have to go on being a regularian moral agent in order to pursue his personal well-being wisely and prudently? If so, then there is a sense in which he is less free than the rational agent at the level of social morality. As a regularian moral agent, he is dependent upon established moral rules in a way in which the latter (who acts according to their spirit rather than their letter) is not. But is this in fact true? What connection, if any, is there between morality and the rational pursuit of personal well-being?

A man who pursues his personal well-being wisely and prudently will necessarily be involved in many forms of co-operation with other people. These extend from family life through economic division of labour to institutionalized political activity. He will have been initiated into many of them in the course of growing up. If he is to provide for his own survival, and over and beyond that, to enhance and enrich the quality of his life, he will find that participation in many of them is indispensable. But there can be fruitful co-operation only where there is mutual trust. Those concerned must deal honestly with one another, and must be able and willing to meet the obligations which their common enterprise involves. It follows that there is a sense in which morality is relevant to rational activity at the level of personal well-being. It will normally be wise and prudent for the rational agent to participate constructively in the various joint activities which directly or indirectly contribute to his personal well-being. That means acting morally in the sense of being a loyal and responsible member of the group concerned. But the extent of his moral commitment will be limited to what he judges to be relevant to his personal well-being. If a particular joint activity ceases to interest him, it will be wise for him to abandon it as soon as he can safely do so, without troubling himself about the effects on the other people involved. If he is comfortable and well provided for, it will be wise for him to enjoy his prosperity without concerning himself about the wretched condition of some of his fellow countrymen, except when it seems prudent to do something to keep them quiet.

More generally: he will be reluctant to incur inconvenience, much less hardship or sacrifice, merely for the sake of acting morally. He may be prepared to incur them for the sake of those he loves, or for a cause in the service of which he finds personal satisfaction, but that is another matter. It is a case of doing what he wants, not of doing what he ought, irrespective of his personal feelings. His attitude towards the established morality of his society will ultimately be governed by his judgement of what is wise and prudent from the standpoint of his personal well-being. If complying with an established moral rule involves him in personal sacrifice, he will do so only if in his judgement it is the lesser evil and hence the path of prudence. In short, his approach to morality is essentially pragmatic, and he cannot therefore be regarded as a regularian moral agent properly so called. Unlike the latter, he is not tied to the letter of established moral rules. But unlike the rational agent at the level of social morality, he does not act in their spirit. He determines his conduct for himself in the light of his judgement of what is most advantageous for his personal well-being. On the face of it, this reinforces our original conclusion. It is at the level of personal well-being that personal freedom is most fully achieved.

But what about the rational agent at the level of social morality? He does not neglect his personal well-being. Within the framework of social morality, he will do his best to promote it wisely and prudently. But just as he is prepared to break an established moral rule for the sake of social responsibility or justice, so for the same reasons he will be ready, if he judges it necessary, to curtail his pursuit of personal well-being, and in the last resort, to sacrifice it altogether. He determines his conduct for himself quite as much as the rational agent at the level of personal well-being. But unlike the latter, he gives priority to considerations of social responsibility and justice over those of wisdom and prudence. This difference may be expressed as follows. In terms of the first sense of 'self-realization', a man can realize his generic capacity for self-determination both at the level of personal well-being and at the level of social morality. But at the lower level, he realizes it in the form of personal freedom; at the higher level, in the form of moral freedom. Of these two forms, moral freedom is the superior. This is because merely personal freedom involves an essentially pragmatic approach to morality. If everyone adopted such an approach, morality would be undermined, and along with it, the social conditions which make personal freedom possible. Regarded as a form of human freedom, merely personal freedom cannot be universally achieved. But moral freedom is what personal freedom becomes after being modified by considerations of social responsibility and justice, and can in principle be universally achieved.

But there is an important reservation. At the level of social morality, the rational agent must accept his society's existing way of life uncritically. His judgements about what is socially responsible and just, must be made in terms of its underlying ideas, beliefs, and values. He does not determine these for himself but finds them already there. His moral freedom is therefore freedom within his society's existing way of life. At the level of social morality, he cannot be free from dependence upon it. But this is an aspect of the problem of moral relativism, and for the present we must leave it. Returning to Green and Bosanquet, and their version of the positive theory: they do not distinguish between personal well-being and social morality as levels of rational activity. Nor do they show any awareness of the problem of moral relativism. Their contention that internal freedom is the condition of mind and character of the rational moral agent will not then do as it stands. It fails to allow for the distinction between personal and moral freedom, and takes no account of the important reservation about moral freedom.

3. THE POSITIVE THEORY CONTINUED: THE IDEA OF A FREE SOCIETY

What about the idea of a free society according to the positive theory? For Bosanquet, the significance of the external side of freedom lies in the context of social and political living. What is important is not the absence of external constraint as such but its absence in the form of interference by anyone with anyone else's rational moral conduct and hence with his self-realization. A free society is one in which this external freedom is secured to all its members through a system of rights maintained by law. It will be a society whose way of life is centred round the idea of the harmonious development by all its members of their native gifts and capacities. According to the negative theory, the idea of a free society is not the idea of a society whose way of life has a peculiar and distinctive character. If there is widespread agreement among the members, it does not matter what the agreement is about. A caste society, a theocracy, even a slave-owning society, can all of them in principle be free societies. But for the positive theory, it does matter what the agreement is about. According to it, the way of life of a free society is of a distinctive and peculiar character. Can this positive idea of a free society be sustained?

A free society must be a self-determining society. It cannot be a colony but must have an independent existence in its own right with its own individual identity as a society. What concerns us here is the character of the way of life of a free society and the status of its members. The last section suggests that its institutions and practices must be of such a nature that they secure to all its adult members adequate opportunities for achieving both moral and personal freedom. They must be able to participate in its way of life as rational agents at the levels of both social morality and personal well-being. It is necessary to stress the importance of moral freedom, as distinct from

154

merely personal freedom. A pragmatic approach to morality will not do if the society is to hold together and maintain its independent existence. The members must be self-determining as moral agents, not merely as individual persons. They must be able and willing to subordinate their individual pursuit of personal well-being to the demands of social responsibility and justice.

The idea of personal freedom is, however, of great importance in a free society. A basic principle in its way of life must be that every adult member should be able to pursue his personal well-being as a rational agent. Subject to considerations of social responsibility and justice, all of them should be able to try to enrich the quality of their lives in whatever ways they think best. In other words: granted that they must also be something more, it is a cardinal principle in the idea of a free society that all its members should be able to become free persons. But all can be free, both as moral agents and as persons, only where all stand on an equal footing. This points to a decisively important characteristic of a free society. There must be equality of status among all the members. There must be no gradations of membership, no first and second class citizens, no privileged group enjoying special favours denied to the other members. A society in which some, by virtue of their status as members, enjoy better opportunities than others for becoming morally and personally free, is something less than a free society properly so called.

How does this compare with the idea of a free society according to Green and Bosanquet? For them, the way of life of a free society is centred round the idea of the harmonious development by all the members of their native gifts and capacities. This fails to take account of the difference between the two senses of self-realization.[1] Consequently it fails to emphasize what is of central importance, that in a free society every member should have adequate opportunities for realizing his generic capacity for self-determination in the forms of both moral and personal freedom. The idea of a free society sketched in the two preceding paragraphs may be regarded as an im-

[1] In my *Social Philosophy of English Idealism*, Allen and Unwin, 1962, this point is not adequately made. I let Green and Bosenquet off too lightly.

provement on that of Green and Bosanquet. We can now contrast it with the idea of a free society according to the negative theory by seeing what its verdict is in the case of a slave-owning society, a caste society, and a theocracy.

In one sense, to say that slaves are not free persons is an obvious tautology. But in another, it is something more. The point is that the status of being a slave is of such a nature that the realization of the generic capacity for self-determination is made almost impossible. The slave is utterly subject to the authority of his master. He is largely confined to regularian activity in obedience to his master's orders and rules. He may have some scope for rational activity at the level of utility, but the ulterior purposes which he serves will mostly be his master's, not his own. It can only be in the interstices of his service to his master that he can formulate ulterior purposes of his own and take steps to execute them. While he may be able to develop some capacity for acting prudently, he will only be able to enhance and enrich the quality of his life in the teeth of the established social order under which he lives. A slave-owning society cannot be a free society properly so called. It makes no difference if the slaves acquiesce in their servitude without complaint. They do not have equality of status with their masters and cannot participate in the society as free persons.

Nor can a stratified society whose members are segregated on the basis of hereditary caste be a free society. The members cannot participate in its way of life on equal terms as free persons. They can participate only as members of their respective castes. Unlike slaves, none of them is utterly subject to the authority of another person. But all of them are subject to the rules of the caste system. The fact that they accept these rules without complaint and want to maintain the system makes no difference. The central idea underlying their way of life is not that each of them should pursue his personal well-being as a rational agent, but that each should follow the traditional occupations and live in the traditional manner associated with his caste. Within this framework, many of them may manage to enhance and enrich their lives to a considerable extent. But they are still something less than a society of free persons, for they all remain subject to the rules of the caste system which sets arbitrarily limits to what each can do to maintain and develop his personal well-being.

Can a theocracy be a free society? We saw that within a theocracy, rational activity at all three levels is possible for all the members. But we also saw that both social morality and personal well-being must be conceived in terms of the ideas and precepts vouchsafed in the divine instructions. The idea around which the way of life of a theocratic society is centred is not that each member should pursue his personal well-being as a rational agent, but that each should live in accordance with the divine instructions. They participate in it as persons subject to the divine instructions without equality of status as members. The members of the priesthood stand in a position of absolute authority over the laity on all matters concerned with belief and conduct. It follows that a theocracy must be something less than a free society. The fact that the members are in full agreement makes no difference. They are not trying to live together as the members of a free society, but as the members of a society dedicated to carrying out the divine instructions. But there is a place for religion in the life of a free society. As a free person each member will work out his own religious position for himself and will be able to join in voluntary religious associations with other like-minded people if he wishes. In a free society, religious diversity and 'free thinking' are open possibilities. In a theocracy these possibilities are excluded.

Because it lacks an adequate idea of both personal and moral freedom, the negative theory is unable to show why these societies cannot in principle be free societies. It does not see that personal and moral freedom involves something more than the absence of constraint because it fails to understand the notion of self-determination and the sense in which it is implied by the concept of constraint. The negative theory has failed to appreciate the implications of its own central tenet. Green and Bosanquet claimed to do better with their positive theory. But while their distinction between the internal and external sides of freedom is a real advance on the negative theory, there are serious defects in their own account of freedom. The theory sketched here is an attempt to go beyond Green and Bosanquet while preserving what is of value in their version. It is still essentially a positive theory because its foundation is the positive human capacity for self-determination. What Mill called 'individuality' falls within the scope of rational activity at the level of personal well-being and hence of personal freedom. A society whose way of life is based on the principle that every adult member should be able to pursue his personal well-being as a rational agent will contain the freedom for individuality which Mill advocates. For Berlin, a free society is one in which all the members enjoy the maximum possible freedom of choice. But this implies not only the absence of constraint but also the ability to make choices, and that is an integral part of the generic human capacity for self-determination. The account given here can include Berlin's idea of a free society and may fairly claim to put it on more secure foundations by linking it to ideas of personal and moral freedom which go beyond the scope of the negative theory.

But Berlin has a serious charge to make against the positive theory. Its proponents are likely to be rationalists. According to him: rationalists are people who believe that there is only one way of life which it is right for human beings to live, and that it can be discovered by human reason. Believing that they have in fact discovered it, rationalists are notoriously prone to conclude that they are justified in compelling those who are unable or unwilling to see the light to live according to it. Such compulsion is not thought of as tyranny but as liberation from error and illusion. But while the account of freedom being developed here is integrally linked to a theory of rational activity, nothing has so far been said which justifies the charge of rationalism in Berlin's sense. On the contrary that theory of rational activity, issuing as it does in the problem of moral relativism, points to a diametrically opposite conclusion. Human reason cannot show that there is one way of life which it is right for human beings to live. It has indeed been a central thesis of this chapter that the way of life of a free society is of a distinctive and peculiar kind. But the question of whether it is a better or worse way of life for human beings than any other is still *sub judice*. It cannot be answered until the problem of moral relativism has been dealt with. Our concern here has been with the idea of what a free society would be like, not with its merits, if any, over other types of society, or with its actual possibility. But Berlin's charge prompts another question, so far neglected and clearly relevant. What would be the scope and limits of socially organized constraint in a free society?

The answer, which may come as a surprise, is that the scope and limits would be those laid down by the negative theory according to its idea of a free society. According to this idea, a society is free if first, there is widespread agreement among its members about the fundamental character of its way of life; second, if the exercise of organized constraint is confined to the enforcing of rules and orders which, in social contexts, have either a pragmatic or a substantive justification; third, if these rules and orders are actually brought within the scope of organized constraint only when there is a net advantage to the life of the society in doing so. What this amounts to is a statement of the justified scope and limits of organized constraint in any society whatever. There is nothing wrong with it so far as it goes, but it must not be taken for more than it really is. This is the mistake of the negative theory. It is logically committed to holding that any society in which the exercise of organized constraint is kept within the justified scope and limits, is *ipso facto* a free society. But something more is necessary. All the members must have adequate opportunities for achieving moral and personal freedom, and they must have equality of status as members. These are essential characteristics of the way of life of a free society. They will affect the content of the rules which are pragmatically and substantively justified. But they do not affect the justified scope and limits of organized constraint which will be the same in a free society as in any other.

In his charge against the positive theory, Berlin seems especially to have had in mind Bosanquet's endorsement of Rousseau's dictum, 'forced to be free'. Bosanquet's point is that freedom is something more than merely the absence of external constraint and that such constraint can sometimes actually contribute to it. Fear of the police may stop me breaking a law which I resent having to obey because it prevents me doing something I want to do. But in a cool hour I may come to see that the law is socially desirable, and be glad that I was stopped by prudential considerations from breaking it. Bosanquet thinks that this is to be forced to be free because it is to be liberated through the threat of police action from the caprice of my merely empirical self. The threat forces me to do what I know in my better moments I ought as a good citizen to do without compulsion. The threat is no doubt a justified exercise of socially organized constraint. But whether I am properly described as being forced to be free, is highly questionable. I must already, at any rate for the most part, be a free moral agent, able and willing to act as a responsible citizen. The most that can be allowed to Bosanquet is that external constraint may keep me up to the mark in occasional moments of weakness. It cannot make me into a free moral agent and responsible citizen. I must have achieved that state already for myself. At the same time, Bosanquet is fundamentally right in his contention that in a free society what is important is not the absence of constraint as such. His thesis is sound if it is amended to read: what is important is the absence of external constraint in the shape of interference by any one with any one else's conduct as a free moral agent and as a free person within the limits of social morality.

Summarizing the argument of this chapter so far, it is possible in terms of the negative theory to answer two questions. Why is socially organized constraint necessary? What are the scope and limits within which its exercise is justified? But the answers to these questions do not by themselves yield adequate ideas of either personal or moral freedom, still less of a free society. The most that can be said is that they draw attention to a necessary condition for both personal and moral freedom: the absence of external constraint. The positive theory claims to do better while preserving what is of value in the negative theory. But we have seen that in the version of Green and Bosanquet this claim is at best only partially successful. Their distinction between the internal and external sides of freedom is a genuine advance on the negative theory. But they fail to distinguish between personal and moral freedom, and their idea of a free society contains some serious defects. My aim has been to develop a theory of freedom which, while still essentially positive in character, is not open to the objections to which the version of Green and Bosanquet is vulnerable. In particular, it tries to give an adequate account of both personal and moral freedom, and of the idea of a free society. It may be said with some justice that the idea of a free society as it has so far been presented is incomplete. More needs to be said about the ideas, beliefs and values which its way of life presupposes. Is it really a possible way of life for human beings? Is it necessarily better than other kinds of society? Here Berlin's point that not all human values are compatible is clearly relevant, as is the problem of moral relativism.

4. THE LAW OF NATURE

In Chapter 2 we saw that while the arguments of the critics of Natural Law are not conclusive, the onus is on its supporters to make good their case. It is up to them to show how we can know that there is such a law, why we ought to obey it, and why there has been so much disagreement about it. What is the bearing of the last two chapters on these questions? For Locke, the idea that there is a Law of Nature which is the supreme moral law for all mankind is of fundamental importance. His whole doctrine of Natural Rights rests upon it. On the face of it, this is a regularian idea of morality. To be moral is to obey the Law of Nature. But this law is clearly not like any human law or rule. It is not conventional in origin, nor was it deliberately enacted by human legislators. To say that it is the law of 'Nature' is at least to say that it did not originate in either of these ways. What then is it and why should all human beings obey it?

Locke's answer is that it is a law made by God and that all human beings ought to obey it because they ought to obey God. He also suggests that human reason can support this answer but he does not develop this suggestion. But if the Law of Nature is the law of God and if our duty to obey it is entailed by our duty to obey God, our discussion of theocracy in the last chapter is directly relevant. While theocratic morality is strongly regularian in character, it permits of rational activity

F   161

at the levels of social morality and personal well-being. But it does not enable the problem of moral relativism to be avoided. The question: 'Why should I obey God?' can be answered in the last analysis only by re-affirming belief in God's existence and in our duty to obey him. This belief is a pre-condition for membership of a theocracy. It is not open to debate within the framework of theocratic morality. It follows that the Law of Nature can be the cornerstone of morality in a theocracy where the members are already in fundamental agreement. But this does not help its supporters. They have still to show that every human society should be such a theocracy. They must establish that there is a God, that all human beings ought to obey him, and that he has enacted the Law of Nature for all human beings to follow. Such propositions are surely a matter of faith rather than rational demonstration. But in matters of faith, human beings notoriously have differed, do differ, and are likely to continue to differ. If supporters of Natural Law try to rest their case on theological grounds they are not likely to be successful.

But need they rest it on such grounds? We saw in Chapter 2 that, according to Margaret Macdonald, many supporters of Natural Law have argued that the existence of the Law of Nature is entailed by human rationality. She rejects such arguments as invalid on the grounds that they involve a confusion between statements of different logical types. The human capacity for rational activity is merely an empirical fact about human beings and statements of empirical fact cannot entail value statements including those which assert the existence of the Law of Nature as a moral law or principle. From the fact that men can act rationally, nothing whatever follows about morality. But in Chapter 2 I questioned this rather cavalier verdict and the whole argument of Chapter 3 suggests that to regard human rationality as merely one more empirical fact is to miss its significance. Rational activity is normative in the sense that the rational agent is committed to certain standards. What he does can be criticized with reference to these standards. But does this help supporters of Natural Law? Only if it can be shown that the Law of Nature is one of the standards to which a rational agent is committed. This means interpreting the Law of Nature not as a moral rule but rather as a general moral principle.

We saw that it is rational to be moral in the sense of acting justly and responsibly. To act justly is to treat the interests and claims of other people as equal in value to your own except where there are relevant grounds for doing otherwise. Relevant grounds can arise out of the nature and purpose of a joint activity or common enterprise in which you and other people are together involved. To act responsibly is to do the best you can to promote and advance a joint activity in the face of its needs and the problems and difficulties which currently beset it. But it is rational to subordinate justice to responsibility. The exigencies of the current situation provide relevant grounds for differential treatment over and beyond those which arise out of its nature and purpose. While it is just for you to play your proper part as a member of the group, it can never be just for you to participate in a way which weakens or undermines the common enterprise. Hence what is responsible can never be unjust and it follows that what is just must be determined in the light of what is responsible, not the other way round. Moreover it is rational to give priority to the responsibilities of the wider more inclusive community if and when a conflict arises. Responsibility is therefore ultimately 'social' responsibility. It is rational to be moral where being moral means being a responsible member of the human territorial society in which you live, and within this framework, acting justly.

At first sight, the Law of Nature as a general moral principle seems not very different from justice. It may be interpreted as laying down that other people are not to be treated arbitrarily. They are always to be treated as ends, never merely as means. 'Other people' includes all mankind since the Law of Nature is a general moral principle for all human beings. So far this is close to justice for it is rational to act justly towards all human beings with whom you have dealings. But to the question: 'how does one treat other people as ends rather than merely as means?' the Law of Nature does not answer, 'by treating the interests and claims of other people as equal in value to your own except where there are relevant grounds for doing other- wise'. The answer which it has been traditionally interpreted as giving is: 'by respecting their natural rights to life, liberty and property'. The only condition admitted is that to qualify for these natural rights, one must be able and willing to respect the natural rights of other people. Subject to this condition, natural rights are regarded as belonging to human beings as such. They are rights which people have simply as human beings, not as members of particular societies. It was this feature of the traditional doctrine to which Ritchie objected on the grounds that rights cannot be divorced from social considerations.

Our discussion of social morality and of justice and social responsibility as standards of rationality gives *prima facie* support to this objection. But we have still to discuss the concept of rights against the background of the last two chapters and until that has been done further comment on the subject of natural rights may be postponed. As a general moral principle the Law of Nature may best be regarded as an inadequate formulation of the idea of justice. It gives no guidance on the question of relevant grounds for differential treatment. The most it can do is to lay down the negative principle: do not act arbitrarily! Moreover its inadequacy as a formulation of justice leaves no room for the transition to social responsibility.

5. THE IDEA OF RIGHTS

To have a right is to be entitled to do something or to have something done: for instance, to vote, or to receive free medical treatment. As Hobbes was careful to point out, it is different from being under an obligation. On any given occasion you have a choice whether or not to exercise your right. You are not obliged to do what you are entitled to do, or to insist on having done what you are entitled to have done. Your decision on a particular occasion not to exercise your right does not prejudice your future exercise of it. You still have the right. Having a right therefore presupposes at least some capacity for rational activity. You must be capable of deciding whether or not you have good reason to exercise your right in the light of the particular circumstances of each occasion. A merely regularian agent is strictly speaking not eligible for rights

since he is incapable of such decisions. He is only eligible for
obligations. While rights and obligations are not the same,
they are nevertheless connected. Whenever you decide to do
what you have a right to do, others have an obligation to let
you do it. Whenever you decide to get done what you have a
right to get done, those concerned have an obligation to do it
for you. Wherever there are rights, there are always correlative
obligations.

But upon what grounds can the claim to have a right be
justified? What entitles me and obliges you? In the case of a
legal right, the answer is simple. The right is conferred and the
co-relative obligation imposed by a law in a society of which
you and I are both members, and to whose legal system we
are therefore both subject. But not all rights are legal rights.
The right discussed by Melden, that of a father to receive
special consideration from his son, is a moral right. The situation is not, however, fundamentally different. Moral rights are
conferred, not by a society's legal system but by its established
morality. People also have rights as members of voluntary
associations. The rights of the members of a club are conferred
by its rules, to which all the members are subject. Rights and
their correlative obligations are essentially social in character.
One has them as a member of a social group. To justify my
claim to a right, therefore, I must show that it is one which the
members of a certain social group have, and that I am a member
of that group. What entitles me is my status as a member,
and what obliges you is that you too are a member. As members
we are both subject to the rules of the group, and these confer
the right and impose the correlative obligation.

But this answer does not allow a distinction to be drawn
between the rights actually recognized in a social group, and
those which its members ought to have. The entire emphasis
is on the fact of recognition. There can be no such thing as an
unrecognized right. Now this is unsatisfactory because it fails
to show how there can be claims to new rights and the revision
of existing ones. But it was pointed out in Chapter 3 that each
member of a group is entitled to insist that the others should
do what is necessary to enable him to share in the common
enterprise upon proper terms, provided that he acts reciprocally

towards them. This points to a revised and expanded answer. A right must be justified in the first place as one which I have as the member of some social group. Secondly what I claim as a right must be something which it is necessary for me to have if I am to play my proper part as a member. Thirdly my claim to have it as a right is justified only if I am able and willing to respect the rights of the other members of the group.

The rights which the members of a social group ought to have are those which are necessary to enable them to participate properly in its joint activity as members. An unrecognized right is one which I am justified in claiming as a member of a group but which is not at present recognized within the group. What justifies my claim is not merely my status as a member but the nature and purpose of the group's joint activity together with what is necessary to enable me to participate in it. In justifying my claim to a right I must show that it is one which as a member I ought to have, whether it is recognized or not. But why is my claim to a right justified only if I am able and willing to respect the rights of the other members of the group? The reason is that if I am unable or unwilling, I am not a participating member of the group. I am not doing what is necessary to enable the other members to share in the common enterprise. I may be physically present among them but I am not a partner in their joint activity. All this presupposes fundamental agreement within the group about the nature and purpose of the common enterprise and about the terms upon which all are to share in it.

But arising out of this, there is something else to be considered. If rights are to be respected, their correlative obligations must be met. Apart from one qualification[1] this means that certain primary rules must be followed which prescribe what must be done to meet them. These rules may be deliberately enacted by legislation, or by the membership of a voluntary association. They may be conventional, being part of a society's established morality, or part of an unwritten body of law like the English Common Law. Whatever their origin, their justification is necessarily substantive not merely pragmatic. What they prescribe is what must be done by the members of

[1] See section 7 of this chapter.

a social group if they are to treat one another as they ought. But while it is normally just to follow substantive primary rules, special circumstances may make a difference. There can be occasions on which it is the lesser evil, and hence just to break them. This applies to rules imposing the obligations correlative to rights, no less than to others. Rights have what may be called a quasi-regularian character. Like rules they take account only of the resemblances between situations, not of what is unique or peculiar about them. You have a right to do something in all situations of a certain kind. But special circumstances on a particular occasion may mean that if you do what you have a right to do in situations of that kind, more harm will result than if you do not. It may sometimes be the lesser evil for you to put up with having a promise broken, with being stopped from saying what you think, or from using your property as you wish.

But all this is allowed for in the concept of a right. You are entitled but not obliged to do something or to have something done. That is why rights are only quasi-regularian in character. If on a particular occasion it is unjust or socially irresponsible to exercise your right you have good reason not to do so. But can it ever be unjust to exercise a right? The answer is that it can, and that the reason why, turns on the difference between the letter and the spirit of justice, that is between justice as a rule and justice as a standard of rationality. Consider an example. I am a landlord and I have the right to evict tenants from my property at the expiration of their lease and may want to do so to get a higher rent than they can afford. But suppose that they have appealed to me to let them stay on a little longer because of serious illness in the family. Suppose that I am not urgently in need of the extra money which the higher rent would bring in. If in spite of this, I insist on my right and evict them, I am not acting unjustly from the point of view of the letter of justice. But from the standpoint of the spirit of justice, I am acting unjustly, for I am choosing the greater evil of their hardship instead of the lesser evil of my temporary inconvenience. The special circumstances of the case constitute relevant grounds for giving their claim preference over mine, and I therefore have good reason not to evict them. In special circumstances it may also be socially irresponsible to exercise a right: for instance during an economic crisis to insist on a wage increase or to increase prices.

More generally: if there is good reason to subordinate the exercise of rights to considerations of social responsibility and justice, it follows that a person is properly qualified to exercise them only to the extent that he is capable of acting rationally at the level of social morality. The acquisition of rights is a gradual process which begins in childhood. So is the development of the capacity to act rationally. They are different facets of the one complex process of growing up to become an adult member of an already existing human society. But what about the distinction drawn earlier, that between the rights actually recognized in a social group and those which its members ought to have? The rights which they ought to have are those necessary to enable all of them to participate in the group on proper terms. But this presupposes agreement about what the proper terms are. In a voluntary association, this agreement can be counted on, since being voluntary, the association will not long survive its absence. There will therefore be no inherent difficulty between the rights actually recognized in the association and those which the members ought to have.

But what about a territorial human society, for instance a modern nation? The rights which one acquires in the course of growing up to be an adult member will necessarily be those which are currently recognized in its way of life. There must be widespread agreement among the members about the fundamental character of that way of life if they are to agree about the rights which they ought to have. But this same agreement is necessary if they are to act rationally at the level of social morality. What makes it possible for them to act responsibly and justly as members of one society, also makes it possible for them to agree about the rights which they ought to have and to co-operate together in removing any discrepancies which from time to time may arise between these rights and those which are currently recognized. It is both socially responsible and just that steps should be taken to remove such discrepancies whenever they are brought to light. But the inherent limitations of social morality as a level of rational activity are equally limitations on the scope and effectiveness of rights as operative ideas in the life of any society.

In a divided society there will be deep and painful disagreement about the terms upon which the members of the various groups composing it are to participate in the common life. Consequently there will be no rational basis upon which agreement can be reached about the rights which the members of each group ought to have as members of the wider society. The rights actually recognized will reflect the views of the dominant group about the fundamental character of the common life. Members of the other groups may protest bitterly that they are being denied their justified rights. But the members of the dominant group will deny that there are rational grounds for this protest. The same will be true of a society in which long established ideas and values, including many recognized rights, are becoming obsolete. The scope and effectiveness of rights as operative ideas in the way of life of a society diminishes as ambiguity about the fundamental character of that way of life increases. This points to a rather depressing conclusion. The more serious the charge that rights are being denied, the less likelihood there is that much can be done about it. Disputes about rights can be resolved only if the issues they concern do not go too deep. Conflicts must be peripheral rather than central.

In the light of all this, what becomes of the traditional doctrine of natural rights? If 'natural' is taken in the scientific or descriptive sense, the answer is nothing. Rights are essentially social in character. They are not natural in the sense of being properties or characteristics which human beings naturally have, like an upright posture or a central nervous system. It may be objected, however, that it is natural for human beings to live socially, and that since rights are essentially social in character, they are natural in at least a derivative sense. But this does not meet the central contention of the traditional doctrine that there are certain rights which it is natural for human beings to have always and everywhere, irrespective of particular social conditions. As a matter of empirical fact this is false. The existence of the institution of slavery is conclusive evidence against it. It may be replied that 'natural' is to be interpreted prescriptively, not descriptively. There are certain rights which human beings always and everywhere ought to have, whether or not they are recognized in actual human societies.

But this runs straight into the problem of moral relativism. It entails the assertion that if in any actual society certain rights are not recognized, its way of life is defective. But the central thesis of moral relativism is that there are no rational grounds on which the members of a society can criticize their common way of life and show that it is defective. They can rationally criticize their own and each other's conduct on the score of its social responsibility and justice, provided that they are in substantial agreement about the fundamental character of their common way of life. But that way of life itself must be accepted uncritically. There are no rational grounds on which it can be shown to be in principle better or worse than any other. Nor will it help to appeal to the law of nature. That law amounts only to the negative principle that human beings ought not to treat one another arbitrarily. Arbitrary treatment is treatment for which there is no morally good reason. But what is to count as a morally good reason can be determined only with reference to the ideas, beliefs and values, underlying the established morality of some already existing human society. There is no escape along these lines from the limitations of social morality. In short, if there is anything to be said for the doctrine of natural rights interpreted normatively as human rights, we are not yet in a position to see what it is. The problem of moral relativism must first be dealt with, and that will occupy us in Part 3 of this book.

6. THE RIGHT TO FREEDOM

According to Hart, if there are any moral rights at all, there must be at least a natural right to freedom. In Chapter 2, I concluded that he shows that freedom may be a residual right but not that it is a natural right. This is because by his own admission, there are systems of morality in which the notion of a moral right does not occur. Unless he can show that this notion is essential to morality as such and that systems which do not employ it are something less than systems of morality properly so called, his case has not been made out. In the last section no mention was made of the right to freedom but if Hart is even partly correct it needs to be discussed. In one sense, every right is the right to a certain measure of freedom. One is free either to exercise it or not to exercise it on any given occasion. But something more than this has normally been meant by the right to freedom. Its advocates have had in mind the right to freedom as such. What can such a right be?

It can only be the right to be free from arbitrary constraint: arbitrary constraint being coercion or interference for which there is not a morally good reason. To put the same point the other way round: no one can be entitled to be free from constraint for which there is a morally good reason. But what constitutes a morally good reason? Here the discussion in Section 1 of this chapter is relevant. Socially organized constraint is necessary to protect the members of a society from inconvenience and injury by those among them who are unable or unwilling to meet the minimum obligations of social living. Constraint is also necessary within the family in order to discipline children. Parents will therefore from time to time have morally good reasons for exercising it against their offspring. So will the police in the course of carrying out their task of law enforcement. Moreover if a man is convinced beyond reasonable doubt that it is the lesser evil for him to coerce or interfere with someone else, he has a morally good reason for doing so. Such a step is a hazardous one for a private citizen to take, but it may sometimes be justified on the score of justice or, in appropriate contexts, social responsibility. The demands of social morality may sometimes give rise to morally good reasons for exercising constraint.

The freedom to which there can be a right is negative freedom, freedom on its external side. To the question: 'What are you free to do?' the answer is: 'Anything you like which no one else has a morally good reason to stop you doing.' But how can the right to freedom be exercised in the face of arbitrary constraint? The answer is by resisting it, using peaceful means if possible but force if necessary, and by seeking redress from the aggressor. Like every other right, there is discretion to decide whether or not to exercise it on any given occasion. Instead of resisting, you can simply submit without protest. To have the right to freedom is to be entitled but not obliged to resist arbitrary constraint. It follows that a slave by virtue of his status cannot have it. He is the property of his master and must subordinate himself entirely to his master's wishes. If someone else interferes with him, that is a violation not of his right to freedom but of his master's right to property. It may well be part of the established morality of a slave-owning society that masters ought not to be cruel to their slaves and ought not to coerce them except to maintain discipline. But this does not entitle a slave to resist cruelty from his master.

According to the logic of the negative theory of freedom, a slave-owning society can in principle be a free society provided that the slaves acquiesce without resentment in their servitude. It follows (according to the negative theory) that a society can be free when a whole class of its members do not have the right to be free from arbitrary constraint. Paradoxical as this may appear, it is at least theoretically possible. Although not having the right to be free from arbitrary constraint, the slaves may nevertheless be free from it. But for this to happen, not only must the slaves accept their servitude without resentment, their masters must never be cruel to them nor coerce them except to maintain discipline. To doubt whether slaves have in fact ever been free from arbitrary constraint is not to be unduly sceptical. The right to freedom is a necessary condition for having any other rights at all. If you are not entitled to resist arbitrary constraint, your other rights can be violated with impunity. You can be interfered with and prevented from doing what nominally you are entitled to do. If you are to be entitled to do anything whatever, you must at least be entitled to be free from arbitrary constraint.

Although a slave has no rights, he has a definite place, albeit a minimal one, in the social order. He is the property of his master and other people must keep their hands off him. They have morally good reasons for interfering with him only if it is necessary to help his master maintain control of him, e.g. catching and returning him if he becomes a fugitive. But if you are not a slave and yet do not have the right to freedom, you have no place in the social order at all. Anyone can coerce you and interfere with you. You do not even have the protection which comes from being someone else's property. Other people may do with you as they please and you are not entitled to resist, much less seek redress. This is in effect what the Nazis did to the Jews. Not only did they refuse to admit that the Jews had the right to freedom; they refused to accord them any status whatever in German life and turned them into social outcasts who could be bullied and humiliated with impunity and, when it became socially expedient, ruthlessly exterminated.

Upon what grounds can the claim to have the right to freedom be justified? The answer is that if you are to be neither a social outcast not a slave but a person, you must have it. If you are to share in the life of your society as a participating member rather than merely as the property of someone else, you must be entitled to be free from arbitrary constraint and to resist it when you are subjected to it. To be a member 'in your own right' is at least to have the right to freedom. It is the fundamental right entailed by participating membership in any territorial human society and, it is a necessary condition for having any other rights. Until a child becomes capable of exercising it for himself, he has the right vicariously. It must be exercised for him by his parents. But this assumes that his parents will not abuse their position, that they will not themselves exercise arbitrary constraint against him. If they do abuse it, there are morally good reasons for authorized agents of the wider society to take over the task of vicariously exercising his right to freedom.

If I arbitrarily interfere with and coerce someone else, police action against me does not violate my right to freedom. There is a morally good reason for it. I have been doing what I am not entitled to do and cannot be entitled to evade legitimate counter-measures. But since I have violated someone else's right to freedom, can I still be justified in claiming it as a right for myself? The argument of the last section suggests not, since according to it, I am justified in claiming something as a right only if I am able and willing to respect the rights of the other members of the group concerned. Does this mean that I have forfeited my right to freedom and have become a social outcast who can be interfered with and coerced with impunity by anyone? Does it mean that in my case other people are relieved of the obligation correlative to the right to freedom, the obligation to refrain from exercising arbitrary constraint against anyone? The answer is that it does not. The obligation still stands even where arbitrary constraint has already been exercised. There is no obligation to refrain from resistance. But there is, not to treat the aggressor arbitrarily once he has been rendered harmless. The obligation is one which while it is the correlative of the right to freedom in the sense that it must be honoured if anyone is to have that right, is not merely its correlative. It stands on its own feet apart from the right and can be justified independently of it.

What is its justification? The answer is that arbitrary constraint is by its very nature anti-social. It is destructive of social relationships as such and the fact that someone has resorted to it is no reason for anyone else to do so. The obligation to refrain from it is the fundamental social obligation and is the necessary foundation for any established morality in any society whatever. It may be expressed as a substantive primary rule with an express exception in the form of a specific moral principle. 'Never interfere with or coerce anyone unless there is a morally good reason to do so!' But if I have broken this rule and my action is not a legitimate exception to it, what is to be done with me? I am not to be treated arbitrarily but I have shown myself to be something less than fully qualified for participating membership. On the score of social responsibility the members of my society have a morally good reason at least to subject me to control and surveillance until there is some evidence that I can be trusted to meet the fundamental social obligation. But they cannot have a morally good reason to bully or torment me, or to subject me to more control and surveillance than is necessary for their protection and my possible rehabilitation.

Admittedly to say this is to do no more than scratch the surface of the philosophy of punishment. But we are here concerned only with the right to freedom. Consider the case of a man serving a prison term for robbery with violence. The constraint to which he is subjected is not arbitrary. There is a morally good reason for it and he is not entitled to escape it much less resist it. His right to freedom is therefore not being violated. But in being sent to prison, is he not being deprived of it altogether? He is being physically confined and made totally subject to the prison authorities. He is no longer free to do the things which no one has a morally good reason to stop him doing. On the contrary, he is now only free to do what the prison authorities permit. He is being deprived of the open possibilities of action and the opportunity for choice and decision which the right to freedom gave him. But this deprivation is the deserved consequence of his own action. In being deprived of the right to freedom, he is not being made a social outcast. He is being placed in a situation in which he is no longer a full participating member of his society and in which, while he is in it, the right to freedom is irrelevant. His status is not unlike that of a slave but it differs in two important respects. He is not the property of the prison authorities and he has the prospect when he has served his term, of resuming full membership of his society and regaining the right to freedom.

But to return to Hart: his doctrine of moral rights is of central importance in his defence of his thesis. Moral rights are of two kinds: general and special. A general moral right is the right to resist constraint which is not justified by a special moral right. This is to say that constraint is arbitrary unless there is a special moral right to exercise it. A special moral right is the right which a man has, to make someone else do what he has freely undertaken to do in a prior transaction to which both of them were parties. Now, according to my account in the last section, a moral right is a right which is conferred by a society's established morality rather than by its legal system. This is in line with what was said by Ritchie on the same subject, as well as at least implicitly with Melden's account. But Hart's doctrine also presupposes it, for he expressly says that not all systems of morality include the notion of a moral right. People can therefore have general and special moral rights in Hart's sense only if they are members of a society whose established morality includes the notion of moral rights.

According to Hart: arbitrary constraint is constraint which there is no special moral right to exercise. According to me:

it is constraint for which there is no morally good reason. Is there a real difference here? On the face of it, no! Hart is in effect saying that there is a morally good reason for constraint only if it is used to resist arbitrary constraint, or to make people do what they have freely undertaken to do. This admittedly overlooks the possibility that the established morality of a given society may authorize the exercise of constraint for other purposes. What counts as a morally good reason will depend upon the provisions of a particular society's established morality. But the main point is clear. Constraint is arbitrary unless there is a morally good reason for it. Something else in Hart's discussion calls for comment. This is what he says about submission to mutual restrictions. This is straightforward enough in the case of a voluntary association, and also in the case of a society in which there is widespread agreement among the members about the fundamental character of their way of life. In the latter case, those against whom socially organized constraint is exercised are only being made to do what they ought to be prepared to do freely without constraint. From Hart's point of view, they are only being made to do what they have freely, albeit tacitly undertaken to do: namely, submit to the mutual restrictions necessary for the society's way of life to be carried on. But what about a divided society? Socially organized constraint will be regarded as arbitrary by its subject groups. They will see it as constraint which, for the most part, there are no morally good reasons. Many of the rules which it is used to enforce will seem to them merely to protect the privileged position of the dominant group, and to lack either substantive or pragmatic justification.

In terms of Hart's position, the situation in a divided society may be expressed thus. The members of the dominant and subject groups are unable to agree about what the mutual restrictions should be, to which they are all to submit. But why are they unable to agree? According to my account: because they are fundamentally divided about the character of their common way of life, and about the terms upon which they are to participate in it. But Hart does not ask this question. He does not inquire into what the agreement to submit to mutual restrictions presupposes. The omission is unfortunate because it prevents

Hart from coming to grips with what is really involved in the idea of rights in general and the right to freedom in particular. His thesis, that if there are any moral rights at all, there must at least be the natural, or better, the residual right to freedom, really amounts to no more than the recognition that the right to freedom from arbitrary constraint is a necessary condition for having any other rights at all. His way of putting the matter is misleading because it obscures the main point. This is that it is possible for the members of a society to have the right to freedom from arbitrary constraint, and therefore all the other rights which as members they ought to have, only if they are in substantial agreement about the fundamental character of their way of life. Rights in general, and the right to freedom in particular, presuppose a common framework of agreement. Hart's account is misleading because it suggests the opposite: that a common framework of agreement presupposes the right to freedom.

7. THEORIES OF RIGHTS: SOME COMMENTS

According to Bentham, the notion of a right is significant primarily in legal contexts. But in these contexts, it is the notion of obligations rather than that of rights which is fundamental. Legal obligations are imposed and enforced by a system of law. You have a legal right to have other people carry out their legal obligations. In other words, legal rights are a by-product of legal obligations. Moral rights are the by-product of moral obligations, moral obligations being those which are recognized by public opinion rather than being imposed and enforced by law. For Bentham, the crucial question is whether the obligations actually enforced and recognized by the law and opinion of a given society are those which ought to be, according to the principle of utility. To ask whether a given right is justified on rational moral grounds is to ask whether the obligation of which it is the by-product really is an obligation from the standpoint of the greatest happiness of the greatest number.

If a right is to be secured and protected by law, a legally enforceable rule must be enacted which imposes the correlative obligation. So far Bentham is correct. But he is surely incorrect in putting the emphasis exclusively on the side of obligations and making rights no more than their by-product. Obligations are as much the by-product of rights as vice versa. In fact both must be determined together. What rights and obligations the members of a group ought to have can be decided only by inquiring into the nature and purpose of their joint activity and the terms upon which they are to participate in it. Why did Bentham fail to see this? For an answer we must go to his principle of utility and more especially to the theory of action from which it derives. The basic error of that theory is to try to represent all action in purely utilitarian terms. Rational activity is conceived of as nothing but rational activity at the level of utility. But at the level of utility, ulterior purposes fall outside the scope of rational thought and decision. Bentham meets this difficulty by introducing psychological hedonism, i.e. the doctrine that all human action is motivated by desire for pleasure and aversion from pain. These twin drives are the two sovereign masters which determine all ulterior purposes. But with the introduction of this doctrine, his theory of action ceases to be normative and becomes descriptive. It is no longer an account of what it is to act rationally but rather an account of how in fact people behave.

But what about the principle of utility? Is it not in some sense a moral principle? No, it is simply the standard of expediency applied to the case of an aggregate of pleasure-seeking, pain-shunning individuals. Bentham is in effect saying that legislation is a technique for securing the conditions which it is expedient for such an aggregate to establish and maintain. Since this technque is represented as a method of influencing behaviour by imposing and enforcing obligations, it is hardly surprising that in its perspective, rights shrink to mere by-products. But there are no good reasons for accepting all this and plenty for rejecting it. Rational activity is more than merely utilitarian action. The ambiguities and confusions latent in psychological hedonism have been exposed many times. Here it is enough to say that treated as an empirical hypothesis about human behaviour, it is false. To regard a human society as merely an aggregate of pleasure-seeking, pain-shunning individuals is not to regard it as a society properly so-called at all. While in one sense legislation may be regarded as a technique, or perhaps better as having a technical aspect, it is certainly not a technique for securing what is expedient for such an aggregate. There are therefore no good reasons for accepting Bentham's emasculated view of rights as the mere by-product of obligations. It is frequently said that if you reject natural law and natural rights, you are necessarily driven into Utilitarianism. That this is not so, at least so far as Bentham's version of Utilitarianism is concerned, should by now be abundantly clear.

But what about D. G. Ritchie's Evolutionist Utilitarianism? He is in effect recommending that for the traditional doctrine of natural rights, we should substitute the idea of morally justified social rights. Moral justification is to be in terms of social utility but social utility is conceived in terms of Evolutionist not Benthamite Utilitarianism. On this view, rights are not the mere by-product of obligations. Something of value in the traditional doctrine is preserved: namely, the idea of certain basic rights which a society ought to secure to all its members. A society is seen as a complex system of human activities and relationships developing over time, a system into which successive generations of human beings are born and within which they grow up, live and die. All this comes a good deal closer to the view developed in this chapter. A person can have rights only as a member of a group and more especially as a member of a territorial human society. The basic rights which such a society ought to secure to all its members, i.e. the rights which as members they ought all to have, are those which are necessary if they are to maintain and develop their common life. What in particular these rights are will therefore depend upon the character of that common life and upon the ideas, beliefs and values which underlie it. So far, Ritchie and I seem to be pretty much in agreement.

But will Evolutionist Utilitarianism bear the weight which he puts on it? Can social rights be morally justified in its terms? I ought to have rights not because it is socially useful but because as a member of a given society, I am rationally and morally justified in claiming them. Others ought to respect them because they ought to treat me as a member and the same applies to me in relation to them. It may be socially expedient to protect morally justified social rights by law but whether certain social rights are morally justified is not a question which has anything to do with what is socially expedient. The fact that you are morally justified in having a certain right does not mean that you must exercise it on every occasion when it is possible for you to do so. The exercise of rights is subordinate to considerations of social responsibility and justice. It is socially irresponsible to do what is socially inexpedient, and if to exercise a right on a given occasion is socially inexpedient, it will be socially irresponsible to do so and the right ought not to be exercised. But this does not mean that rights are justified on the grounds of social expediency. Questions about social expediency are questions about what it is best to do in order to secure the conditions necessary for the continued maintenance and development of a society's way of life. Included in that way of life are the rights of the members. They are part of what is to be maintained and developed and what is socially expedient must be determined with reference to these rights. But all this goes beyond the range and comprehension of Evolutionist Utilitarianism. It is not so much that Ritchie would deny any of it as that his position with respect to it is indeterminate. He has not worked it out and cannot do so unless he goes beyond Evolutionist Utilitarianism and social utility. For these reasons his positive view of rights is unsatisfactory.

Finally there is A. I. Melden. In Section 5 of this chapter, I said that to respect a right is to follow a rule prescribing the correlative obligation. But the right which Melden discusses, that of a parent to receive favourable treatment from his son, suggests that a qualification is necessary. In this case, it is not a matter of following a rule but of implementing a specific moral principle. The right does not call for a specific action but rather prescribes a policy: namely favouring one's parents. It is up to a son to decide, in the light of the particular circumstances, what constitutes giving preferential treatment to his father. This draws attention to the fact that the concept of a right includes the idea of being entitled to have other people act

in a certain spirit and with respect to certain kinds of consideration, using their own judgement and discretion about what in
particular to do on any given occasion. Someone in a position
of authority in a voluntary association has the right to loyalty
from its members. But what they must do in order to be loyal
depends upon the particular circumstances of a given situation.
But it is fair to regard this as an extension of the strict notion
of rights in the same way as acting on specified principles is a
development of strictly regularian activity.

Melden's distinction between obligation-meeting and obligatory actions may be restated in terms of my account in the
last chapter. An obligation-meeting action is either one which is
prescribed by a substantive primary rule or else one which, in
a given situation, successfully implements a specific moral
principle. An obligatory action is one which, in a given situation, is either socially responsible or just. There are occasions
when it may be socially responsible or just to break a substantive
primary rule or not to implement a specific moral principle.
Hence there are occasions when doing what is obligatory means
not doing what is obligation-meeting. There is no fundamental
difference between us here. Nor is there about the way in which
the right of a parent operates in his son's determination of his
conduct. To say that it is a morally relevant consideration is
not fundamentally different from saying that to respect it will
normally but not always be just.

According to Melden, the right of a parent is not something
separate from the status of being a parent which is somehow
derived from it. It is actually a part of that status. To justify
your claim to be entitled to special consideration from your
son, it is enough to point out that you are in fact his father.
But this presupposes agreement about what the status of being
a parent involves and therefore about the nature and purpose
of the family, especially in that phase of its existence when the
children have grown up and are no longer dependent upon
their parents. It is only as a member of a group, the family,
that you can have the rights which are part of the status of being
a parent. What these rights ought to be depends upon what
that status ought to be, i.e. upon the terms upon which as a
parent you ought to participate in the life of the family. Once

more there does not appear to be a fundamental difference between Melden and myself. The account which he gives of the relation between the right of a parent and the status of being a parent can be restated in terms of the general account of the concept of rights developed in this chapter.

But Melden's account fails to bring out the importance of underlying agreement as the foundation for rights. In this respect, the instance which he discusses is not helpful. That a parent is entitled to receive special consideration from his son is not likely to be disputed by anyone. But just what other rights are involved in the status of being a parent may well be a controversial question reflecting underlying disagreement about the parental role in the life of the family. Nor is what he has to say about morality very illuminating. We saw in Chapter 2 that his position is inherently ambiguous. He espouses what appears to be a liberal morality of happiness which he says has superseded an older theistic morality. But whether this is to be regarded as moral progress and if so on what grounds, or whether he is content to accept a position of moral relativism is unclear.

PART 3

Humanism in Morals and Politics

Chapter 6

Individuality and Human Identity

1. INDIVIDUALITY

At the level of social morality, rational agents can criticize their own and each other's conduct on the score of its social responsibility and justice. But there are no rational grounds on which they can criticize and evaluate their common life. This is the problem of moral relativism which, as we have seen, arises at the level of social morality. But whatever else it may be, the way of life of a human society is something in which human beings participate and which they share together. This simple fact suggests a clue to the problem of moral relativism. How far is the way of life of a given society adequate as a human way of life? The humanistic implications of the Law of Nature support this suggestion. So indirectly does the idea of the way of life of a free society according to the positive theory. But there is a difficulty. The suggestion presupposes that we already have a rationally based idea of what an adequate way of life for human beings is. Margaret Macdonald does not think that such an idea is to be had. 'Men do not share a fixed nature. Nor therefore are there any ends which they must necessarily pursue in fulfilment of such a nature. There is no definition of man.' But we have seen that she fails to appreciate the implications of rational activity. We shall therefore explore the notion of humanity and 'the human' on its own merits and our discussion will be centred round the general theme of human identity.

According to Margaret Macdonald: 'It is by having the specific and natural characteristics of being rational that men resemble each other and differ from the brutes.' She also says that: 'There is a more or less vague set of properties which characterize in various degrees and proportions those creatures which are called human.' The general tone of these remarks suggests that she is trying to identify human beings in quasi-zoological terms. Such an approach has its uses but it is deficient in two respects. One is that no special importance is attached to the human capacity for self-knowledge. 'The creatures which are called human', or more accurately, which call themselves human, are able to investigate and reflect upon their own properties and characteristics, and in some degree at least modify their conduct in the light of what they find. The other is that no special attention is paid to human individuality. It is upon the human species rather than upon human beings as individuals that the emphasis is placed. But for Mill, human individuality is something to be welcomed and cultivated. Today in the Western world the term 'an individual' is practically a synonym for 'a human being'. But just what is the import and significance of 'individuality' and 'an individual'? I shall discuss some general features of these notions before considering their meaning in human contexts.

Consider the two questions: 'What is that?' and 'Is that mine?' The first is in effect a request for the classification of something. It is answered by a statement of the form: 'That is an X': i.e. a member of the class of X's. The second is a question about individual identity. It asks whether something is a certain unique object. 'Is that my hat, or only one very like it?' I already know that it belongs to the class of things called 'hats'. I am interested not in its classification but in its identity as an individual. Its identity as an individual is its self-sameness over time. 'It is the very same hat that I bought ten years ago in London and which now all too literally shows signs of wear.' To classify something is to attend to its particularity. It is identified as a particular member of a certain class not as an individual. But it must already exist as an individual if it is to be identified as a particular. It is individuality which is ontologically fundamental rather than particularity.

Every individual is unique. It is itself and not another thing. But what does its uniqueness consist in? Something must first be said about the general character of uniqueness. The unique is the unrepeatable, the once and for all. But what can have this characteristic of unrepeatability? The most obvious candidate is an event. It is a commonplace that every event is unique. It can never literally be repeated. But what is it about an event which makes it unique and unrepeatable? The answer is its spatio-temporal location. It is not what happens which is as such unique but its happening where and when it does. There will be countless thunderstorms in the future but the one which occurred here yesterday afternoon can never be repeated. Its uniqueness does not lie in its being a thunderstorm. Nor does it lie in its spatial location alone. It lies in the fact that of all the thunderstorms which have occurred here, it is the one which happened yesterday afternoon, i.e. what it is together with its spacial and temporal location.

Admittedly there is a relativity about spatio-temporal location. This is because it is we, that is to say human observers, who do the locating. Where something happens is determined by us on the basis of its direction and distance from where we are. We determine when it happened on the basis of its place in the successive order of events which culminates in the present. It happened just now, this morning, a month, a year, or a century ago. This relativity is due to the fact that we human observers are ourselves within the spatio-temporal order of events. But it does not affect the uniqueness of each of the events which make up that order. Each happens before or after each of the others and at a certain distance and direction from each of them.

Events happen: individuals exist. But what exists when an individual exists? The answer is: at the very least, a finite self-maintaining physical structure. In order to be itself and not another thing, an individual must be physically finite. In order to continue to exist through time, it must be a self-maintaining structure. From this it follows that events are ontologically prior to individuals in the sense that there can be events in the absence of individuals but no individuals in the absence of events. The coming into being of an individual is itself an event. So is its dissolution or destruction. Its continued existence through time is its self-maintenance as a physical structure while successive events are happening. Probably the borderline case of an individual is a cloud. Its existence is fleeting and evanescent. But while it exists, it has a rudimentary individuality. It is the cloud now passing across the sun and having a particular shape and colour. Stones, organisms, and artifacts are instances. Each is a self-maintaining finite physical structure. So is the earth, the sun and every other star and planet. All are individuals.

But an individual's uniqueness does not lie in its particular physical dimensions or attributes. These may be duplicated in other individuals. There are many hats of the same material, size, shape and colour as mine. But only one is mine. Nor need physical dimensions and attributes remain unchanged. An individual's physical structure must be relatively stable. It does not have to be static. It may expand and undergo modifications, as in the growth of an organism from infancy to maturity. Where then does the necessary uniqueness of an individual lie? It lies in the fact that every individual is necessarily a unique spatio-temporal continuum.[1] The successive spatio-temporal locations of the one individual can never in their entirety be literally identical with those of any other. Two individuals may co-exist over the same identical span of time. They can be in exactly the same place at different times. But they cannot ever be literally in the same place at the same time. The spatio-temporal continuum of each is made up of a succession of unique spatio-temporal locations. Is this all that individuality amounts to? Is it merely the necessary uniqueness of each individual as a spatio-temporal continuum? The answer is that this is only minimum individuality, the sort of individuality which a stone has. There are, as we shall see later, kinds and degrees of individuality.

Returning to the distinction between individuality and particularity. Individuality rather than particularity is ontologically fundamental because there can be resemblances only between things which are different and therefore individual. But there is also a sense in which individuality as a category of thought, is epistemologically prior to particularity. You can identify things as the same in a certain respect and therefore as particular members of a certain class only if you have already identified them as different things. You cannot think of them as particulars without at the same time also thinking of them as individuals, although your main attention may be focused upon their resemblances rather than upon the self-sameness of each

[1] Cf. P. F. Strawson, *Individuals*.

of them. But you can think of them as individuals without thinking of them as particulars. You can simply note that they are different things in different places without going on to attend to the respects in which they resemble each other.

Margaret Macdonald's quasi-zoological characterization of human beings attaches no special importance to their individuality or their capacity for self-knowledge. But it is only because he is an individual that a human being can have knowledge of himself and of other things. To be able to identify individuals as such and distinguish between them, a human being must himself be an individual in the same world as they and must be able to distinguish himself from each of them. He must be conscious of himself as one individual among others in a common spacio-temporal world. Self-consciousness in its most primitive form is no more than the bare consciousness of the contrast between oneself and what is not oneself. But with the development of some degree of physical co-ordination and of some ability to explore and manipulate what is not oneself, this primitive self-consciousness becomes individual bodily self-consciousness: the consciousness of oneself and one body among others in a spatio-temporal world. It is this individual bodily self-consciousness which is the foundation of all the more sophisticated forms of self-consciousness.[1] It is ubiquitous in all action and is never wholly absent from even the most abstract thought.

But to point out that individuality is epistemologically prior to particularity is not to claim that it is epistemologically superior. On the contrary, particularity is a more advanced category of thought than mere individuality. Thought which was confined to thinking only in terms of individuals would be thought at a pre-classificatory level. It would be confined to the perception of spatio-temporal location. 'This over here is one thing: that over there is another: while this which is now moving between them is a third thing,' would be all that it could manage. It would be thought only in its most rudimentary form. To be able to think in terms of particulars rather than merely in terms of individuals is to be able to compare and contrast different things with respect to their several attributes

[1] Cf. S. Hampshire, *Thought and Action*.

and properties. It is to be able to abstract from spatio-temporal location and attend to the resemblances between different things which have been observed at different times and in different places. The advance which such thought represents needs no stressing. But a word may be said about its significance for the understanding of events.

Every event is unique and the same event therefore cannot literally happen twice. But what happens on one occasion may be exactly like what happens on another. In the sense of being an event of the same kind, the same event may therefore be said to happen again or to recur. In order to apprehend recurrences, thought must be able to abstract from spatio-temporal location and compare what happens on one occasion with what happens on another. It must be able to treat events as particulars, attending to the respects in which they are the same, rather than to their uniqueness. Two types of recurrence are of special importance. One is cyclical: the regular recurrence of the same events in the same order; e.g. the cycle of the tides, of days and nights, of the seasons. The other may be described as 'law-like' recurrence: where two events of different kinds are regularly conjoined but not as part of a regular cycle. The second happens only when the first happens but the first does not happen with uniform frequency at regular intervals: e.g. the freezing of water when its temperature falls below 32°F. It is the apprehension of cyclical recurrence which makes possible the envisagement of the future. It is only because we can apprehend it that we can have the idea of 'tomorrow', 'next week' and 'next year'. The apprehension of law-like recurrence makes possible the investigation of the different properties of things, of how they behave in different circumstances and how they may be adapted to human purposes.

Particularity is superior to mere individuality as a category of thought, but it is not an exclusive category. The epistemological priority of individuality remains. You cannot think of things and events as particulars without recognizing that they are also individual and unique, even though your main focus of interest is on the former aspects. Moreover you can abstract from spatio-temporal location and attend to resemblances and recurrences only if you are yourself an individual. You can compare your own observations made on different occasions and in different places only if you are the same self-conscious observer throughout. Nor does the ability to think in terms of particularity mean that you cannot turn your attention away from resemblance and recurrence to individuality and uniqueness. So far we have seen only what minimum individuality is, what about those kinds and degrees of it which are of more direct human significance?

2. INDIVIDUALITY AND PERSONAL IDENTITY

Personal identity is individual identity. It is a man's identity as the unique person that he is. But what does his uniqueness consist in? What constitutes his individuality as a person? It must be something more than merely the uniqueness of a spatio-temporal continuum. That is the uniqueness not of a person but of a physical individual. A person is unique not only as a physical individual, but also as a finite centre of experience. His sensations and feelings are his alone. No one else can literally suffer his pain or enjoy his pleasure. But while this is important, it does not answer our questions about the uniqueness of personal identity. Animals as well as persons are unique sentient subjects. A person is not merely a finite centre of experience. He is also a self-conscious subject who thinks and acts as well as feels and desires. A man's identity as a person is bound up with his individuality as a self-conscious agent rather than with his uniqueness as a finite centre of experience. But having recognized this, it is necessary before going further to say something about actions in relation to the general topic of individuality.

Every action is an event in the sense that when it is done, something happens. But it is important to distinguish between natural events and actions. Sneezing is a natural event: blowing one's nose is an action. Natural events happen: actions are done or performed. Where there is an action, there is always an agent. Every action is somebody's action. But while natural events happen to people, they are not done or performed by anybody. This points to the presence in every action of some degree of self-conscious initiative on the part of the agent whose action it is. He is aware of it as something which he has originated and is carrying out, and he always has at least some idea of what he is trying to do. Not all action is premeditated. When a man stretches, or turns over in bed, he acts on impulse not from prior deliberation. But an impulsive action is still an action. When a man stretches he is aware of what he is doing. Impulses can be resisted. Feeling an impulse to do something is one thing: acting on it is another. You do not have to do what you feel an impulse to do.

As an event, every action is unique in virtue of its spacio-temporal location. What was done here yesterday afternoon can never literally be done again. But an action is also unique in another respect. Not only is it done on a unique occasion. It is consciously done on that occasion by a unique person. Every action is an individual action in the sense of being the action of an individual agent. Events can be abstracted from their spatio-temporal locations: so can actions. When a man ties his shoe-laces, he is performing a unique action. But what he is doing is an action of a kind which he has performed innumerable times in the past. The significance for human life of this abstraction from spatio-temporal locations needs no stressing. It is the basis of all habitual action. But actions can be abstracted not only from their spatio-temporal locations but also from the unique persons who are their agents. It is this which makes possible the formulation of rules. Rules are addressed to all who are in a specified kind of situation, regardless of who they are. Rules, that is to say, deal with persons as members of classes not as unique individuals.

The exercise of self-conscious initiative in habitual actions and in regularian activity may be very slight but it is never wholly absent. When a man ties his shoe-laces, he performs an action of a kind which he learned to do in childhood. But however mechanical his performance may have become, he is never wholly unaware of what he is doing. On each occasion when he ties up his shoes, he must have decided to do it, albeit spontaneously and without conscious forethought. When a man follows a rule, he does what the other people following it are doing. On the face of it, he is acting not as an individual but as a particular: i.e. as a member of the class of persons who are subject to it. But again albeit spontaneously and without conscious deliberation, he must have judged that he is in a situation to which the rule applies, must have classified himself as a member of the class of persons subject to it and must have decided that he will follow it. All this involves the exercise of self-conscious initiative on his part.

In rational activity and in the implementation of specific principles, the exercise of self-conscious initiative is sufficiently obvious. In Chapter 4 discussing self-determination, the emphasis was upon the degree to which an agent determines his action for himself as distinct from having it determined for him by the precept or example of other people, or by established rules. It was pointed out that rational activity is a more developed form of action than regularian activity and represents a greater degree of self-determination. The implementation of specific principles is intermediate between them. The present discussion brings out the sense in which, even if what the agent does is determined for him, e.g. by an established rule, it is still his action. Without the exercise of self-conscious initiative on his part, it would not have taken place.

But there is another aspect of the notion of self-determination. Wherever there is an action there is an agent. But one cannot be an agent without acting. One determines oneself as an agent, that is to say, through the actions which one does. The exercise of self-conscious initiative is the assertion of oneself as an agent, and not just as any agent but as the individual agent of this unique action. There are then two meanings of 'self-determination'. The first is that of Chapter 4. It is concerned with who decides what is done. To the extent that it is the agent, his action is 'self-determined' rather than 'other-determined'. The second is concerned with what is involved in the fact of action as such. When what happens is an action rather than a natural event, an agent is 'determining himself'. This second sense is relevant to the problem of personal identity. It suggests that a person's uniqueness lies in his being an agent. His actions are unique and through them he has determined himself as a unique agent. In what he has done we have the answer to who he is as a unique person. His personal identity, that is to say, is revealed in his biography as an agent.

But this is to equate being a person with being an agent. Being a person involves at the very least being able to communicate with other persons. Being an agent necessarily involves being able to exercise self-conscious initiative. A rudimentary form of its exercise occurs in the development of individual bodily self-consciousness. The human infant becomes conscious of himself as an individual body among other bodies in a spatio-temporal world as he becomes able to explore and manipulate his immediate physical environment. He is an embryonic agent before he is a person in any meaningful sense. But he cannot become a regularian agent, let alone a rational agent, until he learns to communicate with other persons for instruction and guidance. His individual bodily self-consciousness develops into personal self-consciousness as his powers of communication develop and he becomes able to talk with and listen to other persons. More generally: personal self-consciousness is generated in the consciousness of the reciprocal relationship between oneself and someone else to whom one speaks and listens. In its simplest form, it is the consciousness of oneself as an individual speaker and listener among other speakers and listeners with each of whom one can enter into the reciprocal relationship of communication. But speaking and listening involve the exercise of self-conscious initiative. Speaking is doing something and listening is attending to what is being said. Hence personal self-consciousness even in its simplest form is the consciousness of oneself as an agent, albeit not yet a regularian or a rational agent.

Personal self-consciousness does not normally however remain in its simplest form for long. The persons with whom a young child first establishes communication are the members of his immediate family circle whom he sees every day. He soon finds that he is himself included in that circle. It is not long before his personal self-consciousness expands into the consciousness of himself as a member of a family. But this is only the first step. As a child grows up, he is gradually initiated into the wider life of the territorial society within which his family has its being. While still in the bosom of the family, he becomes a regularian agent and embarks on the first stages of rational activity. He becomes a schoolboy, then probably a trainee and finally a worker. Later he gets married and starts a family of his own. His personal self-consciousness expands and develops with each successive phase of his up-bringing and education. Moreover this development is cumulative. As an adult, he is conscious of himself not only as the man he has become but also as having been the child he was. He remembers his past life in broad outline and can vividly recall many of its episodes in detail.

It is this cumulative development of personal self-consciousness which gives continuity to personal existence. A person is always conscious of himself as being the same person throughout all the fortunes and vicissitudes of his life. Now the hall-mark of individuality is self-sameness. An individual is and continues to be itself. It follows that it is in virtue of his personal self-consciousness that a person is an individual, for it is his personal self-consciousness which gives continuity to his personal existence. But individual bodily self-consciousness is a necessary component of all personal self-consciousness. A man's consciousness of himself as having been the child he once was, is at the same time his consciousness of his own physical continuity as an individual body among other bodies in a spatio-temporal world. The world which he now inhabits as a man is the same world which he inhabited as a child. He has a practical consciousness of himself as a unique spatio-temporal continuum within that world, even though he might be hard put to find words to express it. This is not merely his consciousness of being the same body. It is his consciousness of being the same agent and sentient subject who on a series of past occasions did certain actions and had certain experiences. An action is unique not only because it is an event but also because it is the action of a unique agent. But according to the second meaning of 'self-determination', an agent gets his uniqueness from his actions rather than the other way round. He becomes the agent he is because of the actions he does. To clear up this difficulty, we must return to the early stages in the development of human self-consciousness. An infant's first random movements are not yet actions properly so called. But as he becomes aware that they are his movements and that he can in some measure control them, he begins to convert them into actions by the exercise of self-conscious initiative. In the early stages, the uniqueness of each of his actions and his uniqueness as their agent are two sides of the same thing: the exercise of his self-conscious initiative. But as his individual bodily self-consciousness develops and he becomes increasingly aware of his own continuity as a sentient subject and agent, the two sides begin to diverge. Each fresh action he performs is unique in virtue of being done by him. But he is unique not only as its agent but as the agent of an accumulating series of past actions. With the development of personal self-consciousness, this divergence becomes clear-cut. Each of his subsequent actions is unique because done by him. But he is already unique before he does it.

To return to the suggestion that a person's identity is revealed in his biography. His biography is the record of a series of actions, each of which is unique in virtue of being done by him on a unique occasion. It is not however a series of totally disconnected discrete actions. Each of them springs from the exercise of his self-conscious initiative on a given occasion. But on each occasion, he is aware that he is the same agent who acted on previous occasions. What he does on any given occasion always reflects in some measure, his cumulatively developing personal self-consciousness. Each of his actions contributes to his identity as a unique agent as it takes its place in the accumulating series of his actions. But what makes him the unique person that he is, is that he is the agent of the entire series of his actions, not merely of any one of them taken separately. It follows that a man's identity as a person remains incomplete until his death. At any given moment in his life, he is the person he has so far become in the series of his actions up to that moment. But his biography is as yet unfinished and his determination of himself continues in his subsequent exercise of self-conscious initiative. There is however nothing strange about this. It serves only to emphasise that personal identity is individual identity: i.e. the identity of something which remains the same while it changes.

But the first meaning of 'self-determination' is also relevant. It is concerned with who decides what is done. To the extent that it is the agent, his action is 'self-determined' rather than 'other-determined'. It is in rational activity, more especially at the levels of personal well-being and social morality, that self-determination in this sense is most fully achieved. Moreover it is at the level of personal well-being that the agent must act with the greatest awareness of his own personal individuality. It is his life not anyone else's that he is trying to enhance and enrich. No doubt he can only do so if the well-being of certain other persons is an integral constituent of his own well-being. But this being granted, it is what is wise and prudent for him, he being the person he is, situated as he is, which is his leading consideration. There is a sense therefore in which, to the extent that he acts wisely and prudently in shaping and directing his life, he positively develops his own personal individuality. His life becomes his own and bears upon it the stamp of his authority as a self-determining agent. It is something like this that Mill seems to have had in mind in his conception of individuality.

But before anyone can become a rational agent, he must first become a regularian agent. No one can become a regularian agent until he has learned to communicate with other persons. Individual bodily self-consciousness develops into personal self-consciousness as a young child's powers of communication develop. But these powers can develop only as he learns for himself to follow the conventions of the language being spoken around him. The earlier statement must therefore be qualified. In learning to communicate, he is already becoming a regularian agent as his mastery of simple linguistic rules gradually develops. But in order to become a self-conscious and advanced regularian agent, he must learn from the guidance of those with whom he has already learned to communicate. What concerns us here however is that if he is to learn to follow linguistic rules, he must have learned for himself how to abstract from immediate spatio-temporal locations and attend to resemblances. He must already have begun to think in terms of particularity rather than mere individuality. His ability to think abstractly further develops as he becomes a self-conscious regularian agent. Recalling the relation between individuality and particularity as categories of thought, we can see that development in terms of particularity is necessary for further development in terms of individuality. One must first achieve the abstract thinking necessary for regularian activity before one can reach the self-conscious individuality of rational activity.

3. INDIVIDUALITY AND THE IDENTITY OF SOCIAL GROUPS

Our theme in the last section was the identity of a human being as an individual person. But being a person necessarily involves being able to communicate with other persons. No one can be a person on his own, he must be a member of a social group. We have still to consider this social aspect of personal identity and the implications for the general theme of human identity of the social character of life. Social groups vary enormously in size, composition, and activities, but they always consist of two or more people involved together in some joint activity or common enterprise. Membership of a social group necessarily involves participation. Each member must think of himself and the others as 'we'. He must have at least some idea of what 'we' do together and must play a part in it however slight. In some cases participation may be so slight that membership is merely nominal: for instance trade unionists who do nothing beyond paying their dues. But whenever it is more than nominal, membership contributes to a man's personal identity through the exercise of the self-conscious initiative which his participation requires. Being a member makes a difference to his conduct and to his consciousness of himself as an agent and a person. But this is not all. A child's personal self-consciousness first develops in the bosom of his family. 'We' is the group which includes himself and his parents and his idea of what 'we' do is derived from his day to day relationship with them. It is as he becomes aware of who they are that he first becomes aware of who he is. Membership of the domestic social group does not merely contribute to his personal identity. It is a necessary condition for his developing any personal identity at all.

Every social group has an individual identity. It is the group which it is and not another group. But what constitutes its individual identity? What makes it the group which it is? The short answer is: its membership, together with the nature of its joint activity and its spacio-temporal location. Its members are all individual persons. Their joint activity must necessarily be carried on in some place over a period of time. Its individual identity therefore lies in its being the group of persons who do what they do where and when they do it. But this presents a purely external view of the matter. The members themselves, are aware of their individual identity as a social group, and membership may mean different things to different members of the same social group.

To a young child, the individual identity of his family is bound up with his relationship to his parents. They are his providers, comforters, and guides. 'We' are the members of 'our' family and 'our' family is the group of which his parents are in charge and to which, as their son, he naturally and properly belongs. His idea of what 'we' do together is a composite of his impressions of the day to day life of his home. In like manner, when he first goes to school the school's individual identity is bound up with his relationship to the other children, and more especially to individual teachers. 'We' are the group which includes himself, the other children, and the teachers. His idea of what 'we' do together is a composite of his impressions of what goes on from day to day in the classroom and the playground.

But to his parents, his family is something more than merely the group of which they are in charge. It is an extension of their marriage, something which they have together created through the children they have brought into being. 'We' are the group which includes themselves and their children but in which their relationship to each other remains distinct from their relationship to their children. What 'we' do together embraces their shared activities and experiences as husband and wife, as well as what they do as parents both for and with their children. Similarly to a teacher, his school is something more than merely the place where he teaches children. His awareness of his school's individual identity is bound up with his own part in the overall programme and with his relationships to his colleagues and to the children.

The joint activity of a social group necessarily takes place over a period of time. During this period the group may undergo many changes without losing its individual identity. A family increases in size as each of the children are born. It may move to a completely different area. As the children grow up, their relationship with their parents and with each other change. But the family retains its individual identity. It continues to be the same family. Pupils in a school are constantly changing, and from time to time, a teacher leaves. Over the years, the curriculum is revised. But the school does not lose its individual identity. It continues to be the same school even after generations of pupils have passed through it and none of the original teachers remain.

But what is still the same? What is the individual identity which is retained? The answer turns on two necessarily related characteristics of any social group. The first concerns membership. Any changes must be piecemeal and gradual, not wholesale and abrupt. 'We' must be a continuing 'we' to which new members can adhere and from which individual members can drop out. The second is continuity of its joint activity. The family must continue living together from day to day and from year to year through good times and bad. Each year the school must carry out its annual programme. What is done on any given occasion in the group must be related to what was done before. Far-reaching changes may be introduced from time to time but they must be changes in something already going on and must be relevant to the problems and difficulties which currently beset the group in maintaining and developing its common enterprise.

It is the continuity of the joint activity of a social group, together with a continuing although not necessarily unchanging 'we', that makes a social group the same group after many years. It is the group which embarked on a certain enterprise, on a certain occasion in the past and which has been carrying it on ever since. Its individual identity as a social group is revealed in the history of that enterprise. This history is the record of the actual course which the group's joint activity has taken. Each of the actions which have shaped that course is necessarily unique, however much it may resemble what the members of a similar group have done in similar circumstances. The group's individual identity lies in its being the same group whose joint activity has taken the unique course which it has taken. But just as a man's personal identity remains incomplete until his death, so does a group's individual identity, until its existence comes to an end.

A family's history as an individual social group begins when the parents first set up home together. That of a school begins when the first pupils are admitted. In each case the group comes into existence *de novo* at a specific time. The same is true of a business firm, a trade union, and a club. But what about the territorial human societies within which these groups come into existence and have their being? Do they come into existence at a specified time? The British nation is such a society, but it did not come into being *de novo*. 1776 may be given as the beginning of the American nation, but the American nation was created out of the thirteen British colonies in North America. It appears that these human territorial societies did not come into being *de novo*. How far then does what we have said about the individual identity of social groups apply to nations?

4. INDIVIDUALITY AND NATIONAL IDENTITY

It is sometimes said that the family is the basic social unit. If this means that the existence of the family or an equivalent domestic social group is a necessary condition for the initial achievement of personal identity, it is true. But if what is meant is that the family is a self-sufficient social group, it is false. Human life can go on only in a social group which is greater than a single family. Otherwise there would be no one for the daughters to marry. To be self-sufficient, a social group must at the very least be one in which the children of the various families can inter-marry. It must also have a viable economy either by making everything it needs itself or by engaging in trade and barter with other groups.

But this is to view self-sufficiency in predominantly biological terms and would be applicable to an animal herd. The members of the herd must be able to interbreed. If a herd cannot strictly be said to have an economy, it must at least have continuous access to sources of food. Our concern however is with self-sufficiency for human, not merely animal, life. Many contemporary philosophers appear to suggest that what distinguishes human life from merely animal life is language. On this view, a self-sufficient human group, whatever else it is, must be a group whose members use language and communicate with each other. But while this is true, it follows that the members of such a group must have achieved at least some degree of personal self-consciousness. Each must be aware of himself not merely as an individual body in a spatio-temporal world of bodies but as an individual speaker and listener among other speakers and listeners. What makes them a self-sufficient human group rather than a self-sufficient animal herd is that they are not only maintaining a common life together but are conscious of themselves as doing so. This social self-consciousness is expressed and articulated in their use of language.

Today, the typical form of the self-sufficient human group is the nation: a settled territorial society with a large population and a complex, highly organized way of life. But it was not always so. In the past, itinerant tribes of food-gatherers, hunters and pastoral nomads have been self-sufficient social groups and cases of each still survive. No doubt it is only as a settled territorial society that a human group can develop more than a merely subsistence economy. But whether it is a nomadic tribe or a modern nation, every self-sufficient social group has an individual identity, the basis of which is the continuity of its common life. Each new generation is initiated into that life as it grows up and in its turn initiates its progeny. The successive generations constitute a continuing, gradually changing 'we'. What 'we' do together is to carry on the common life bequeathed to us by our forbears and prepare our children to carry it on in their turn. To adapt Burke's phrase, a self-sufficient social group whatever its economy and organization, 'is a partnership between those who are living, those who are dead and those who have yet to be born'.

But if 'we' are to prepare our children to carry on our common life, 'we' must teach them what they need to know. Each generation must transmit to the next the accumulated body of knowledge and skills necessary for maintaining the group's economy. It must also transmit the rules and principles as well as the ideas and values connected with the institution of marriage as it is practised in the group. The rising generation must learn to think, feel and act as members of the group. They must learn to respect the system of authority recognized in it. Some system of authority is necessary in every self-sufficient social group to enable decisions to be made about matters which concern the group as a whole. It will normally be organized round a ceremonial office, the chief, the monarch, the head of state, which symbolizes the continuing identity of the group. But even where it is not, e.g. in a small nomadic tribe, there will be *de facto* authority exercised by certain persons in virtue of their age or their prowess in war or hunting. As the members of the rising generation learn to respect the prevailing system of authority and to follow the secondary rules which confer it, they will become aware of the individual identity of their group, whether it be tribe, kingdom or nation. The common life into which they are being initiated is carried on within the framework of this system. As they learn to conform to it, they learn to think, feel and act in terms of the ideas, beliefs and values which underly it and the common life which it sustains.

Human life can go on only where there is a common life into which the next generation can be initiated. As long as there has been human life, there have been self-sufficient social groups. But these have not remained the same. Tribes, kingdoms and empires which once existed have lost their individual identity and disappeared. Human history is the record of the changing identity of self-sufficient social groups. But what is the nature of these changes? How does a self-sufficient social group lose its individual identity? The crudest and most obvious way is by physical destruction. A tribe may be destroyed by famine or disease. It may be massacred at the hands of its enemies or conquered and enslaved.

But physical destruction is not the only way in which a self-sufficient social group can lose its individual identity. It may be absorbed into and assimilated by a larger social group. For this to happen, three conditions are necessary. The system of authority of the original group must either be replaced by or made totally subordinate to that of the larger group. Its economic life must be incorporated into that of the larger group so that it no longer has a distinct economy of its own. Its members must cease marrying only among themselves and must be able and willing to marry into the larger group. The first of these conditions may be brought about by conquest. The second may be facilitated by conquest although something more than the replacement of one system of authority by another is necessary. The members of the original group must have something to contribute to the economic life of the larger group. If they are not already able to participate in it, they must learn how to do so. The third, intermarriage, is bound to take time, perhaps generations, to accomplish.

If there is no intermarriage absorption remains partial and assimilation incomplete. A formerly self-sufficient social group may be brought under the system of authority of a larger society to whose economy its own is progressively linked. But its members may cling tenaciously to their old way of life, continuing to speak their own language, to marry only among themselves and to maintain as much as possible of their traditional institutions and practices. The old system of authority will be retained although now subservient to that of the larger society. Although no longer self-sufficient, the group has retained its individual identity. The members continue to think of themselves as 'we' while the members of the larger society are 'they'. 'We' continue to maintain our common life although it is now that of a minority group, not a self-sufficient social group. This is graphically illustrated by the history of the Jews.

It was said that no human group can be self-sufficient unless the children of its families can inter-marry. This statement now needs qualifying. What is necessary is that there should be some other families into which to marry. The existence of a minority in its midst whose members only marry among themselves does not prevent a territorial society from being a self-sufficient social group. But this restriction upon the marriage opportunities of the members of the minority group effectively preserves its individual identity within the larger society. Not every minority was once a self-sufficient social group. Religious conflicts generate religious minorities. Immigration, the transfer of territory after a war, and the emancipation of slaves generate linguistic and ethnic minorities.

The process of absorption and assimilation is not a one way affair in which the host society remains unaffected. Where the population of the group being absorbed is small in relation to that of the host society, there may be few if any significant changes in the latter's way of life. But if it is relatively large or if the acquisition of new territories and populations becomes a deliberate policy, changes may be far-reaching. Enlarged economic opportunities will lead to changes in economic life. The old system of authority will have to be extended and adapted to embrace the new territories. Old ideas, beliefs and values will have to be revised and modified to accommodate the new social and political relationships resulting from expansion. In the course of time the old way of life will be gradually transformed as the society itself turns into something different.

Ancient Rome is a case in point. The Roman Republic achieved supremacy in the Mediterranean world through military conquest. But with its conversion into an empire, the conquered territories became provinces and with the extension of Roman citizenship to them, absorption and assimilation became official policy. Over a period of some 400 years, one self-sufficient social group had turned into another. The city-state of the third century B.C. had become the empire of the second century A.D. During this period there was a continuing 'we': the successive generations of Roman citizens. There was also a continuing common life into which each generation was initiated. But as Roman expansion proceeded, this common life began to change its character. As absorption and assimilation progressed, 'we' began to change in composition and scale. The Empire under the Antonines was a very different society from the Republic which fought the Punic wars. It was different not only in size and complexity of organization, but also in the nature and character of its way of life.

A social group such as a family or a school can retain its individual identity through many years and many changes. While its joint activity continues, it is still the same family or school. Rome was no longer the same self-sufficient social group after 400 years. It had ceased to be a city-state and had become an empire. It had not lost its individual identity but rather changed it. This change was the outcome of a cumulative development. There was continuity in the carrying on of a joint activity from day to day and from year to year. But this joint activity, the maintenance of a common life, was itself gradually transformed, and so therefore was the individual identity of the social group which carried it on. What the history of Ancient Rome reveals is not an individual identity which is retained through change but rather an individual identity which itself undergoes change. Ancient Rome was neither the city-state nor the empire exclusively. It was the city-state which over some 400 years turned into an empire and which thereafter continued as an empire until it was destroyed by the Germanic invasion of the fifth century A.D.

Can a social group which in its nature cannot be self-sufficient, change its individual identity as distinct from retaining it through change? The answer turns on whether its joint activity can be continued while being transformed in character. A monogamous family which became polygamous might be described as having changed its individual identity rather than as having retained it. The same may be said of a school which radically changed the content of its curriculum and the composition of its pupils and staff. Eton was founded in the reign of Henry VI as a school for poor scholars. Its contemporary character suggests, to put it mildly, that in the intervening 500 years Eton has changed rather than retained its individual identity. A business firm which from small beginnings expands to a monopolistic position, absorbing and assimilating its competitors becomes a commercial 'empire'. More generally: in the case of many social groups, changes in individual identity over a period of time are normal, its retention is somewhat exceptional.

Today we are accustomed to the deliberate creation of new nations by successful nationalistic movements in former colonial empires. But this is not how self-sufficient national territorial societies first came into being. They originated in Europe and were not deliberately created at all. Rather they were what the feudal kingdoms, principalities and duchies of Medieval Europe gradually turned into, following the upheaval of the Reformation. It involved gradual changes in the individual identities of the larger feudal kingdoms as the lesser principalities and duchies were absorbed. What this means is that the nations of modern Europe, like social groups in general, have a historical identity. They are not merely natural phenomena which regularly recur in situations of the same kind. Still less are they metaphysical entities which somehow embody eternal essences. Their ontological status is that of emergents. They are the outcome of the cumulative effects of changes in the ways of life of earlier societies, changes which were themselves the outcome of the attempts by the members of those societies to deal with the problems which currently faced them.

But what about nationalism and the deliberate attempt to create new nations? Nationalism began to be an influential political doctrine only after the American and French Revolutions. Its inspiration was the social and political development which had already taken place. But can a new nation be deliberately created at all? The answer is that the nation itself cannot be, but the conditions for its emergence may be. There must already exist a territorial social group capable of becoming a self-sufficient territorial society. It may then be possible to deliberately create the conditions under which it can do so. What cannot be deliberately created is the already existing social group. A colony can become a nation only if it already has an individual identity as a social group. There must be at least the nucleus of a continuing 'we' and a common life already in being. Like their European counterparts, new nations are emergents with a historical identity. This being their ontological status, they will in the course of time turn into something else just as they themselves are what earlier societies have turned into.

5. HUMAN IDENTITY

Consider the hypothetical case of a self-sufficient society which is totally isolated, its members having no knowledge of any other societies. To them it will be 'the society'. They will contrast it with other social groups which exist within it but will be unable to contrast it with other self-sufficient societies. They will have no concept of foreigners and, it might seem at first sight, no need for the concept of humanity, since being human will be the same thing as being a member of their society. But they will need it to distinguish between themselves and all other animal species. They will recognize that they too are animals but will also know that as self-conscious agents and persons they are something more. Their concept of humanity will be their concept of themselves as something more than merely animals. In the case of a self-sufficient society which is not totally isolated, the need for a concept of humanity is more obvious. Its members will need the concept of foreigners to distinguish between themselves and the members of other self-sufficient societies. Their concept of humanity will be their concept of what they and foreigners have in common and of what differentiates both of them from all other animal species.

Human beings have not always and everywhere had the same concept of humanity. How we think of ourselves depends upon how we understand the world we inhabit and our place in it. The concept of humanity points beyond itself to a wider theory of human identity, and of the nature and significance of human life in the general scheme of things. In the course of human history there have been a number of different theories of human identity, some of which have been ethnocentric. An ethnocentric theory is one which gives pride of place among mankind to a particular human group. This group may be a single self-sufficient society; or it may consist of a number of such societies inhabiting a certain region and sharing a common culture which gives them an individual identity as a people; for instance the Ancient Greeks. An ethnocentric theory holds that there are different grades of humanity, and that the members of the group in question constitute the superior grade. The rest of mankind make up the inferior grades. Thus the Old Testament Jews drew a distinction between themselves as 'the chosen people' and all Gentiles. The ancient Greeks distinguished between themselves and all non-Greeks, whom they considered barbarians. The Chinese traditionally distinguished between themselves and all 'foreign devils'.

There are however serious difficulties about ethnocentric theories. If the doctrine of grades of humanity is saying only that human beings are variously and unequally endowed, it is true enough as far as it goes. If however, the doctrine is a racist one, maintaining that some races are inherently superior, then there are fundamental objections to it. There are no grounds in anthropology upon which one race can be said to be more human than another. All the available evidence is against there being any inherent connection between race and native capacities. Moreover an ethnocentric theory would have to show that races and human social and cultural groups were invariably empirically correlated, and here again the available evidence is to the contrary. There is a provincial arrogance about ethnocentric theories. To give pride of place among mankind to a particular human group, to claim that 'we' its members, are superior, suggests conceit born of ignorance rather than the mature wisdom of experience.

A theory of human identity, if it is to be adequate to its task, must be cosmopolitan, not ethnocentric in character. Stoicism and Christianity are notable instances of cosmopolitan theories in Western history. Stoicism provided the Roman Empire with a cosmopolitan intellectual foundation. But while it emphasized the common humanity of all human beings and preached an austere code of ethics, as a theory of human identity, Stoicism suffered from excessive abstractness. Indeed it amounted to little more than the assertion that human beings are fundamentally the same and that the diversity and variety of human life at different times and places is only superficial. Christianity as it was practised in the early Church, did not suffer from excessive abstractness. What it had to say about human identity and about the nature and significance of human life in the world was couched in personal terms and was concrete, vivid and dramatic.

Now Christianity is a religion and Stoicism was fundamentally religious in spirit. Buddhism and Islam are also religions with cosmopolitan theories. The claims of these different religions cannot all be literally true. Upon what rational grounds, if any, can a choice be made between them? The concept of revelation does not help. If the truth or falsity of what is revealed can be established on independent grounds, the concept of revelation is superfluous. If it cannot, how can the genuine revelation be distinguished from the spurious? The genuine character of a given revelation cannot itself be a matter of revelation, for that would involve a vicious infinite regress. Revealed truth can only be a matter of personal conviction. It cannot be demonstrated to those to whom it has not been vouchsafed.

But can the particular tenets of any religion ever be literally true? Surely not if they purport to give an ultimate explanation of the nature of things. Any explanation must presuppose certain categories in terms of which it is framed and these categories of necessity fall outside the scope of the explanation. An ultimate explanation, if that means one which explains everything and leaves nothing unexplained, is strictly inconceivable. We may be able progressively to deepen our understanding of ourselves and of the world we inhabit, and in the light of such an understanding, discover more and more explanations for more and more of what happens in the world. But an explanation of why there should be a world at all must in the nature of the case lie beyond us. To say that its existence is due to the will of God, that he created it for his own purposes, is to give an allegorical account of the world not an ultimate explanation of its being. Concepts such as 'will', 'purpose' and 'creation' are intelligible within the sphere of human thought and action. They presuppose an already existing world in which ends can be willed, purposes formulated and executed, works of rat created. They cannot be used to explain the being of what they themselves presuppose as a condition for themselves being meaningful.

All this is another way of saying that the ultimate nature of things is necessarily shrouded in total mystery. Our human self-consciousness is always the consciousness of ourselves as being in an already existing world. The scope of our knowledge is necessarily limited to what we can find out from our position within that world. We cannot go beyond it or outside it. A theory of human identity which is to be adequate to its task must start with the recognition that this is the fundamental character of the human predicament. It must not be geared to any religious tenets which offer an ultimate explanation since such an explanation is not to be had. It must be non-theological, its account of the nature and significance of human life not being couched in terms of any theological creed or doctrine. This should not be interpreted as an attack upon religion as such. No religion can know the ultimate truth about the nature of things, but religion has value and significance for human life. It is just because the ultimate nature of things is wrapped in an impenetrable mystery that human experience has a religious dimension. What is called 'religion' is our human response to that mystery, and the various religions of mankind are attempts to come to practical terms with it. Failure to realize that these attempts must necessarily be allegorical generates the idea that religion contains the ultimate truth.

To be adequate, a theory of human identity must be cosmopolitan not ethnocentric. It must answer the questions: 'What is it to be human?' and 'What is the nature and significance of human life in the general scheme of things?' without being geared to the particular tenets of any religion, while avoiding the excessive abstractness of Stoicism. But if the ultimate nature of things is mysterious, can the second of these two questions be answered at all? Can anything be known about the general scheme of things, let alone the nature and significance of human life within it? The answer has already been foreshadowed in an earlier paragraph. We may not be able to know why there should be a world at all but from our position within it, we can at least try to find out what it consists of and how it is constituted. The achievements of the natural sciences is eloquent testimony to what in fact we have already accomplished in this direction. From their work an over-all picture of the general scheme of things can be extracted. It is of a vast and complex spatio-temporal order of natural events and processes. Within the framework of this order, multitudes of living species have come into being and among these the human species is one of the latest.

This suggests that human life has no special significance. It is only the life of one more zoological species among many others. But the human species is a very unusual one. Its members are not merely animals. They are self-conscious agents and persons who wonder about the general scheme of things and their own position in it. We can say somewhat elliptically that human life has whatever significance in the general scheme of things human beings themselves are able to give it. More specifically: human life is subject to the conditions of the natural world. It has emerged within the spatio-temporal order and must be lived inside the framework of that order. It is whatever human beings can manage to make it. It is not merely natural life but self-critical life: the life of beings who have some capacity for understanding themselves and their situation in the world and of acting in the light of that understanding.

Human life emerged out of animal life with the evolution of the human species from pre-human ancestors. After this emergence, what human beings have in fact made of it is revealed in the record of human history. That history is the record of the changing identities of the self-sufficient societies within which human life has always been carried on. But it is also the record of the many and various ways of life which human beings have developed within the framework of these societies. Human life itself is historical in character. No generation of human beings in any society ever starts from scratch. It is always at once the beneficiary and the victim of the deeds and misdeeds of preceding generations. It is heir not only to their achievements but to their unfinished business; to their unsolved problems and difficulties no less than to their institutions, skills and knowledge.

Mankind has not so far become a single social group, much less a single self-sufficient society. Unlike a nation, a kingdom or a tribe, it has no individual identity. But there is nevertheless a sense in which any self-sufficient society, just because it is a society of self-conscious agents and persons, is a microcosm of mankind. Its way of life at a given time and place represents what the current generation of its members are in fact making of human life in the conditions of that time and place. The ideas, beliefs and values in terms of which its way of life is framed, reflect their understanding of themselves and their situation in the world. It is a concrete embodiment of the universal human predicament, that predicament arising out of the fact that the ultimate nature of things is totally mysterious and that whatever significance human life is to have must be given to it by human beings themselves. This inevitably prompts further questions about any individual self-sufficient society. What does its way of life, as it is being carried on by a

212

given generation at a given time and place, really amount to? What sort of a job are they making of the task of giving significance to human life in the conditions of that time and place? How well are they coping with the universal human predicament as it is concretely embodied in their society? And these questions raise issues which bring us back to the central problems of moral relativism, the point of departure for the present chapter.

Chapter 7

Critical Humanism

An approach by which the problem of moral relativism might be overcome was suggested at the beginning of the last chapter. It was that the common life of a given society should be criticized and evaluated from the point of view of its adequacy as a way of life for human beings. What bearing has our subsequent discussion of human identity on this approach? Human beings are self-conscious agents and persons. They are members of individual self-sufficient societies but are not irrevocably confined within them. Each of these societies is a concrete embodiment at a given time and place of the universal human predicament. As self-conscious agents and persons, human beings are capable of understanding their predicament. From their vantage point within the world, they can investigate what it consists of and how it is constituted, and can explore its possibilities for human living. This suggests a standpoint from which a society's way of life may be rationally evaluated. At any given time the ideas, beliefs and values which underlie its way of life, reflect the understanding which the members of the current generation have of themselves and the world. The better this understanding, the more adequate the society's way of life as a way of life for human beings. This standpoint may be called the standpoint of critical humanism. But much more needs to be said to explain and justify it, and to show how it meets the problem of moral relativism.

The problem of moral relativism arises from the fact that at the level of social morality there are no rational grounds upon which the members of a society can evaluate their common life. If they are to act responsibly and justly, there must be widespread agreement among them about its fundamental

214

character. But given this agreement, it does not matter what that character is. At the level of social morality, that is to say, one way of life is as good as another. But according to critical humanism, this is not so. One way of life is better than another to the extent that its underlying ideas, beliefs and values, reflect a better understanding of the world and of human identity. But why should the standpoint of critical humanism be accepted? What reasons are there for maintaining that the better the understanding, the better the way of life? The short answer is that it is the distinctive characteristic of human beings to act in the light of that understanding. The better the understanding therefore which a given way of life reflects, the more it is a distinctively human way of life. This is by no means a revolutionary idea. It is implicit in the Socratic doctrine that an unexamined life is not worth living. Mill's famous aphorism that it is better to be Socrates discontented than a fool satisfied expresses it elliptically.

There is, however, an objection. According to critical humanism, the better the understanding of the world and of human identity, the better the way of life. But how is this understanding to be appraised? What are the grounds for judging that it is better or worse? Anyone who attempts such a judgement is himself a member of a society at a given time and place. It seems therefore that he is precluded from making such a judgement in the case of his own society, since as a member, he is already committed to understanding the world and human identity in terms of the ideas, beliefs and values, which underlie its current way of life. If he attempts it in the case of another society, he will have to appraise its understanding in the light of that which currently prevails in his own, and that would be to beg the main question. This suggests that the standpoint of critical humanism is untenable as far as human beings are concerned, and this conclusion seems to reinforce the position of moral relativism.

An individual's first understanding of the world is necessarily in terms of standards currently prevailing in his society. But as a self-conscious agent and a person, he is not irrevocably committed to understanding it in these terms for the rest of his life. He can try to understand the world and what it is to be human for himself. He need not be tied down to the received ideas, beliefs and values, in terms of which his first understanding was formed. He can test them in the light of his growing knowledge and experience: asking to what extent the ideas are meaningful, relevant and mutually consistent; what evidence there is that the beliefs are true; what reasons there are for respecting the values. He can appraise his own society's standards and such an appraisal is an integral part of his attempt to understand for himself. The same is true of societies other than his own. They are microcosms of mankind and their members are equally involved in the universal human predicament. He has good reason to appraise the various ways in which they understand the world and human identity as a contribution to his attempt to understand them for himself.

The understanding which an individual being can achieve for himself is necessarily his own but it is not on that account private. He can share it with others who can reciprocate by sharing theirs with him and both sides can learn from each other. All human beings live in the same world and are equally involved in the universal human predicament. Each of them who tries to understand the world for himself is aiming at something universal which must be the same for all human beings everywhere. No doubt it is only a minority of the members of each generation in a society who seriously try to understand for themselves. The majority for the most part will be content to accept the understanding bequeathed to them by former generations. But that understanding itself is the outcome of the efforts of minorities in previous generations to understand for themselves and to communicate what they have understood. It is when the practical relevance of new ideas, beliefs and values, become apparent that the conservative majority may come gradually to accept them without perhaps being fully aware that they are doing so. The new idea may point to wider horizons, or to ways in which present burdens may be alleviated and present discontents remedied. Thus what is at first revolutionary may come over a period of time to be accepted as orthodox.

But to aim at an understanding which is universal is one thing; to achieve it is quite another. At different times human beings who have tried to understand the world for themselves, have in fact understood it in ways which in various respects have been very different. Thus is hardly surprising. Human beings are always limited in the attempt to understand the world and human identity for themselves, by what they know and have experienced. Both the scope of the knowledge and the range of the experience which human beings have had to go on, have been very different at different times and in different places. Differences in the ways in which they have understood are therefore only to be expected. Not that sheer quantity of knowledge or sheer variety of experience is the whole story. Knowledge must be interpreted, integrated and systematized, if there is to be understanding. But the wider such knowledge and experience, the better the understanding which it is possible for human beings to achieve. Different ways of understanding are therefore not merely different. They are also better or worse, depending upon the scope of the knowledge and the range and variety of the experience from which they spring.

The appraisal of the prevailing understanding must be made in the light of the fullest knowledge and the widest experience that the person making it can command. Consider the case of a society in whose way of life witchcraft figures prominently. Its members believe that some of their number are witches and alternate between persecuting and trying to propitiate them. A mid-twentieth century Western European has good grounds for judging that so far as their attitude towards witchcraft is concerned, their understanding of the world is defective. On the basis of the knowledge and experience available to him, he has good reason to conclude that there is no evidence which supports a serious belief in the existence of witches, while there is massive evidence to the contrary. If there really are witches, then the world must be very different from the picture of it presented by the natural sciences today.

This does not mean that the modern scientific picture of the world is final and authoritative in all matters. It can only be a provisional picture which remains open to modification in the light of new scientific discoveries. Nor can it be a complete picture, since the scientific perspective takes account only of natural events and processes, and so presents only a partial and one-sided view of human thought and action. But being provisional and incomplete does not make it irrelevant. No one who wants to understand the world and what it is to be human, can afford to neglect the modern scientific perspective. To do so would be to ignore the knowledge acquired by a sustained, many sided, critical inquiry into what the world consists of. The picture of the world entailed by witchcraft is in radical conflict with the modern scientific world picture. It does not derive from a body of knowledge acquired through critical inquiry but is the product of uncontrolled imagination.

What is true of witchcraft is true of magic and astrology. Anyone who seriously believed in any of them cannot have understood the modern scientific perspective. To the extent therefore that any of them figures prominently in a society's way of life, a modern Westerner has good grounds for judging that the society's prevailing understanding is defective. In the discussion in the last chapter of ethnocentric theories of human identity, it was said that all the evidence of physical anthropology and genetics is against ethnocentrism. To the extent therefore that the way of life of any society is ethnocentric, a modern Westerner once more has good grounds for judging that its prevailing understanding is defective. But it is important to emphasize that all these appraisals are limited and piecemeal in character. They are appraisals only of some particular feature of a given way of life, for instance, witchcraft, astrology or ethnocentrism.

The understanding prevailing in a given way of life is necessarily that of the conservative majority of the current generation, not that of the minority who try to understand for themselves. To find out what it is, one must go to the ideas, beliefs and values underlying the way of life. These will be embedded in the various institutions and practices which make up that way of life and any relevant well-grounded appraisal must start from a specific institution or practice. The appraisal must be directed towards the understanding reflected by those ideas, beliefs and values, integral to that institution. Different institutions and practices within the same way of life may involve different and even incompatible ideas, beliefs and values. There can be many latent ambiguities and contradictions of which people are hardly aware and which can be discovered only by appraising each of its institutions and practices in turn.

It follows that in a large and complex society such as a modern nation, the prevailing understanding is likely to be an amalgam of a number of ways of understanding the world and human identity, some of which are mutually inconsistent. Astrology and modern science may co-exist in the same way of life at the same time and place. But the standpoint of critical humanism can take this fully into account since its appraisals are limited and piecemeal. If those who believe in witchcraft come to see that there are no good reasons for their beliefs and so proceed to abandon them there will be an improvement. Whatever its merits and defects in other respects, their way of life on that score will have become a better one for human beings. It is because it furnishes the rational basis for such evaluations (limited and piecemeal though they necessarily must be) that critical humanism enables moral relativism to be overcome. Such evaluations are of course relative to the knowledge, experience and understanding of whoever undertakes them, but this relativity does not make them any the less rationally grounded.

It was argued in the last chapter, that an adequate theory of human identity must not be geared to the particular tenets of any one religion. From the standpoint of critical humanism, to the extent that a given way of life is shaped in terms of one particular religion, it must be inadequate for human beings because reflecting an inadequate theory of human identity. But it was also pointed out that human experience has a religious dimension arising out of the fact that the ultimate nature of things is totally mysterious. To the extent that in any way of life the religious dimension is ignored, the way of life is in that respect inadequate for human beings; the more the true character of the religious dimension is understood, the better the way of life. What counts according to critical humanism is the degree to which the religious side of a given way of life shows insight into the universal human predicament and displays imagination and sensitivity in coming to practical terms with it. The more tolerant and undogmatic the religious side of any way of life, and the more widespread the recognition that the particular tenets of any religion can only be allegorical in character, the better that way of life. From the standpoint of critical humanism, there can be many different ways of responding to the religious dimensions of human experience, not all of which necessarily involve membership in a church or equivalent corporate organization.

Suppose that someone says that he does not care if the understanding currently prevailing in his society is defective in various ways. He is quite content with its way of life as it now is and remains unmoved by the argument that there are good grounds for judging that in a number of respects it is inadequate for human beings. In his opinion it is good enough not only for him but for the other members of his society. Suppose further that he produces convincing evidence to show that this opinion is shared by his fellow members. What can critical humanism say in reply? The short answer is that it does not have to say anything. The fact that people are indifferent to its rational evaluation of their way of life does not invalidate that evaluation. Nor does it follow that because people are in general contented with their way of life, it is on that account an adequate way of life for human beings. Whether people are contented with something is an empirical question to be answered in the light of empirical evidence. Whether something is adequate is a question of value to be answered by a rational evaluation according to an appropriate standard. But perhaps general contentment rather than critical humanism is the appropriate standard. Not 'the better the understanding, the better the way of life', but rather 'the greater and more widespread the contentment, the better the way of life', should be the basis of rational evaluation. This will not do. The capacity to be contented and discontented is not a distinctively human characteristic. Animals have it as well. A way of life is not distinctively human simply because those who live it are contented with it. Understanding, because it is a distinctively human characteristic, is a better standard.

Granted that the capacity for understanding is a distinctively human characteristic, it is not the only one. Why should it be singled out as specially important? Laughter is also a distinctively human characteristic. Human beings are the only creatures who can appreciate comedy. Why not, 'the more plentiful the opportunities for comedy, the better the way of life'. But there can be no comedy, and for that matter no tragedy, without understanding. It is because they are capable of understanding themselves and their situation that human beings can appreciate the comic and the tragic. The choice of the capacity for understanding is not arbitrary. It is what distinguishes man as *homo sapiens* from all other species, and is the foundation of the other distinctively human characteristics.

2. ESTABLISHED MORALITY AND THE SOCIAL ORDER

The established morality of a self-sufficient society consists of moral rules both primary and secondary, of specific and general moral principles, and of moral virtues. We saw that the justification of moral rules is substantive rather than merely pragmatic. It is a society's prevailing understanding of the world and of human identity which furnishes its official justification for its established morality. But within this prevailing understanding, the members' ideas and beliefs about the individual identity of their own society will be especially relevant. Their general ideas about what it is to be human will be embedded in their explicitly formulated and consciously held ideas of who 'we' are and of what is important and valuable in 'our' way of life. These consciously held ideas will shape their attitudes towards other societies. They will also play an important part in the substantive justification of secondary moral rules. Such rules are substantively justified because the social order which they shape is part of the fabric of the society's way of life. Without them, it would not have the specific character which it has.

As we saw, self-sufficient societies are not eternal entities. Human history is the record of their changing identities and of how those existing at one time have turned into those existing at another. To the extent that this is not recognized in the ideas which the members of a given society have about its individual identity, their prevailing understanding of what it is to be human is defective. Ethnocentric ideas betray a lack of historical perspective as well as erroneous anthropology and genetics. So do delusions of national grandeur such as 'Manifest Destiny',

'The White Man's Burden', or 'The Herrenvolk'. To the extent that such ideas infect a society's prevailing understanding, its way of life is corrupted. History and more especially the light which its perspective throws on human social living is no less relevant than science to the attempt to understand the world and human identity. The same is also true of philosophy and the social sciences.

To be a person is to be a finite centre of experience. More especially it is to be capable of suffering. This suggests that to the extent that the established morality of any society condones suffering, its prevailing understanding is defective. War and the martial virtues may be extolled while the misery and pain which they involve are played down. But officially sanctioned indifference to suffering may take less blatant forms. The misery and degradation of the poor in a society may be dismissed on the grounds that poverty is the result of laziness, or that those concerned have never known anything different. The same judgement of a defective understanding is applicable wherever there is indifference or acquiscence in the suffering inflicted by human beings on animals, or on non-human sentient creatures of any kind that are capable of suffering.

There is and always will be much suffering in the world which is unavoidable. Poverty may sometimes be the result of laziness. It may be necessary for human beings to exploit animals but to try to cover up these unpalatable facts and pretend that what is in fact suffering is really something else to betray a defective understanding of the world. It may be objected that this is only to say that to the extent that a society's prevailing understanding involves self-deception, it is defective. What about the case of a society in which the reality of suffering is fully recognized but in which nothing is done to prevent or alleviate it? What can be said from the standpoint of critical humanism about such a society? Can its prevailing understanding be branded as defective if there is no self-deception on the subject of suffering and full awareness of its presence?

The answer is that it can, and that this can be seen by considering the nature of sympathy. Sympathy is always sympathy with the individual experience of other persons. One sympathizes when one imagines oneself to be in their place experiencing what they are experiencing and when one feels in oneself something of the emotions which they are feeling. Some capacity for sympathy is a native human trait. But it is a capacity which can be either cultivated and fostered or blunted and warped by the influences to which a human being is exposed in the course of his life. It is a capacity the importance of which can hardly be exaggerated.[1] It is a necessary condition for mutual understanding, for shared experience, and for effective co-operation in any joint activity. Without it, human life would indeed be 'solitary, poor, nasty, brutish and short'. When it is blunted human communication is impoverished and the possibilities open to human beings through co-operative activity are correspondingly reduced.

No one can sympathize with someone else's suffering and at the same time be indifferent to it. Sympathy will always generate a desire to try to remove the cause of suffering. A society in which the present reality of suffering is frankly acknowledged but in which there is widespread indifference to it, is therefore a society in which the capacity for sympathy has been blunted or warped. It will be a society in whose established morality sympathy does not rank high as a virtue to be cultivated. If anyone fails to appreciate the nature and importance of sympathy, his understanding of what it is to be human is necessarily one-sided and inadequate. To the extent therefore that a society underestimates and undervalues sympathy as a human capacity, its prevailing understanding of human identity is defective. Thus from the standpoint of critical humanism, there are good grounds for judging that a society in which there is widespread indifference to acknowledged suffering is a society whose way of life is inadequate for human beings.

In appraising a society's understanding attention must be paid to its social order. Consider the case of slavery. Slaves are exposed to the very real danger of suffering at the hands of their masters in addition to any which their consciousness of being slaves may cause them. To condone or even to acquiesce in slavery is to be indifferent to the suffering of a certain group of human beings. From what has been said about suffering,

---

[1] In Hume's *Enquiry concerning the Principles of Morals* and in Adam Smith's *Theory of the Moral Sentiments* sympathy is the central ethical concept.

there are good grounds for judging that the way of life of a slave-owning society is inadequate for human beings. But this is not the whole story. As we saw, to be a slave is virtually to be confined to regularian activity. A slave can become a rational agent only within the interstices of the social order. His status as a slave officially denies him the opportunity of becoming an independent person able to pursue his well-being as a rational agent. The justification for slavery as an institution must therefore be the belief that those who are slaves belong to a special class of human beings who lack the capacity for rational activity. They must, as Aristotle put it, be 'natural' slaves who are by nature precluded from anything more than regularian activity. But modern science affords no empirical support for this. Cases of congenital and pathological defects apart, the findings of genetics, psychology and physical anthropology are all against the belief that certain human beings are inherently limited to regularian activity and lack all capacity for rational activity. Aristotle's class of natural slaves is therefore an empty class. It has no members. A society in which slavery is believed to be justified is therefore one whose prevailing understanding is defective.

But what about a hypothetical case of a society in which it is admitted that slavery has no justification but in which slavery is actively maintained. Such a society is condoning in its social order something which is acknowledged to be arbitrary. It is acquiescing in the unjust treatment of certain human beings. In maintaining slavery, the free members of the society are acting irrationally at the level of social morality since they are doing what they know to be unjust. Now a society whose social order fosters irrationality at this level is one in which, to put it mildly, the nature and significance of both rational activity and morality are seriously underestimated. This betrays a seriously defective understanding of what it is to be human, and more especially of what is entailed in human social living. Indeed it reflects an attitude of mind which is inimical to understanding as such. In virtue of its cynical support of slavery the way of life of such a society is not merely inadequate for human beings. It is in this respect fundamentally anti-human in character.

Slavery is an extreme case but what has been said about it

applies to other social institutions. Consider the case of a multi-racial society whose social order is based on racial segregation. The members believe that there are inherent differences between the races and that in particular intermarriage must be prevented if the physical, intellectual, and moral calibre of future genera-tions is not to deteriorate. Modern genetics and psychology however lend no support to this belief and the concept of the 'natural' which it implies has no support in the modern scientific perspective. There are grounds for judging this part of the society's way of life to be inadequate and the development of an open social order untramelled by the barriers of racial segregation would be an improvement. The same conclusion is applicable to the case of a society whose social order is based on a hereditary caste system. It is also applicable although for different reasons to a theocracy. The way of life of a theocracy is inadequate for human beings because it betrays a defective understanding of the nature, scope, and limits of religion, and therefore of the world and of human identity.

The existence in a multi-racial society of widely different cultural standards and attitudes of mind may well give rise to social problems which seem to those concerned to be intractable. But that is not a good reason for maintaining a social order based on false beliefs about human beings. Still less does it justify cynical acquiescence in a social order known to be unjust to the members of certain races. What has just been said about a slave-owning society, a caste society, and a theocracy, recalls what was said in Chapter 5 about the idea of a free society. It suggests that from the standpoint of critical humanism, the more a society's social order approximates to the equality of status integral to the idea of a free society, the more adequate will be its way of life for human beings. Discussion of the relation between critical humanism and the idea of a free society will be one of the main themes of Chapter 9.

For the present it is important to emphasize again the piece-meal character of the appraisals made from the standpoint of critical humanism. The social order of a given society may reflect a defective understanding but that does not mean that its way of life can be condemned wholesale. It may contain other features which would enhance and enrich the way of life of any human society. The social order of classical Athens was based on slavery and its prevailing understanding was coloured by ethnocentrism. But when attention is focused upon Athenian achievements in art, in philosophy and in politics, its prevailing understanding and way of life appears in a different and very much brighter light. From the standpoint of critical humanism, a society's non-moral intrinsic values, and its attitudes towards human creativity and human achievements, are no less relevant than its established morality and social order.

3. INTRINSIC VALUES

A self-sufficient society must be able to provide and maintain the conditions necessary for its own continued existence. It must have a viable economy. In an obvious sense a society's economic activities are utilitarian in character. They are the means which its members adopt to bring about certain ends. But as we saw in Chapter 3, utilitarian activity is pointless unless directly or indirectly it prepares the way for activities and experiences which are intrinsically valuable. What is important about a society's economy therefore is not whether it enables the members to stay alive but what sort of lives it enables them to lead. The greater its wealth and the more efficient its technology, the greater the possibilities which are open to the members. This does not mean that wealth is itself intrinsically valuable. But it does mean that a rich society is in a better position than a poor one to establish the conditions necessary for the widespread enjoyment of intrinsic values.

But so far as the individual agent is concerned, rational activity at the level of utility forms an integral part of rational activity at the level of personal well-being. There is a parallel in the case of a self-sufficient society. Much of the time and energy of the members will necessarily be devoted to economic activities. What these are, and how much time and energy they demand will be an important factor in establishing the terms upon which the members are able to participate in the society's way of life. In other words, how a society earns its living cannot be separated from how it lives. Its way of life is comparable not to an individual agent's specific ulterior purposes but to his over-all personal well-being. There are then two ways in which a society's economy affects its way of life. One is indirect, arising out of the utilitarian character of economic activities. The greater the productivity of these activities, the better the opportunities for intrinsically valuable activities. The other is direct and arises out of the fact that a society's methods of production and technology are not separate from but form an integral part of its way of life.

Whether and to what extent all this is understood are relevant questions in appraising any society's prevailing understanding. In William Morris's novel *News from Nowhere*, the attitudes of the members on the subject of work was a central theme. In the utopian society which he imagined, it was the view of the members that whatever work was done must be fit for human beings to do. If certain goods and services could be produced only by work which was degrading to those who did it, or which was inherently dull, affording no scope for imagination, skill, and intelligence, then they would do without those goods and services. But the benefits of scientific technology and advanced division of labour, high productivity of a range and diversity of goods and services can be had only at the cost of methods of production which involve much repetition and routine labour. A society which tried to dispense with them would be sacrificing the opportunities for the enjoyment of intrinsic values which they make possible.

This objection to Morris's view is sound enough in the case of the indirect way in which a society's economy affects its way of life, but what about the direct way? If people have to spend their time doing dull and unimaginative things, they are likely to become dull and unimaginative people. Work is necessarily utilitarian in character but utilitarian activities can also be worthwhile for their own sake. To fail to appreciate that how a society earns its living cannot be separated from how it lives, is to betray a defective understanding of both human action and of human social living. A society which tolerates methods of work which degrade the workers by blunting their sensibilities is betraying this defective understanding. Its way of life is on that score inadequate for human beings. According to Morris, this was true of Victorian society.

It was pointed out in the last chapter that whatever significance human life is to have, must be given to it by human beings themselves. But if they are to give it significance, they must incorporate into it, activities and experiences which are intrinsically valuable. It was suggested in Chapter 3 that what makes an activity or an experience intrinsically valuable is that it affords scope for the development of some native human gift or capacity. An adequate theory of intrinsic value would have to go a good deal further.[1] Here what is important is the sense in which intrinsic values are empirical discoveries. That various sorts of activity and experience are intrinsically valuable is something which human beings can find out only by engaging in them. While each generation can pass on to the next knowledge of the activities and experiences which it has found intrinsically valuable, the new generation still has to rediscover their intrinsic value for itself. They will appropriate from the preceding generation what they themselves find intrinsically valuable but they will modify these values in the light of their own experience. Human beings have always found intrinsic value in sensuous and aesthetic experiences and in friendship and love. Broad limits are set to the range of experiences and activities which they can find intrinsically valuable by the nature of the human organic and physical constitution. But within these broad limits there is no reason to expect uniformity. Human beings differ in the degree to which they are endowed with particular gifts and capacities, so that activities and experiences which to some human beings are worthwhile for their own sake, are to others devoid of intrinsic value.

In societies of comparable size the combinations of different degrees of natural endowments will be roughly duplicated but the extent and richness of the range of intrinsic values in each society will depend in part upon the efficiency of the society's economy and in part upon its prevailing understanding of the world. A society which lives close to the margin of subsistence will lack the material resources necessary for the cultivation of elaborate and sophisticated tastes and interests. One whose way of life is centred on the stern teaching of an ascetic religion

[1] For such a theory see C. I. Lewis *An Analysis of Knowledge and Valuation*, Open Court Press, 1946. Especially Book 3.

will find no intrinsic value in amusement or conviviality, and will dismiss as mere frivolity whatever does not directly contribute to the cultivation of the austere virtues enjoined by its creed.

The reason that contemporary Western societies display roughly the same range of intrinsic values lies in the fact that their economic efficiency is roughly similar, and also because they share more or less the same understanding of the world. These two factors are not independent of one another. Technological productivity and economic efficiency can be raised through the application of scientific knowledge. But how far the members of a given society will be able and willing to make this application will depend upon the extent to which their understanding includes an appreciation of the scientific perspective and its relevance to utilitarian activity and upon their understanding of utilitarian activity in the wider context of human action. This in turn will depend upon their prevailing understanding of what it is to be human, and more especially of the fact that if human beings are to give human life significance, they must incorporate into it activities and experiences which are intrinsically valuable.

It follows that in appraising a given society's prevailing understanding, critical attention needs to be paid to its members' attitudes towards intrinsic values. How far do these attitudes reflect a true understanding of the nature of intrinsically valuable activities and experiences and of their relevance to human life? Puritan condemnation of the theatre and of dancing sprang from religious zeal. The Puritan version of Christianity was supposed to give to human life all the significance it needed, and the contribution of activities and experiences intrinsically worthwhile for their own sake irrespective of religious considerations was discounted. But this monolithic attitude betrays a defective understanding of intrinsic values in general and of religion in particular. It fails to appreciate the empirical character of intrinsic values and the necessarily allegorical character of all religious creeds and doctrines. Failing to understand these things, it arbitrarily restricts the attempt to give significance to human life, and is therefore inadequate as a way of life for human beings.

Intrinsic values are not as such moral in character, they belong to the level of personal well-being. But are all intrinsic values equal or are some more valuable than others? In his 'Utilitarianism', Mill in effect answers this question through his distinction between 'higher' and 'lower' pleasures. According to him the pleasures of the intellect and of the arts are superior in quality, not merely in quantity. Stripped of the psychological hedonism which encumbers his entire discussion, what he is saying amounts to this. Certain sorts of activity and experience are intrinsically more valuable than others by virtue of the kinds of activity and experience which they are. Intellectual and artistic pursuits are intrinsically valuable: so are sport and entertainment. But the intrinsic value which can be found in the former is at once different in kind from and greater in degree than the intrinsic value which can be got from the latter. To anyone who has had genuine experience of both, no amount of entertainment and sport can compensate for the loss suffered in being cut off from intellectual and artistic pursuits. But the converse does not hold.

Empirical evidence supports this reformulation of Mill's doctrine. Wherever intrinsic values have been cultivated with any degree of sophistication, some sort of hierarchy has been recognized among them. The important point is that each value should be appreciated for what it is worth. A way of life in which no room was found for the enjoyment of sport or entertainment would be drab and colourless. But one in which there was no room for artistic or intellectual pursuits and in which, apart from economic activities, there was an unending round of amusement would be inadequate by reason of its triviality and lack of understanding of the richer possibilities in human life. From the standpoint of critical humanism therefore a relevant consideration is the degree of sophistication and depth displayed in a society's prevailing attitudes towards intrinsic values. To the extent that these attitudes are naïve or crude, to the extent that they display ignorance of the achievements of human beings at other times and in other places, and a lack of awareness of present possibilities, the society's way of life is inadequate.

All sorts of combinations of natural gifts and capacities occur among human beings. They will differ in their ability to appreciate and enjoy the more sophisticated and subtle intrinsically valuable experiences. Intellectual and artistic pursuits are not for everyone. But it is only by trial and error that human beings can find out what capacities they in fact possess. In the absence of adequate opportunities such capacities as there may be for appreciating higher intrinsic values are likely to remain undeveloped. Whether or to what extent this is understood are relevant questions in appraising a given society's prevailing understanding. Securing opportunities for every member to develop whatever capacities he has for appreciating higher intrinsic values, is a problem which faces the society as a whole and which requires concerted social action. The extent to which this is recognized is an important indication of the society's understanding.

4. THE NATURE OF EVIL

It is of the essence of evil to be destructive of good. To be justified therefore in branding anything as evil, one must be able to show what the good is which it threatens. According to critical humanism, the better a self-sufficient society's prevailing understanding the better its way of life. This suggests that anything which threatens the efforts of human beings to understand themselves and the world, and to act in the light of that understanding is evil. But this is not all. An adequate understanding of what it is to be human shows that whatever significance human life is to have must be given to it by human beings themselves. They must incorporate into it activities and experiences which are intrinsically valuable. It follows that anything which is destructive of human beings' appreciation and enjoyment of intrinsic values is an evil.

According to Hobbes, the greatest of evils is death. This is plausible because death is final. It puts an end to the appreciation and enjoyment of intrinsic values. But death is inevitable. 'All men are mortal.' Is the fact of human mortality in itself an evil? If so, there must be some intrinsic value, appreciation and enjoyment of which is made impossible by the fact that human life always and everywhere has a finite temporal span. But whether there is, and if so what it is, are questions which we human beings are precluded from answering by the fact of our mortality. It follows that for us, death is not as such an evil. Paradoxically enough it is a fact of life, albeit an unpalatable one, and we have no alternative but to accept it.

But why should death be an unpalatable fact of life? The answer is that the prospect of his impending annihilation is not one which any human being can normally view with equanimity. Apart from cases of merciful release, the typical reaction is one of fear. When it is not mastered and controlled, fear is always an evil. It is destructive of good because it inhibits all other feelings and distorts judgement. A man in the grip of fear is dominated by the desire to escape from what he fears. He is in no condition to appreciate and enjoy intrinsically valuable activities and experiences. That is why courage is a virtue. To be courageous is to master fear, and through mastering it to overcome its evil tendencies. When it gets out of hand the fear of death is an evil. While human mortality is not as such an evil, an individual human being's death on a given occasion may very well be. It will be if it is premature so that the person concerned is cut off from the appreciation and enjoyment of intrinsic values which would have otherwise been open to him. It will be an evil if it is an irreparable loss to those who love him, a loss from which they never fully recover, so that their capacities for enjoying intrinsic values are permanently impaired.

A lingering and painful death is always an evil. But what makes it an evil is the suffering which is involved rather than the death itself. Suffering is always an evil because while it lasts, the sufferer's capacity for enjoying intrinsic values is always impaired. But there are occasions on which suffering is unavoidable. That is why fortitude is a virtue. It consists in bearing unavoidable suffering with resolution and composure. Both suffering and uncontrolled fear or panic are states into which human beings get, not activities or attitudes. Because they are states, panic and suffering are evils which befall human beings rather than evils which they commit. They are natural evils rather than moral evils, although they may be caused by human sins of commission and omission as well as by natural events.

This points to a distinction between intrinsic and extrinsic evils. States such as panic and suffering in all its forms are intrinsic evils. They directly impair their victims' capacities for enjoying intrinsic values and so are directly destructive of good. Natural disasters such as earthquakes and crop failures, human failings such as carelessness, negligence, and selfishness, may be extrinsic evils. They are extrinsic evils when they cause intrinsic evils but they are not evil in themselves. Earthquakes do not always cause and destruction. Not all crop failures result in famine. Human carelessness, negligence, and selfishness are nearly always a nuisance, but they by no means always cause suffering. But in the last paragraph reference was made to moral evils and to human sins. Are these extrinsic evils, intrinsic evils, or a combination of both? They can hardly be merely states but must in some way either be or involve actions and attitudes. Our account of evil must be expanded to embrace them.

The hypothetical case of a society in which slavery was maintained although it was admitted to have no justification, was discussed in Section 2 of this chapter. In maintaining slavery the free members of the society were acting immorally since they were doing what they knew to be unjust. Immorality properly so called consists in doing that you know to be morally wrong. At the level of social morality it is to do what you know to be socially irresponsible or unjust. In terms of regularian morality it is knowingly to break an established moral rule which you acknowledge ought to be obeyed. The attitude manifested in immorality is one which is inconsistent with itself. The claims of morality are acknowledged but at the same time they are repudiated. It is an attitude which is inherently destructive of morality, whether in the shape of social morality as a level of rational activity, or in the simpler form of regularian morality. Because it is inherently destructive of morality, it is an intrinsic moral evil. Admittedly this assumes that morality as such is good since only then can what is inherently destructive of it be an intrinsic evil. Provisionally we will take this for granted.

This account of moral evil is in direct conflict with the famous Socratic doctrine that virtue is knowledge. According to Plato, Socrates maintained that no one would knowingly do wrong. If that was true there would be no such thing as immorality properly so called. There could only be moral error arising out of ignorance or imperfect understanding. The immoral attitude would be a psychological impossibility and hence there could be no such thing as intrinsic moral evil. But the Socratic doctrine is false as each of us surely knows from his own personal experience. But although false, it is nonetheless illuminating for it draws attention to an important feature of immorality. If I really believe something to be morally wrong, I am likely to have qualms about doing it however strongly I am tempted. In order to allay these qualms I will therefore pretend to myself that it is not in fact wrong although I know that I really believe that it is. The immoral attitude, that is to say, is fundamentally dishonest or in contemporary jargon, inauthentic. It involves me in the strain of conscious self-deception, a strain from which I can escape only by repressing its cause: my belief that what I want to do is wrong. The Socratic doctrine would have been much more plausible if it had been confined to the proposition that: No one will be willing to admit to himself that what he is doing is wrong.

A distinction is drawn between immorality and amorality. Consider the conduct of the psychopath. He is indifferent to moral distinctions. The claims of morality mean nothing to him. He is not immoral but amoral. But what about the rational agent at the level of personal well-being with his essentially pragmatic approach to morality? Is he amoral or immoral? To call him amoral is misleading because it suggests that he is incapable of acting morally. But this is not so. Unlike the psychopath, he is not indifferent to moral distinctions. He knows how to act morally and does so, provided that major personal inconvenience or sacrifice is not involved. But to call him immoral is also misleading. It suggests that he acknowledges that he ought to give priority to moral demands irrespective of personal inconvenience or sacrifice. But this is precisely what he does not acknowledge. The truth is that on the subject of morality he is fundamentally equivocal. He is trying to have it both ways: to have the benefits of morality without meeting its costs. It is therefore less misleading to call him immoral since he is so implicitly if not explicitly. The term 'amoral' can then be reserved for the man who is altogether devoid of moral capacity.

Persistent immorality may degenerate into amorality. The repeated repression of moral qualms is likely to produce an increasing insensitivity to moral distinctions culminating in a state of mind approximating to the psychopathic. Like immorality, amorality is an intrinsic moral evil since it is inherently destructive of morality. But of the two, amorality is the greater moral evil. The immoral man is not wholly beyond the reach of rational appeal. He still acknowledges the claims of morality even though he inconsistently repudiates them and tries to conceal this inconsistency from himself. Since he is in other respects a rational agent, the hope still remains that he may be brought to recognize the truth about himself. But the completely amoral man is out of reach. He cannot be touched and is truly a 'lost soul'. To blame him is pointless for he has no idea of responsibility. Whatever relevance the concept of blame has in moral contexts is confined to the case of the immoral man who may still be able to overcome his inauthentic attitude.

But is morality as such good? Let us recall why there has to be morality at all. An established morality is an integral part of the way of life of any self-sufficient society which is not torn by internal dissention. Rational activity at the level of social morality is something more than merely regularian morality. It involves acting in the spirit rather than the letter of an established morality. But it necessarily remains anchored to some way of life of which an established morality is an integral part. Human life is necessarily carried on in individual societies. If there is to be human life, there has to be morality. But what about its goodness? According to critical humanism: the better the understanding, the better the way of life. Now much of a society's prevailing understanding will be embedded in its established morality. While therefore any established morality is better than none, it follows that a given established morality will be good to the extent that the prevailing understanding which it embodies is good. The better therefore the established morality, the better will be the regularian morality which is carried on in terms of it. The same is true of social morality as a level of rational activity. It is always better to be a rational agent at the level of social morality than to be a merely regularian moral agent. But the better the way of life in terms of which you are socially responsible and just, the better is your conduct as a rational moral agent. Social morality as a level of rational activity is good, that is to say, to the extent that the way of life to which it is anchored is good.

There are also extrinsic moral evils, for instance, hatred, jealousy and envy. They are not in themselves inherently destructive or morality. But their tendency is to induce a frame of mind in which moral distinctions cease to be significant. A man dominated by hatred is in a state bordering on amorality. But anything which dominates or obsesses a man may either make him insensitive to moral distinctions or induce him to repress moral qualms. Moreover, an extrinsic moral evil is likely also to be a non-moral intrinsic evil. A man dominated by jealousy or envy is in a state in which he cannot properly cultivate, appreciate, and enjoy intrinsic values.

There are degrees of intrinsic evil, both moral and non-moral. Immorality on a given occasion may be more or less serious depending upon the degree of irresponsibility or injustice involved, or upon the importance of the moral rule which is broken. The suffering experienced may be more or less severe. It was pointed out in Chapter 4 that it is always just to choose the lesser rather than the greater evil when these are the only alternatives. But this choice can only be between greater or lesser non-moral intrinsic evils, for instance, between greater or lesser suffering. There cannot be a moral choice between greater or lesser degrees of immorality. To do something one knows to be morally wrong, can never be a moral alternative in any situation whatever. Admittedly it is by no means always easy to decide what is the lesser evil, but in a morally difficult situation one can at least do one's best.

Evil cannot be wholly eliminated from human life. It is possible that one day amorality as a psychopathic state may prove amenable to clinical treatment. It is also theoretically possible that human beings may be able to overcome their inauthentic attitude of immorality to such an extent that immorality is reduced to insignificance. But susceptibility to suffering is an integral part of being human. In the nature of the case suffering cannot be totally eliminated, therefore some degree of non-moral intrinsic evil is an inevitable feature of human life. How far all this is appreciated is relevant in appraising the prevailing understanding embedded in the established morality of any society. The better the understanding of evil, the better to that extent the society's way of life. Moreover since it is the essence of evil to be destructive of good, a society's ideas about evil will be an important clue to its understanding of good.

5. CRITICAL HUMANISM AND RATIONAL ACTIVITY

There is a well-known aphorism of Marx. 'Hitherto philosophers have tried to interpret the world. But the problem is to change it.' Our preoccupation so far has been with understanding, but nothing has yet been said about action. Now the standpoint of critical humanism is implicit in rational activity. It was argued in Chapter 3 that what makes one level of rational activity higher than another is that it embodies a better understanding of human life and the world in which it is lived.

This suggests that we must think of rational activity not merely in terms of social morality, still less merely in terms of personal well-being or utility, but in terms of the standpoint of critical humanism. It means that above social morality there must be another level of rational activity the perspective of which is co-extensive with the standpoint of critical humanism, a level which may appropriately be called the level of critical humanism. But what are the implications of the standpoint of critical humanism for action? What is the rational agent at this level, the critical humanist, as we may henceforth call him, to do? He will evaluate his society's way of life from the point of view of its adequacy for human beings through a piecemeal appraisal of its prevailing understanding. He will not repudiate the demands of social morality. The perspective of social morality is included within the larger perspective of critical humanism and the critical humanist knows that he has good reason to act responsibly and justly. But unlike the rational agent at the level of social morality he will not interpret these demands in terms of his society's prevailing understanding. He will interpret them rather in the light of his appraisal of that understanding and hence of his evaluation of his society's way of life.

It may be objected that because the critical humanist's appraisals are piecemeal, his evaluation will always be provisional and incomplete. Consequently his interpretations of the demands of social morality will be tentative and will lack the confidence and decisiveness of those of the rational agent at the level of social morality. But this objection misses the point. It is not necessary that the critical humanist's evaluation should be final and complete. What is fundamental is that he understands that his society's way of life requires evaluation, that it is not sacrosanct and beyond the reach of criticism. Wherever he has no reason to think that it is inadequate he will act like the rational agent at the level of social morality. But unlike the latter, he will be ready to challenge and question rather than merely take existing institutions and practices for granted. What the critical humanist lacks is not confidence or decisiveness but dogmatism. But nothing has yet been said about how the critical humanist is to interpret the demands of social morality in cases where he judges his society's prevailing understanding to be defective. Nor is it clear what the positive focus and direction of his conduct is to be; nor again what the relation is, if any, between this and his interpretation of the demands of social morality.

Each of the other three levels of rational activity has a positive focus and direction. At the level of utility, the rational agent must act efficiently and expediently: at the level of personal well-being, wisely and prudently; at the level of social morality, responsibly and justly. In each case this positive focus and direction springs from the understanding of the world and of human identity which is specific to the perspective of the level in question. This suggests that the positive focus and direction of critical humanism must spring from the understanding which is specific to its own perspective.

This understanding is contained in the theory of human identity sketched in the last chapter. That theory is the foundation of the standpoint of critical humanism and therefore of its perspective as a level of rational activity. It is a theory which makes clear that every self-sufficient society is a microcosm of mankind in the sense of being a concrete embodiment at a given time and place of the universal human predicament. It also makes clear how that predicament arises: namely out of the fact that the ultimate nature of things is totally mysterious and that therefore whatever significance human life is to have must be given to it by human beings themselves. This points to the conclusion that a rational agent has above everything else good reason to make the best contribution he can in his individual situation to the enterprise of giving human life significance. We have seen that if human beings are to give human life significance they must incorporate into it activities and experiences which are intrinsically valuable. This is an integral part of the understanding specific to critical humanism, as is a grasp of the sense in which intrinsic values are empirical discoveries. A rational agent has therefore above everything else good reason to make the best contribution he can in his individual situation to the discovery of intrinsic values and to their appreciation and enjoyment by as many human beings as possible. This is the positive focus and direction of critical humanism as a level of rational activity.

It has something in common with the conclusion reached by G. E. Moore in *Principia Ethica*. He in effect maintained that a rational agent has above everything else good reason to bring about the existence of as many intrinsically good things as possible. This was his answer to the second of what he considered to be the two fundamental questions in ethics: namely, 'What kinds of action ought we to perform?' But the position being developed here differs from Moore's in some important respects. Intrinsic values are not confined, as they were for Moore, to the enjoyment of friendship and the appreciation of beauty. What makes an activity or an experience intrinsically valuable is not that it possesses a simple non-natural quality but that it affords an opportunity for the exercise and development of some native human capacity. Nor is action thought of in purely utilitarian terms as it is by Moore. Moreover there is no reference in *Principia Ethica* to the social character of human life, much less to social morality. Considerations of social responsibility and justice apparently have no relevance to human conduct. At all events Moore had nothing to say about them, perhaps because his exclusively utilitarian view of human action did not permit them to be taken into account. But this is not so for critical humanism.

The critical humanist does not repudiate the demands of social morality. He interprets them, however, in the light of his piecemeal appraisal of his society's prevailing understanding. But what is the relation between this interpretation and the positive focus and direction of critical humanism? This brings us back to the question which was raised earlier. How is the critical humanist to interpret the demands of social morality in cases where he judges his society's prevailing understanding to be defective? The answer is that before interpreting them he must decide what the best contribution is that he can make in his individual situation to the enjoyment of intrinsic values. His first concern, that is to say, is with the positive focus and direction of his conduct as a critical humanist, and it is with reference to this that he must decide what is socially responsible and just. That is why in cases where he has no reason to think that his society's way of life is inadequate, he will act like the rational agent at the level of social morality.

It might be thought that in cases where his society's way of life is inadequate, it would be socially responsible for the critical humanist to try to make it more adequate. But while this is true, it is misleading unless certain qualifications are added. Consider a case where the inadequacy lies in the indifference of many members of a society to the suffering which is being endured by certain of their number. The critical humanist certainly has good reason to do all he can to alleviate the suffering. By doing so he will be making at least an indirect contribution to the greater enjoyment of intrinsic values by a greater number of people. But if his society's way of life is to be made more adequate, the defect in its prevailing understanding manifested in the indifference to the suffering must be remedied. If this indifference is due to sheer ignorance, remedying it may not be too difficult. But it may be due to a reluctance to admit the fact of the suffering, or to prejudice and a blunted capacity for sympathy. 'They are Negroes, Jews, or Irish.' In either case, remedying the defective understanding will be an uphill task. But he can go ahead with efforts to relieve the

suffering without waiting for success in the long-term enterprise even though only when that enterprise is successful will
his society's way of life have become more adequate.

An obvious example is racial segregation. There may well
be little or nothing that the critical humanist can do in the
immediate future to remedy this defect. He can only accept the
fact that his society's way of life is inadequate and is likely to
remain so. But the positive focus and direction of critical
humanism remains relevant. He can still do the best he can in
a painful situation to contribute to the discovery of intrinsic
values and their enjoyment by as many human beings as
possible even if he is limited to the sphere of personal relations
and private undertakings. So far as social responsibility is
concerned, he does what he can towards loosening the social
order and preparing it for eventual change. To destroy it and
provoke social anarchy cannot however contribute anything
to the greater enjoyment of intrinsic values. To do so would be
socially irresponsible. He may however sometimes have good
reason to join a revolt against established authority. In a
society which is deeply and painfully divided along racial or
religious lines to do that might be the lesser evil. But that can
only be where there are reasonable prospects of avoiding
anarchy and of replacing the existing régime by one which holds
out more hope of eventual improvement.

But what about considerations of justice as distinct from
social responsibility? False beliefs about what it is to be human
can never constitute relevant grounds for differential treatment
between human beings. Consequently a social order based on
racial segregation involves injustice since it is maintaining
differential treatment on the basis of false beliefs. But we have
seen that what is just must be determined in the light of what is
socially responsible. Considerations of social responsibility
constitute relevant grounds for differential treatment. In the
last paragraph we saw that it will be socially responsible for
the critical humanist in a racially segregated society to accept
its social order rather than destroy it. Does this mean that
racial segregation is not after all unjust since it is for the time
being socially responsible to accept it? The answer is that it
does not. A distinction must be drawn between the justice or

injustice of the social order and what it is just for the critical humanist to do. At the level of social morality, this distinction cannot be drawn. The rational agent can only accept the racially segregated social order as an integral part of his society's way of life. But in the wider perspective of critical humanism it can. To accept the social order for the time being is the lesser evil and it is therefore both socially responsible and just for the critical humanist to do so. But the social order itself remains unjust for reasons which can be understood at the level of critical humanism although not at the level of social morality. The critical humanist has to accept the fact that his society's way of life is inadequate for human beings and is likely to remain so for the foreseeable future. That means tolerating its unjust social order.

A rather different case is that of a society in which prevailing ideas about intrinsic values betray a defective understanding of what it is to be human, for instance where they have been infected by Puritanism. On the face of it, the positive focus and direction of critical humanism and the demands of social morality seem to go hand in hand. By doing what he can to improve his society's prevailing understanding on the subject of intrinsic values, the critical humanist will be contributing to their greater appreciation and enjoyment. But this will be an uphill task and it may well be possible for him to make a more immediate contribution in spite of the unenlightened attitude of the majority in his society. He can take part in the private cultivation and development of intrinsic values joining with others among the minority who share his outlook. Nor need he be confined to his own society for he can join with like-minded members of other societies for the same purpose.

This last point recalls the cosmopolitan character of the theory of human identity underlying the standpoint of critical humanism. That cosmopolitanism must be reflected in the positive focus and direction of the critical humanist's activity. His horizon must not be limited to the way of life of his own society. If he can do more abroad than at home to contribute to the greater enjoyment of intrinsic values by more human beings, then he has good reason to take advantage of any opportunity to go abroad. This does not mean that his own society has no claim upon his loyalty, but this loyalty must be interpreted in terms of his wider loyalty to mankind, not the other way round. That wider loyalty is summed up in the positive focus and direction of his activity as a critical humanist. It is directed to the greater appreciation and enjoyment of intrinsic values by all human beings, not merely by his fellow countrymen. This may sometimes present him with difficult and painful problems but then the life of the critical humanist is not always an easy one.

The rational agent at the level of social morality does not give up trying to enhance and enrich the quality of his personal life. But he knows that he has good reason to subordinate considerations of his personal well-being to the demands of social morality. The same is true of the critical humanist but there are two respects in which his attitude is different. One is this different interpretation of the demands of social morality. The other springs from his better understanding of what it is to be human. Like the rational agent at the level of personal well-being he wants to make the most of his individual life. But his ideas about what making the most of it means are different. He knows that whatever significance human life is to have must be given to it by human beings themselves. He also knows that his own individual life like that of every other human being has a finite temporal span. If it is to amount to anything as an individual human life, it must contribute something to the over-all enterprise of giving significance to human life as such. He must make the most of the opportunities in his individual situation to contribute to the discovery of intrinsic values and their enjoyment by as many human beings as possible. In other words, the positive focus and direction of his activity as a critical humanist provides the rational basis not only for his interpretation of the demands of social morality but also of the claims of his own personal well-being.

At each of the other three levels of rational activity there are corresponding standards of rationality. For critical humanism there is one appropriate standard which may be expressed in the phrase 'enlightened humaneness'. The critical humanist will be the more likely to realize the positive focus and direction of his activity, the more his conduct is humane. It will be humane to the extent that it shows sympathy for and understanding of the difficulties facing other human beings and helps them to make more of their lives as human beings. But the humaneness must be enlightened. It must reflect an adequate understanding of the world and of human identity, and also of the obstacles to, and the opportunities for, the enjoyment of intrinsic values. At the level of critical humanism, therefore, the more the rational agent's conduct displays enlightened humaneness, the more rational it is. This is the relevant standard for criticizing what he does. It takes precedence over the standards of the other levels. What is socially responsible and just must be determined in the light of the requirements of enlightened humaneness. The same holds of decisions about what is wise and prudent, and about what is efficient and expedient.

6. SOME AMPLIFICATIONS AND IMPLICATIONS

Anyone who makes a rational appraisal of his society's prevailing understanding must try to understand for himself. But why should he arrive at the theory of human identity which is the foundation of critical humanism? The short answer is: because in the light of the knowledge and experience available in the twentieth century it is a better theory than any alternative. This does not guarantee that he will arrive at it. What he comes up with will depend upon his intellectual capacity, and upon how far he approaches the task with goodwill and without prior commitment to any particular doctrine. But it is a theory which tries to do justice to all the dimensions of human experience and to take full account of the perspectives of scientific and historical knowledge. It is itself neither scientific nor historical. Rather it may properly be described as a philosophical theory. It is an 'open-ended' theory. It does not try to prejudge the detailed results of future empirical research. Its concern is not with empirical detail but with the general character of the world and of what it is to be human. Nor does it claim to have said the last word on these matters but simply that what it has to say is true so far as it goes.

The standpoint of critical humanism is essentially modern,

involving as it does an appreciation of the perspectives of science and history. Men tried to understand for themselves before the rise of modern science and modern historical research. The record of ancient and medieval philosophy is eloquent testimony to this. They tried to evaluate their own society's way of life and to make it more adequate for human beings. Both Stoicism and Christianity challenged accepted ideas, beliefs, and values, and advocated ways of living which were believed by their adherents to derive from a more profound understanding of the world and of what it is to be human. But in neither case had that understanding the advantage of the perspectives of modern science and history. Critical humanism enjoys this advantage. Its standpoint embodies an understanding which is not only different from but better than those contained in Stoicism and Christianity. Consequently while there is a sense in which Stoicism and Christianity each pointed to a level of rational activity above social morality, it was in each case something less than rational activity at the level of critical humanism properly so called.

Does this mean that a critical humanist cannot be a Christian? As we have seen, the standpoint of critical humanism is not hostile to religion as such. It appreciates that human experience has a religious dimension. But it recognizes that religious creeds and doctrines cannot be literally true and that they can have only allegorical significance. If being a Christian means believing in the literal truth of a particular creed, then a critical humanist cannot be a Christian. But is it not possible to appreciate that religious creeds and doctrines can only have allegorical significance and yet at the same time to find in Christian ritual and practice a personally satisfying way of coming to terms with the religious dimension of human experience? If there are Christian churches to which such an attitude is acceptable, then being a critical humanist is not incompatible with being a Christian and from the standpoint of critical humanism the more such churches the better.

The better a society's prevailing understanding, the better its way of life. But what about the individual human being? There is an apparently straightforward corollary. The better the understanding and hence the greater the degree of enlightened humaneness with which he acts, the better he is as a human being. In other words, the higher the level of rational activity a man habitually achieves, the better he is and since critical humanism is the highest level of rational activity, the critical humanist is the best type of human being. It has been suggested that only a minority in each generation are likely to try to understand for themselves. The conservative majority will be content for the most part with received ideas about the world and human identity. If this is true, only a minority can become critical humanists. Therefore the best type of human beings will be a minority in each generation but this needs some qualification.

A distinction must be drawn between personal criticism and evaluation. A man may be fairly criticized for failing to do his best according to his lights but not for having the lights which he has. How good these are, is a matter for evaluation rather than personal criticism. Consider an extreme case: the Christian fundamentalist. He sincerely believes in the literal truth of Christian doctrine and does his best to live up to its precepts. From one point of view, he is being a good man. He is doing his best according to his lights and no one can do more. But in being a fundamentalist, he is betraying a defective understanding of the world. Fundamentalism makes the mistake of taking literally what can only have allegorical significance. In trying to live according to fundamentalist teaching, he is being human in the best way he knows but it is not the best way. He cannot however be blamed if temperamentally and intellectually he is incapable of a more sophisticated attitude. More generally; personal sincerity is one thing, the merits of what one is sincere about, another. The most that anyone can do is to be human in the best way he knows. But that does not alter the fact that some ways of being human are better than others.

At the level of social morality the rational agent's way of being human is in terms of his society's prevailing understanding of human identity. But because of the limitations of the perspective of social morality it will always be inferior to the critical humanist's way. The rational agent at the level of social morality takes his society's prevailing understanding of human identity for granted. He does not try to make a rational appraisal of it. But the critical humanist does. His way of being human is in terms of a theory of human identity which takes full account of the perspectives of science and history and a mature understanding of all the dimensions of human experience. But there is an exception. This is where a society's prevailing understanding substantially embodies the theory of human identity specific to critical humanism. Such a case is not wholly fanciful. If contemporary Western societies are not yet in this position, it is one towards which many of them are tending to move as the meaning of the perspectives of science and history come more and more to be appreciated. In such a society, it would seem on the face of it that there is no difference between the critical humanist's way of being human and that of the rational agent at the level of social morality. It is not clear that there is any longer any difference between critical humanism and social morality as levels of rational activity.

But this is not the whole truth. Like the critical humanist, the rational agent at the level of social morality will try to make the best contribution he can to the greater enjoyment of intrinsic values by as many human beings as possible. But he will do it because it is authorized by his society's prevailing understanding and is therefore part of what is involved in being a good member rather than because he understands for himself that above everything else he has good reason to do it. In Platonic language, he will have true opinion rather than knowledge. He will recognize that he should do it but will not understand why. But the critical humanist will have knowledge rather than true opinion. He will know why he should do it, having arrived for himself at the theory of human identity from which it springs and having understood the reasons for it. In such a society, that is to say, the rational agent at the level of social morality will typify the conservative majority, the critical humanist the minority who try to understand for themselves. The conservative majority will be dependent upon the minority of critical humanists to keep their understanding of human identity alive. Without them it will soon degenerate into a formal dogma more honoured in the breach than the observance. In such a society there will still be a difference between being a rational agent at the level of social morality and being a critical humanist properly so called, a difference marked by the Platonic difference between knowledge and true opinion, the critical humanist's way being better than that of the rational agent.

If a society's prevailing understanding substantially embodies the theory of human identity specific to critical humanism, its way of life is to that extent the more adequate for human beings. If it is true that many contemporary Western societies are moving in this direction, it follows that their ways of life are gradually improving. But such rational evaluations are piecemeal. The fact that in Britain or the United States today a better understanding of what it is to be human is gradually becoming more widespread is to be welcomed. But this does not mean that everything in the garden is lovely. A society's prevailing understanding consists of an amalgam of ideas, beliefs and values, among which there will be latent ambiguities and conflicts. While the general tendency may be towards more enlightened ideas, old ones are likely to linger on. Certain sections of the population who fear the effects of change will cling tenaciously to old beliefs and practices unwilling to accept the fact that they betray a defective understanding. The present rearguard action by white Americans in some states of the old South, to preserve racial segregation, is a case in point. But resistance to change may take more subtle forms and while these may not be able to halt a general tendency towards improvement, they may well slow it down and be the cause of much suffering.

Is the best type of human being the genius? Great artists and scientists, great statesmen and reformers, great inventors and engineers contribute most to the discovery and appreciation of intrinsic values. But there is no necessary connection between excellence in a particular field and a high degree of enlightened humaneness in the general conduct of life. Notoriously some geniuses have been impossible people. Being a genius does not automatically qualify one as a critical humanist. A man's personal identity is revealed in his biography. What has he made of his life? What sort of human being has he managed to become? His biography must be evaluated if these questions are to be answered. One way of evaluating it is in terms of the level of personal well-being. How far has he directed his life wisely and prudently? Another is in terms of the level of social morality. How far has he been a responsible and just member of his society? But neither of these ways are satisfactory. Both reflect a defective understanding of the world and of human identity. The best way is in terms of the level of critical humanism. How far and with what degree of enlightened humaneness has he tried to contribute to the greater enjoyment of intrinsic values by more human beings? His performance as a rational agent at the levels of social morality and personal well-being, and at the level of utility will be interpreted in the light of his overall performance as a human being. An individual man's life is no more likely to be a coherent whole than is the way of life of an individual society. It will be a case of how far and to what extent his way of being human in successive periods of his mature life approximates to the best way.

It was said that the theory of human identity underlying critical humanism was philosophical not scientific or historical. Scientific theories are concerned with natural events and processes, historical theories with the human past or with some phase or aspect of it. Philosophical theories are concerned with general ideas and concepts, and with general principles, standards and values. They always contain a normative or appraising element. A philosophical theory of knowledge is a theory of what counts as knowledge and why, and about the scope, limits and possibilities of knowledge. A philosophical theory of morality is a theory about what it is to be moral and about why there should be morality at all. More generally: a philosophical theory is an attempt to say what a concept, a value, or a principle amounts to, not in some limited context but from the point of view of its overall significances and relevance to human experience of the world. Thus a philosophical theory of human identity is a theory about what it is to be human and about the place and significance of human life in the general scheme of things. It is a theory about ourselves and about our general situation, its scope, limits and possibilities.

In the opening chapter of his *Mind and the World Order*, C. I. Lewis writes: 'It is, I take it, a distinguishing character of philosophy that it is everybody's business. A man who is his own lawyer or his own physician is poorly served. But everybody both can and must be his own philosopher.' Whether or not this is true of everybody, it is certainly true of the critical humanist. He has to try to understand the world and what it is to be human for himself. He must work out for himself a philosophical theory of human identity. He can learn from and take advantage of the work of others and should take what help he can get from academic philosophy. If he is unable to get very much, that may well be the fault of academic philosophy rather than his own. The main justification for academic philosophy as a subject in higher education is that it helps those who study it to become their own philosophers. Its proper business is with those general ideas and concepts, and those general principles, standards and values, which must be understood if the world and human identity are to be understood. To the extent that it neglects its proper business, it betrays its calling. This book is an attempt to contribute to the proper business of academic philosophy. Its aim is to work out a philosophical theory of freedom and of rights. Discussion of other topics such as rational activity, rules and principles, individuality, and above all the pervasive problem of moral relativism, have been undertaken in the interest of this specific aim. There is however one topic which is certainly relevant and which has so far largely been neglected, namely, government.

Chapter 8

Government

1. SELF-INTEREST AND THE CORPORATE INTEREST OF A SOCIAL GROUP

Government is, or at least ought to be, carried on in the interest of the governed not the governors. But what is the interest of the governed and what is it to govern? A clue is suggested by the idea of the public interest. The interest of the governed is the public interest, that is their interest not merely as private persons but as members of the public. Government is the activity of identifying, maintaining and developing the public interest. But if this clue is to bear fruit more must be said about this activity and the idea of the public interest. Something must also be said on the subject of self-interest and the interest of a social group.

A man's self-interest is his interest in all the conditions necessary for the maintenance and development of his personal well-being. After the satisfaction of his bodily needs what these necessary conditions are will depend upon his personal character-istics and idiosyncrasies, and upon his individual circumstances. His judgement of his self-interest will be enlightened to the extent that it reflects a wise conception of his personal well-being. The latter will be wise to the extent that it rests upon a candid recognition of his own capacities and limitations, a mature understanding of his own tastes and propensities, and a true appreciation of the possibilities open to him in his in-dividual circumstances. The pursuit of self-interest, the activity of securing the conditions necessary for personal well-being, is utilitarian. It is a matter of ends and means in the special sense of 'ends' defined in Chapter 3 in which an end is a state of affairs or a process. A man's pursuit of his self-interest will therefore be enlightened to the extent that two requirements are satisfied. The first is that his judgement of his self-interest be enlightened, the second that he act efficiently and expediently in bringing about the ends which it is in his self-interest to secure.

In what way can a social group have an interest? Social groups vary enormously in size, composition and in the nature of their activities. But they always consist of a number of persons involved in some joint activity. Every social group therefore has an interest in the conditions necessary for the successful carrying on of the joint activity which is its *raison d'être*. Membership of a social group necessarily involves participation. If its joint activity is to be successfully carried on as the activity of a social group, all its members must be able to participate in it upon terms which are appropriate to their status as members. The interest of a social group is the corporate interest which 'we' its members have in the conditions which are necessary for all of us to participate in 'our' joint activity upon proper terms. Membership of a social group involves responsibility. Each member must make the best contribution he can to advancing the common enterprise and surmounting current difficulties. Each member therefore has a responsibility to assist in promoting the group's corporate interest.[1]

As an illustration, consider the case of a tennis club. Certain conditions are necessary for the successful carrying on of the joint activity which is the club's *raison d'être* as a social group, the playing of lawn tennis. There must be rules about the use of courts and amenities and provision for the maintenance of the club's premises and the handling of its finances. Rules will be necessary about membership and subscriptions. It is in the corporate interest of the club as a social group to maintain these conditions. They are necessary if all its members are to share in and enjoy the opportunities it affords for playing tennis. Each member therefore has a responsibility to assist in maintaining them. He must observe the rules, pay his subscriptions regularly, co-operate with the management committee and if necessary serve on it. For the club to be a success, there must

---

[1] This concept of a social group's corporate interest may be part of what Rousseau had in mind in his doctrine of the General Will.

not only be enthusiasm on the courts but co-operation and consideration on the part of the members.

But does every social group necessarily have a corporate interest? What about a trade union? Its basis as an association is common self-interest, the interest which each of the workers has in better wages and working conditions. It may be thought that the interest of the union can only be the interest which its members have in common. But this is not so. The purpose of the union is to improve wages and working conditions through concerted action. This concerted action is the joint activity which is the union's *raison d'être* as a social group. Its interest as a social group is therefore the corporate interest which its members have in the conditions which are necessary to enable all of them to carry on concerted action efficiently. Among these conditions will be a system for electing leaders, procedures for regular contact between leaders and rank and file, arrangements for administering union funds, and the maintenance of effective discipline within the union. Each member has a responsibility to play his part in maintaining these conditions. How concerted the action of the union is in pursuit of better wages and working conditions will depend upon how well its members discharge their responsibilities.

The suggestion that the interest of a union can only be the interest which its members have in common, points to a confusion between a social group and a class. The interest of a class can indeed only be the interest which its members have in common. But classes are not social groups. Social groups are concrete existents. Classes are not, they are abstractions. The members of a class do not as such do anything together. If they do, they cease to be merely a class and become a social group. Only when the members of a class begin doing something together can they begin to have an interest as a social group: namely a corporate interest in the conditions necessary to enable them to do what they are doing together successfully. But this corporate interest cannot be the interest which they had in common merely as the members of a class because as merely the members of a class they did not do anything together and had not yet become a social group. The workers in a given industry constitute a class in virtue of a common interest in better wages and working conditions. But that does not make them a trade union. They must associate together for the sake of concerted action. When they do, their interest as a union is their corporate interest in the conditions necessary for this concerted action. But that is something different from the interest they had in common merely as a class of unorganized industrial workers.

To make the same point in another way: classes do not as such have an individual identity. The members of a class must have something in common but they need not be aware of it. They do not have to think of themselves as 'we', nor do they have any responsibilities merely in virtue of being members. But a social group necessarily has an individual identity. Its members must think of themselves as 'we' and of its joint activity as 'ours', and they have responsibilities arising out of their involvement in the common enterprise. It is its individual identity which gives a social group an interest which is *sui generis*, a corporate interest which its members can have only as members of the group and not merely in virtue of belonging to a particular class. Matters are made somewhat complicated in the case of a trade union by the fact that a trade union is an essentially utilitarian association. As a social group its *raison d'être* is concerted action as a means to certain ends which its members already have independently of their membership of the union. But their corporate interest as members of the union is in the conditions necessary for their concerted action, not in the ends to which this concerted action is the means. Their responsibilities as members of the union arise out of the demands of this concerted action. Merely as the members of a class having certain ends in common, they have no responsibilities.

A trade union was earlier described as an association, the basis of which is common self-interest. This description is appropriate because the joint activity which is its *raison d'être* as a social group is utilitarian in character. It is the means to ends which the members already have independently of their membership and which it is in their self-interest as individual men and women to establish and maintain. But the same description would not apply to a tennis club. Tennis is a game, not a utilitarian activity. Like any game it is worth playing, if at all, for its own sake. The club is an association of people who have come together to do something which they enjoy, not something which is a means to ends which it is in their self-interest as individual men and women to establish and maintain. The basis of the club as an association is not mutual self-interest but mutual enjoyment of a certain activity. The joint activity which is its *raison d'être* comes under the head of intrinsic value not utility. Of course there may be a subsidiary utilitarian characteristic. A man may join the club not so much because he likes tennis but because he wants the exercise as a means to keeping fit. A girl may join in the hope of finding a husband. But these must be minority motives, otherwise it would be a gymnasium or a marriage bureau, not a tennis club.

2. THE IDEA OF THE PUBLIC INTEREST

Can what has been said about the corporate interest of a social group be applied to the case of a self-sufficient society? Such a society is 'a partnership between those who are living, those who are dead, and those who have yet to be born'. It is not a voluntary association. A society founded by voluntary emigrants might seem to be an exception, but it is only after a new generation has grown up who never knew the 'old country' that a self-sufficient society with an identity of its own has come into being. If a self-sufficient society is not a voluntary association, can it have a corporate interest? The *raison d'être* of a self-sufficient society is its common life, for it is this common life carried on from generation to generation which gives it an individual identity as a self-sufficient society. Its members therefore have a corporate interest in the conditions necessary for the carrying on of their common life. This common life is always a way of life of a certain kind, expressed and articulated in a body of institutions and practices. What 'we', the members of the present generation therefore, have a corporate interest in, is the conditions which are necessary not merely for any form of common life but for the successful maintenance and development of 'our' present way of life with all its distinctive features and characteristics. However there is an important proviso. A

self-sufficient society can have a corporate interest only if there
is widespread agreement among its members and the fundamental character of its current way of life. Lacking this agreement, there can only be the corporate interest which the
dominant group in the society have in the conditions necessary
to enable it to maintain its privileged position.

If the public interest is to be a significant idea, there must
be private interests with which the public interest can be con-
trasted. This suggests that the public interest is the corporate
interest of a self-sufficient society in whose way of life private
interests have a legitimate place. But what is it for an interest
to be private? The concept of privacy and the 'private' points
to two requirements which must be satisfied. There must be
a person or persons whose proper interest it is. There must
also be other people whose proper interest it is not. A man's
self-interest can be a private interest properly so called only
in a society in which his pursuit of it is held to be his own affair
and not the business of his fellow citizens. By the same token,
in a society in which voluntary association on the basis of common
self-interest or common enjoyment is recognized to be legitimate,
the corporate interest of a social group such as a trade union
or a tennis club is a private interest, the proper concern of the
members.

If a society is to be self-sufficient in human life, must a
legitimate place of some sort be found in its way of life for
private interests? In a small tribe with a subsistence economy
there will be no scope for the private pursuit of self-interest,
much less for voluntary associations. Everything will be everybody's business and even in family life there will be little or no
privacy. But this does not prevent the tribe being a self-
sufficient society and maintaining its way of life from generation
to generation. In a theocracy where the spiritual welfare of
each is considered to be the proper concern of all, a man's self-
interest will not be regarded as merely his private business.
Nor will the corporate interest of any voluntary association
permitted by the theocratic morality be regarded as merely
the private concern of its members. Because of the monolithic
character of a theocracy, the legitimate place, if any, accorded
to private interests in its way of life will necessarily be a lowly

and subordinate one. But there is an important difference between the two cases. In the tribe, life is too close to the margin of bare subsistence to make the development of private interests a practical possibility. But in the theocracy it is the theocratic morality which assigns a low degree of importance to private interests.

Does it matter if a low degree of importance is assigned to private interests? It means that a low degree of importance is being assigned to the private pursuit of self-interest, that is the attempt by individual men and women to pursue their own self-interest according to their own judgement whether that be enlightened or unenlightened. This is in effect to hold that it is not very important that human beings should try to take personal responsibility for the shape and direction of their individual lives. It also means that a low degree of importance is being assigned to the joint activities of voluntary associations, these joint activities being what give rise to private corporate interests. Now if human beings are not expected to take personal responsibility for the shape and direction of their individual lives, if they are not encouraged to associate together on the basis of mutual self-interest and mutual enjoyment, they are not likely to make much headway in giving significance to human life as such. To fail to appreciate this, or to be indifferent to it, is in either case to betray a defective understanding of the world and what it is to be human. From the standpoint of critical humanism therefore there are good grounds for judging that a society in which private interests are undervalued is one whose way of life is on that account inadequate for human beings. But private interests can also be overvalued. When they are, this means that the public interest is being undervalued.

This brings us back to the suggestion made earlier: that the public interest must be the corporate interest of a self-sufficient society in whose way of life private interests have a legitimate place. Subject to the proviso of widespread fundamental agreement, this corporate interest is the interest which the members of the current generation have in the conditions which are necessary for the maintenance and development of their present way of life. More precisely: it is their interest in the conditions which are necessary for all the members to participate in the society's way of life on terms which are consistent with its established morality and social order. But if private interests are to have a legitimate place in that way of life, their pursuit must be authorized by the society's established morality and social order. It must be an accepted moral principle that people ought to take personal responsibility for the shape and direction of their individual lives. All this suggests that the public interest and private interests are essentially complementary.

But matters are not so simple. A man's private interests are the interests which he has, not as a member of a self-sufficient society, but as an individual person and as a member of voluntary associations. He is also a member of a self-sufficient society and pursues his private interests within the framework of its way of life. But so far as his private interests are concerned, it does not matter to him whether all the members are participating in its way of life on terms consistent with its established morality and social order. All that matters is that the general conditions prevailing in the society should be such as to enable him to pursue his private interests successfully. He can afford to be indifferent to the many members of his society who are not directly involved in his private interests so long as they do not bother him by interfering with his private pursuit of his self-interest, or with the joint activities of the voluntary associations to which he belongs. This points to a flaw in the suggestion that the public interest and private interests are essentially complementary. What it overlooks is that when a man thinks about the way of life of his society solely from the point of view of his private interests, what concerns him is not that there should be conditions in which the private interests of all the members can have a legitimate place; but that there should be conditions in which his own particular private interests can prosper.

The suggestion that the public interest and private interests are complementary is misleading in another way. It encourages the idea that a self-sufficient society should be thought of as a kind of voluntary association writ-large, the basis of which is mutual self-interest. Now we have already seen that a self-sufficient society cannot literally be a voluntary association.

Nothing is gained by trying to think of it as one in some metaphorical sense, still less as one whose basis is common self-interest. People can associate together on the basis of common self-interest only if each of them already has some idea of what his self-interest is independently of his membership of the association. They must already be social beings who can communicate with each other and become aware of what they have in common. They must already be moral agents who can give and receive trust and meet the responsibilities involved in belonging to a voluntary association. In other words they must already be members of a self-sufficient society before they can form a voluntary association based on common self-interest. Such an association is possible only within a self-sufficient society and to try to think of the latter as if it were a kind of association possible only within itself is therefore fundamentally misleading. In contemporary philosophical jargon, it is a case of a category mistake. The basis of a self-sufficient society at a given time and place is neither common self-interest nor common enjoyment. It is its current generation's prevailing understanding which furnishes them with such reasons as they need for continuing to maintain and develop their present way of life.

If private interests are to have a legitimate place in the way of life of a self-sufficient society, their pursuit must be authorized by its established morality and social order. But this authorization cannot amount to a complete *carte blanche*. It can only be that private interests may be pursued in ways which do not infringe any of the other principles and rules of the established morality and do not undermine the social order. The members must not lie, steal or cheat nor use violence. They must respect each other's status as members and uphold the society's system of authority. In other words: if private interests are to have a legitimate place in a self-sufficient society's way of life, their pursuit must be subordinate to all the obligations and responsibilities involved in membership of that society, including helping to promote the society's corporate interest. It follows that the pursuit of private interests must be subordinate to the public interest, since the public interest is the corporate interest of a self-sufficient society in which private interests have a legitimate place. Therefore any private interest pursued at the expense of the public interest ceases to have a legitimate place in the way of life of the society concerned.

But it is not always clear when a private interest is being pursued at the expense of the public interest. The larger the scale and the greater the complexity of a society's way of life the greater the complexity of the conditions necessary for all its members to participate in its way of life on terms consistent with its established morality. In many contexts of modern life the public interest is not something immediately and obviously apparent. It has to be discovered and may often be a problem rather than a datum. In a modern industrial society the steps which need to be taken to promote the public interest include the organizing of services in fields such as health, education, housing, communications and transport as well as fostering cultural activities of many kinds. They are also likely to include the over-all guidance and supervision of the economy. All this involves constructive initiative and persuasion as well as the making of rules. But in what fields there should be initiative, what form it should take and most of all how far it should be carried, will be controversial questions. It was suggested that governing is the activity of identifying and taking steps to maintain and promote the public interest. Because the public interest is not always obvious, the members of a society cannot be left to maintain and promote it by their own individual efforts. If they are, it will tend to go by default. If this is not to happen, responsibility for identifying and taking steps to promote the public interest must rest with a single agency, the government, which acts on behalf of the whole society. Members have responsibility in the matter and must give it priority over their private interests. But they must know what they ought to promote and in what ways they ought to restrict their pursuits of private interests. The greater the complexity of the society's way of life, the greater is the need of the members for authoritative direction and guidance. This is in effect an answer to the question 'Why should there be government at all?'

But governing can be something less than the sophisticated activity of identifying, maintaining and promoting the public interest. We saw in Chapter 6 that in every self-sufficient society some system of authority is necessary to enable decisions to be made about matters which concern the society as a whole. This suggests that such decision making on the basis of recognized authority is the generic activity of governing. Promoting the public interest is one species of this activity. Making decisions about the corporate interests of small tribes with little place for private interest is another. These two species of the generic activity are not however co-ordinate and mutually exclusive species. They do not stand on the same level. It is another of those cases of a difference of kind which is also one of degree. Government in terms of the corporate interest of a small tribe is a rudimentary form of the generic activity. Government in terms of the public interest of a complex national society is a sophisticated form of the generic activity.

This idea of the public interest emphasizes those conditions within a society which are necessary for the maintenance of its way of life. But conditions abroad may be as important as those at home and are also the concern of the government. We will be discussing this topic later. Another matter is the use of force by government. It was argued in Chapter 5 that if socially organized constraint is not to be arbitrary, its exercise must be controlled by two considerations. The first is that it should never be used except to enforce obedience to orders and rules which in social contexts have either a pragmatic or a substantive justification. The second is that it should be used to compel obedience to such rules and orders only when there is a net advantage to the life of the society in doing so. It is these two considerations which ought to control a government's use of force in taking steps to maintain and promote the public interest. More will be said on this topic, especially on law and its relation to government.

3. SELF-GOVERNMENT AND FORMS OF GOVERNMENT

That self-government is better than good government is a well-known political maxim. The concept of self-government is normally understood in two senses. The first is where the aim is to contrast self-government with imperial government. A colony seeking independence demands to be allowed to govern itself rather than be governed by its imperial masters. The second is connected with forms of government. Self-government is that form of government in which the people govern themselves. Any self-sufficient society which has a government is self-governing in the first sense. It is not a colony and is not subject to alien imperial rule. But it need not be self-governing in the second sense. Government may be in the hands of a single class or a clique, or of a single person aided by a group of followers, while the broad mass of the people play no part in it. As our present theme is forms of government, it is the second sense of the concept of self-government which primarily concerns us here.

According to the second sense, to say that self-government is better than good government, is to say in effect that the best form of government is the one in which the people govern themselves. But in what way, if any, can the people govern themselves? What was said in the last section suggests that this is not literally possible. It was there pointed out that if the public interest is not to go by default, the task of identifying it and taking steps to maintain and develop it must be entrusted to a single agency authorized to act on behalf of the whole society. Another question also needs to be considered. Has the notion of the best form of government any meaning in the abstract? There are prima facie grounds for thinking that it has not. Any form of government is necessarily the form of government of an individual self-sufficient society at a given time and place. It must be geared to that society's system of authority and hence to its established morality and social order. One must therefore always ask: 'best for whom, where, and when?' if the question: 'What is the best form of government?' is to be significant. That form is best for a given society which is best suited to its established morality and social order. To make the same point in another way: the best form of government for any society is that which enables the public interest to be identified, maintained and developed most successfully. In the case of a given society this will therefore be the form which best harmonizes with its established morality and social order, and *a fortiori* with its prevailing understanding of the world and of human identity. No form of government is the best *per se*.

It may be readily granted that the form of government which is best for one society may not be best for another. It does not however follow that there are no rational grounds for maintaining that one form of government is better as such than another. Suppose that there are such grounds and that form of government *A* can be shown to be better than form of government *B*. It could still be the case that *B*, although inferior to *A*, is nevertheless the best form of government for a given society *S* because it harmonizes best with *S*'s established morality and social order. What this means is that *S*'s established morality and social order are of such a character that it has to make do with *B*. These being what they are, the best it can manage in the way of a form of government is *B*. Although *A* is as such a better form of government, it lies beyond the reach of *S*. In other words, it does not follow that because one form of government is as such better than another, it is therefore the best form of government for every society always and everywhere. The best is always the best which is possible in the circumstances of a given case. But the best in one case may be inherently better than the best in another.

Are there rational grounds for this contention? If the matter is approached negatively, it can be seen that there are. Rational grounds, that is to say, can be adduced for maintaining that one form of government is inherently defective in various respects and that another is inherently better because lacking some of these defects. Consider despotism: its basis is a secondary rule which prescribes absolute obedience to a single man. The people's duty is simply to obey without question whatever rules and orders he chooses to make. But he himself is not subject to any secondary rule. Everyone is subject to his authority but there is no authority to which he is subject. That is what makes him a despot. In other words, what characterizes despotism as a form of government is not merely that the activity of governing is in the hands of a single man aided by subordinates. Rather it is that the government is not subject to any form of control or limitation. The despot's authority is absolute. He is answerable to no one and his subjects have no redress against him.

A despotic government need not necessarily be a bad government. The despot may be benevolent. He may try to promote the public interest honestly and intelligently, choosing his subordinates well, taking advantage of wise counsel and good advice, and lending a ready and sympathetic ear to the problems and grievances of his subjects. But whether or not a despot turns out to be benevolent is a matter of chance. There is nothing in despotism as a form of government which ensures that he will be. He must enlist and retain the loyalty and active support of enough subordinates to enforce obedience to his will, but apart from that, he is subject to no sanctions. If he is lazy and incompetent, if his subordinates are brutal and corrupt, the people must simply put up with it. Despotism as a form of government affords no protection to the governed from the vices of the governors. Nor does it make any provision for ensuring that the public interest is promoted intelligently. The governed are at the mercy of the stupidity of the governors no less than of their vices. These defects in despotism are due to its neglect of human fallibility. As a form of government, despotism is open to the serious objection that it fails to take account of human shortcomings.

In view of this, it is not surprising that despotism has traditionally been regarded as the worst form of government. The remedy traditionally suggested for it is constitutionalism. If a government is not to be despotic, it must be constitutional. The best way of understanding constitutionalism as a form of government is through what is known as the rule of law. This is the principle that everyone in a given society, the governors no less than the governed, should be equally subject to its law. No one must be above the law in the sense of being exempt from its authority and no one must be below it in the sense of being denied its protection. Without the rule of law, there can be no law properly so called. It is of the essence of law that its authority should be paramount throughout the society whose law it is. A system of rules to which all are not equally subject is something less than a system of law. It is also necessary that if everyone is to be equally subject to the law, everyone must be able to find out without too much difficulty what the law is. Its content therefore must be relatively stable, changes in it being made according to secondary rules which are themselves part of the law. There cannot be a system of law properly so called in a despotism. A despot is not bound by any secondary rules. He can issue decrees, making and unmaking rules how and when he likes. He does not have to obey the rules he makes for his subjects and can capriciously exempt any subordinates or subjects from doing so.

The basic principle of constitutionalism is that the government itself must be subject to rules. In Aristotle's phrase, 'government must be of laws, not of men'. This is possible only in a society in which there is a system of law and the rule of law. In such a society, as we have just seen, there must be secondary rules which prescribe the procedures to be followed in changing the law, rules which are themselves part of the law. These rules must confer authority upon the holders of designated offices to make such changes and there must also be other rules which provide for law enforcement and for a judicial system. Such rules form the nucleus of a constitution. The government derives its authority from them and it must conform to them, as it must to the system of law as a whole. If it wants to change the law in the course of promoting the public interest, it must do so lawfully, that is in accordance with the provisions of constitutional rules. The rule of law, together with the specific provisions of constitutional rules, provide the governed with a measure of protection from the vices of their governors. Unlike despotism, constitutionalism takes some account of human fallibility.

But what about the stupidity of the governors as distinct from their vices? Does constitutionalism as a form of government make provision for the intelligent promotion of the public interest? Merely as constitutionalism, it does not. There can be such provision only in a form of government which is not merely constitutional but representative in character. The basic principle of representative government is accountability. Responsibility for governing must rest with representatives who are elected from time to time by a wider citizen body. They are ultimately accountable to the members of this body who, if they are dissatisfied with the way in which the public interest is being promoted, can dismiss them and replace them by others. More will be said about what this involves when we discuss democracy, which may be provisionally characterized as fully developed representative government. Constitutionalism is a necessary but not a sufficient condition for representative government. Government can be constitutional without being representative, as for instance when it is in the hands of a hereditary monarch who is subject to constitutional limitations upon the scope of his authority. There may be a representative element in the constitution without representative government properly so called, as when a monarch consults the elected representatives of a wider citizen body without being himself subject to election by that body. But genuine representative government must be constitutional government. Constitutional rules are necessary to provide for elections and for the ultimate accountability of the government to a wider citizen body.

The argument of the last five paragraphs may now be summarized as follows. The inherent defects of despotism as a form of government are due to its failure to take account of human shortcomings. Constitutionalism is a better form of government than despotism because by providing a measure of protection against the vices of governors, it shows at least some awareness of the fact that all human beings are fallible. But a fuller grasp of this is shown by representative government which through the principle of accountability provides a measure of protection against the stupidity as well as the vices of governors. A form of government which is representative in character is therefore inherently better than one which is merely constitutional without being representative, while one which is constitutional whether or not it is representative is as such better than one which is despotic. Now to fail to be aware that all human beings are fallible is to betray a defective understanding of what it is to be human. From the standpoint of critical humanism there are therefore good grounds for judging that a society whose form of government is despotic is one whose way of life is in that respect inadequate for human beings. If and when it becomes capable of constitutionalism, that will be an improvement.

Some qualifications are however necessary. What form of government a given society actually has, is an empirical question. The three forms we have been discussing are ideal types or theoretical constructs, not empirical descriptions. But they are not arbitrary constructs. They are empirically relevant because they abstract and focus upon important considerations concerning government in any human situation. Taken together, they furnish a conceptual framework in terms of which actual forms of government can be classified and evaluated. Concrete human institutions as they exist historically are not usually fully self-consistent and an actual form of government may be a hybrid of two, or all, of the three forms. The form of government in Czarist Russia was largely despotic in character. But the Czar was a hereditary monarch and the rule of hereditary succession to the throne was a fragment of constitutionalism within the despotism. The United States today has what appears to be a representative form of government. But Negro Americans in Alabama and Mississippi live under a despotism. The rule of law does not operate for them and they are at the mercy of the vices of their governors and their white fellow citizens. An actual form of government is likely to be predominantly representative, constitutional, or despotic in character rather than a pure instance of any one form. It will therefore be better to the extent that it is predominantly representative rather than merely constitutional, or constitutional rather than despotic.

It may be thought that the inherent defects of despotism as a form of government are sufficiently obvious and no self-sufficient society would willingly accept it. Where it exists, it must therefore have been imposed from outside by conquerors upon a vanquished people, or in a divided society by the dominant group upon the subject groups. But this is not necessarily so. An established morality and social order permeated by theocratic beliefs and ideas may predispose a people in favour of a personal system of authority and a despotic form of government. The despot will be accorded a quasi-divine status and will occupy a position at the apex of the social pyramid. A predominantly despotic form of government may also be willingly accepted following a successful nationalist revolution in the course of which an able and ambitious leader has come to command unquestioning personal allegiance. A period of social upheaval and conflict may lead to despotism with a personal dictatorship being accepted as the price of social stability. This may seem to be only a variant of the case of a divided society. But the conflict may be due not to the division of the society into antagonistic racial or religious groups but to an intense and prolonged economic crisis provoked by external events and aggravated by the incompetence of a constitutional government.

It was said that the best form of government for a given society is that which harmonizes best with its established morality and social order. This now needs qualifying. It assumes that the established morality and social order are a going concern and not in imminent danger of disintegration. When that danger becomes real, as it is likely to in the face of social upheaval and conflict, resort to a despotic form of government may well be the only alternative to complete social collapse. What remains of the established morality and social order will then have to be accommodated to the requirements of despotism. It will be a question, not of what form of government harmonizes best with the established morality and social order, but rather of what morality and social order can harmonize best with the only possible form of government. This does not affect the conclusion that despotism is as such an inferior form of government to constitutionalism. It serves only to emphasize that in some cases, the inferior is the best that can be managed. Despotism may sometimes be the necessary price of social survival.

What about the original question: in what way, if any, can the people govern themselves? Clearly under despotism, they cannot at all. Their duty is simply to obey. Nor is constitutionalism necessarily any better. Being protected from the vices of governors is not the same thing as having a positive part to play in the work of government. But in representative government an element of popular participation is essential. The government is in the hands of representatives elected by an ultimately accountable to a wider citizen body. The people play a part in governing themselves by being members of the wider citizen body. Only in a society whose form of government is representative in character is there anything which can properly be called politics. Only where the government is accountable to a wider body can there be room for debate and discussion of issues in the public interest and competition for popular support.

4. SELF-GOVERNMENT AND FORMS OF GOVERNMENT CONTINUED: DEMOCRACY

There is a semantic point which must be cleared up. Most Western nations today profess to be democracies. But contemporary communist societies also claim to be democratic and some officially style themselves 'People's Democracies'. Western aspirants to the title of Democracy have in common the fact that their forms of government are predominantly constitutional and representative in character. This is not true of communist societies. No communist government today is accountable to a wider citizen body, nor is the rule of law in effective operation in any communist society. They all have forms of government which are predominantly despotic in character. Our concern here is with democracy as a development of representative government not as a variety of despotism. It is therefore the Western model not the communist that we shall be discussing.

Constitutional opposition is an integral part of representative government properly so called and may be conveniently summarized in terms of three principles. The first is that there can be public criticism of the government without reprisals. The second that opposition candidates can stand for election on equal terms with members of the government. The third that elections should be frequent enough to be an effective sanction. The relevance of these three principles to representative government is readily apparent. Unless there can be uninhibited public criticism of the government, the members of the wider citizen body to whom it is accountable will find it difficult to make informed appraisals of its performance in promoting the public interest. Unless there are opposition candidates, there can be no alternative to the government of the day, no possibility of replacing it without rebellion. If the interval between elections is too long, the incentive to govern well will be reduced. If there is to be genuine accountability and therefore representative government properly so called, the three principles of constitutional opposition must be implemented in constitutional rules. These must regulate the timing of elections and the details of electoral procedure. They must also make the status of opposition candidates legitimate and provide safeguards for public criticism of the government.

The party system is indispensable for the practical working of constitutional opposition. It enables political leaders to be recruited, issues in the public interest to be publicized, and a practical alternative to the government of the day to be permanently available. But something else more fundamental is also necessary. This is a practical grasp not only by political parties but also by the members of the citizen body generally of the difference between opposition and rebellion. Public criticism of the government of the day and opposition to its policies must be carried on within the limits of the law. There must be no question of undermining the government's authority or of inciting disobedience to it. An opposition candidate is in effect saying in one breath: 'This government is doing an incompetent bungling job and the sooner we get rid of it the better', and in the next: 'I respect the authority of this government and will loyally obey whatever rules and orders it sees fit to make.' It is by going to the polls, that is to say, not the barricades, that the government is to be got rid of. All this implies a certain degree of sophistication on the part of the members of the citizen body. It also implies that there is broad agreement among them about the fundamental character of their society's way of life. Differences between them must not run too deep if they are to be willing to abide by the verdict of the polls. It must not be a vital matter who wins the next election.

Universal suffrage, or 'one man, one vote', is commonly regarded as the hallmark of democracy, but without constitutional opposition universal suffrage is worthless. A better criterion is that the citizen body should be co-extensive with the adult population. To be an adult is to be a citizen, and to be a citizen is to be entitled to a vote, to join a political party and to stand as a candidate at the elections. Democracy is therefore representative government developed to its fullest extent.

When the citizen body does not include all adults there is representative government without democracy. Britain in the early nineteenth century is an example. The citizen body to which the government was accountable included only a minority of the adult population. It took a hundred years for Britain to be transformed into a democracy as the citizen body was gradually widened through a succession of Reform Bills.

What should be the composition of the citizen body to which a representative government is accountable? There is a prima facie case that it should be co-extensive with the adult population. If it is not the interests of those who are excluded from the citizen body will not receive proper consideration. The government has an incentive to pay attention to the interests of people to whom it is accountable but none to those who have no vote and cannot affect the result of the next election. For such people, the government may be constitutional but it is not representative since it is not accountable to them. They are protected neither from the stupidity of the government nor from the selfishness of the members of the citizen body since the latter will naturally be inclined to think of their own interests when appraising the government's performance. Representative government without democracy is little if at all better than constitutionalism without representative government. Under the latter all stand on an equal footing so far as the government's stupidity is concerned while the government itself has no inducement to favour the interests of one section of the population.

But while this is plausible, it overlooks the fact that the government's task ought to be to promote the public interest, that of the members of the citizen body to pass judgement on its performance in doing so. The public interest is the corporate interest of a self-sufficient society in whose way of life private interests have a legitimate place. This corporate interest is the interest of all the members of the society in the conditions necessary to enable all of them (non-citizen as well as citizen where the form of government is representative without being democratic) to participate in its way of life on terms consistent with its established morality and social order. It is with how well the government is promoting these conditions that the members of the citizen body should be concerned in appraising its performance, not with how well it is promoting conditions favourable to their respective private interests. They must not do what they are naturally inclined to do; think of their own private interests when appraising the government's performance, or rather they should think of them only to the extent that it is in the public interest that their private interests should prosper.

If the members of the citizen body think only of their private interests when appraising the government's performance, democracy will not help much so far as the public interest is concerned. The government will have an incentive to promote conditions favourable to the interests of a majority of the population. But these conditions are by no means identical with those necessary to enable all the members of the society to participate in its way of life on terms consistent with its established morality and social order. The most that can be expected is some degree of overlap. Admittedly, under democracy, the government has an inducement to search for common ground between the interests of all the population rather than only of a section within it. But that hardly amounts to an incentive to promote the public interest vigorously and intelligently. This is neglected by the doctrine that democracy is government in accordance with the will of the majority. The relevance of the majority principle is in the sphere of electoral procedure. What the doctrine fails to bring out is that the members of the democratic citizen body must think as public not merely private persons. To the extent that they do not, the public interest tends to go by default and democracy degenerates into a struggle between competing interest groups.

In a society with a hierarchial social order based on hereditary status, only those in the upper ranks can form a citizen body. It will be out of keeping with the established morality for those of lower status to debate and discuss with their betters, still more to criticize them. There may be a representative form of government but without democracy. Such a hierarchial social order imposes arbitrary restrictions upon human relationships and enjoyment of intrinsic values. It is therefore one whose prevailing understanding of the world and what it is to be human is defective, from the standpoint of critical humanism its way of life in this respect is inadequate for human beings. Changes in the direction of an open social order in which people can find their own level instead of having it determined for them by their parents' status would be an improvement. A citizen body co-extensive with the adult population is possible only in a substantially open social order. Democracy presupposes a substantially open social order and therefore a more adequate way of life.

The following objection, however, may be made. In an open social order not all the adult population are equally capable of citizenship. Human beings are unequally endowed with ability. Although an open social order enables them to make the most of their capacities, it does not follow that all will have the intelligence and understanding to make rational appraisals of the government's performance. Democracy overlooks the fact of human inequality and so betrays a defective understanding of what it is to be human. A representative form of government in which the citizen body is restricted to those qualified to meet the demands of citizenship is free from this defect. But democracy does not have to assume that all the adult population are equally capable of appraising the government's performance rationally, much less that they are all equal in ability or intelligence. It must assume only that with negligible exceptions they have a practical grasp of the difference between opposition and rebellion, and that there is sufficient agreement among them not to make it too serious a matter who wins an election. Whether these assumptions are true in a given case is an empirical question. If they are not, then democracy will not be the best form of government in that case.

It may still be objected however that while all this may be granted, the citizen body should nevertheless be restricted to those with the requisite degree of intelligence and understanding to appraise the government's performance rationally and this will always be less than the whole adult population. Why include those who have nothing to contribute and who can only be passengers? But does it matter if some passengers are included so long as no potential citizens are excluded? How is the line between them to be drawn? Just what degree of intelligence and understanding is requisite for rationally appraising the government's performance? How is its presence to be reliably ascertained? In a society with a substantially open social order including provisions for mass education, precise and unambiguous answers cannot be given to these questions. If potential citizens are not to be arbitrarily excluded, the citizen body must be co-extensive with the adult population. This in brief is the case for democracy. It does not betray a defective understanding of what it is to be human. On the contrary, by reason of its appreciation of the difficulties involved in trying to separate passengers from potential citizens, it may fairly claim to rest upon a deeper and more adequate insight than the objection.

The objection then cannot be sustained and the original suggestion stands. Democracy is as such inherently better than undemocratic representative government. Moreover, by making the citizen body co-extensive with the adult population, it is the nearest thing possible to self-government. It does not enable the people literally to govern themselves. No form of government can do that. But it does make the government accountable to all of them and through the party system it enables all among them with the aptitude and taste to participate actively in politics. This brings us back to the maxim: self-government is better than good government. We can now see that it involves two assertions. The first is that the form of government is more important than the quality of the government's day-to-day performance. The second that self-government is inherently better than any other form of government. If we interpret self-government as democracy, the second is true. But what about the first?

It amounts to saying that a democratic government which governs badly is better than a despotic government which governs well. In support of this it may be argued that if a democratic government governs badly, the remedy lies with the people. They can replace it with a better alternative. But this assumes that a better alternative is available, and more generally that in the society in question the conditions necessary for democracy are present. If these assumptions are false, if the best that can be managed is a despotic form of government, the question of whether a bad democratic government would be better does not arise. What has been overlooked is that the best form of government is always the best which is possible in a given case. But the best which is possible in one case may be inherently better or worse than the best which is possible in another. It follows that the assertion that the form of government is more important than the quality of the government's performance is false. The two cannot be separated. The best form of government for a given society is that which in the circumstances of that society will best enable the public interest to be promoted intelligently and vigorously.

The maxim that self-government is better than good government will not then do as it stands. The most that can be allowed is that self-government in the shape of democracy may be better than merely good government. The discussion of this section has shown that democracy is not a simple straightforward form of government. On the contrary, it is a complex and sophisticated one, presupposing as it does a substantially open social order and a practical grasp throughout the adult population of the difference between opposition and rebellion. It can therefore be the best form of government only for a society in whose way of life the standpoint of critical humanism is at least on the way to being substantially embodied. That so far only certain Western nations should have managed to achieve a form of government which is even predominantly democratic in character is hardly surprising.

5. POLITICAL OBLIGATION

We have managed so far without any mention of 'the state'. But the problem of political obligation is sometimes posed in the form of the question: what is the nature and ground of the individual's obligation to the state? Originally the 'State' meant the 'King's estate' in a feudal monarchy. But it has subsequently come to mean simply a society with an organized government: for instance, a nation-state. In terms of the argument of this chapter then, a state is a self-sufficient society organized for the purpose of promoting the public interest. The organization may be complex as in a federal state. The form of government may be predominantly despotic, constitutional, representative, or democratic. Our concern however is not with how states differ but with what makes them all states. It follows that only a self-sufficient society in whose way of life private interests have a legitimate place can be a state, since only in such a society can there be such a thing as the public interest properly so called. Admittedly this has the apparently awkward consequence that a totalitarian state cannot really be a state because it is of the essence of totalitarianism to deny any legitimacy to private interests. But we shall discuss this later.

We can now see that the question: 'What is the nature and ground of the individual's obligation to the state?' is really a convenient abbreviation of a more cumbersome question: 'What is the nature and ground of the individual member's obligation to a self-sufficient society, with respect to its organization for promoting the public interest?' We said in Section 2 that the members of a self-sufficient society have a responsibility to co-operate with the government in its work of promoting the public interest. This suggests that so far as its nature is concerned, the obligation is one of co-operation: specifically, it is an obligation to co-operate with the government in the performance of its task. Its ground lies in the responsibilities involved in membership of a self-sufficient society and in their relation to the public interest. But while this way of putting the matter locates the problem of political obligation in its proper context, further questions still remain. What is involved in co-operating with the government? Must the government always be obeyed no matter what? Or is disobedience sometimes justified? If so, when and for what reasons?

Consider another question. What is the justification for the secondary rule which prescribes obedience to the government? No government can govern unless it is obeyed. But are those who govern to be obeyed because of who they are, or merely because of the consequences to be expected from their being obeyed. In other words, is the justification for the rule substantive or merely pragmatic? There is a prima facie case for the view that it is merely pragmatic. Without government, the public interest will go by default and it is desirable that this should not happen. But having a government necessarily involves having the rule. Since therefore the consequences of having a government are better than those of not having one, it follows that the consequences of having the rule are better than those of not having it: and this is to justify the rule on pragmatic grounds.

But rules do not exist in the void. They necessarily have their being in the context of human activities. The rule which prescribes obedience to the government is always addressed to the members of an individual self-sufficient society. The obedience which it prescribes is always to the legitimate government of that society. But what makes a government legitimate? If a single agency is to have responsibility for promoting the public interest on behalf of a whole society, its authority to do so must be respected. The members must think of it as their legitimate government. But if this recognition is to be forthcoming, a system of authority organized round a ceremonial office and geared to the society's established morality is a necessary prerequisite. Government must be carried on either by the incumbent of the ceremonial office or by others acting in its name: as in the case of 'The Queen's Government'.

In other words: what makes a government legitimate is its society's system of authority. We saw in Chapter 6 that a self-sufficient society must always have some system of authority to enable decisions to be made about matters which concern it as a whole. It follows that if it is to have a legitimate government, its system of authority must become an organization for promoting the public interest. But if this is to happen, the system of authority must have a stable and enduring basis. It must rest not upon the personal prestige of a single man but upon a ceremonial office which symbolizes the individual identity of the society. Now a self-sufficient society's established morality puts its members under an obligation to respect whatever system of authority it has. When this is an organization for promoting the public interest, the members are therefore under an obligation to respect that organization and *a fortiori* the government which is both the apex and the driving force of the organization. But this is to say that those who govern are to be obeyed not merely because of the good consequences which may be expected to result, but because of who they are, the legitimate government of the society: 'Her Majesty's Ministers'. The secondary rule which prescribes obedience to them is then justified on substantive not merely pragmatic grounds. It is part of the society's established morality. Being a member involves being under an obligation to follow it.

It was argued in Chapter 4 that to break a substantive secondary rule can never be socially responsible. This is because to do so is to strike at the way of life which gives the rule its substantive justification, and to do that can never be the lesser evil. It suggests the rather depressing conclusion that the answer to our earlier question: 'Must the government be obeyed, no matter what?' is: 'Yes!' To break the secondary rule which prescribes obedience to it is to repudiate the system of authority and established morality of the society in question, and so to strike at its way of life. There is however a qualification. The rule prescribed obedience to a society's 'legitimate' government. If a constitutional government deliberately violates the constitution, it ceases to be the legitimate government. It has itself repudiated the society's system of authority and established morality. Resistance to it may then be the lesser evil because offering the best chance of preserving something of the society's way of life. Such resistance does not involve breaking the secondary rule because the government is no longer legitimate. But where the form of government is despotic, this qualification does not apply. A legitimate despotism, just because it is a despotism, can do anything and therefore cannot make itself illegitimate. Under a legitimate despotism, for instance an absolute monarchy, resistance can never be the lesser evil. The government must be obeyed, no matter what!

But the argument of Chapter 4 was conducted in terms of the perspective of social morality as a level of rational activity. How do matters appear from the standpoint of critical humanism? The short answer is that the depressing conclusion of the last paragraph does not follow. At the level of social morality, a society's way of life is sacrosanct. It must be accepted uncritically. To strike at it, whether by breaking substantive secondary rules or in any other way, can never be the lesser evil. But at the level of critical humanism, this is not so. A society's way of life is no longer sacrosanct. It can be subjected to a rational piecemeal evaluation on the basis of its adequacy for human beings. If such an evaluation shows that in certain respects it is seriously inadequate, to strike at it may be the lesser evil because necessary to prepare the way for making it more adequate. If this involves breaking certain substantive secondary rules, then to break them will also be the lesser evil.

From the standpoint of critical humanism then, the answer to our earlier question is: 'No!' It is not the case that the government must be obeyed no matter what. Disobedience to a legitimate government is justified if it is the lesser evil. But when is it likely to be the lesser evil? Disobedience may be in the form of rebellion or of civil disobedience. If rebellion is to be the lesser evil, the overthrow of the legitimate government is necessary as a step towards making the way of life of the society concerned more adequate. But the probable aftermath of rebellion in the circumstances of the individual case must be taken into account in estimating whether it is the lesser evil. Has it a reasonable chance of success? If so, is the ensuing situation likely to be better so far as the society's way of life is concerned? There must be good grounds for answering both these questions with a confident 'Yes', if rebellion really is to be the lesser evil. The most that can reasonably be expected as the immediate political outcome of a successful rebellion is some kind of despotism. If anarchy is to be avoided, there must be unconditional obedience to the successful rebels. But the despotism of successful rebels may be preferable to that of a legitimate government which has degenerated into a brutal tyranny. It may prepare the way for the spread of a better understanding and for the eventual development of constitutional government. Again it may be preferable to an inept and corrupt constitutional régime under which the society's way of life is rapidly disintegrating. But the new despotism may turn out to be as bad or worse than the legitimate government it has superseded. Historical evidence shows that all too often this has happened in spite of noble ideals and high hopes.

There may be situations, such as a divided society, in which rebellion would be morally justified if there was any chance of success, but the chances are nil. Contemporary South Africa is

an example. Nothing can apparently be done. An evil situation
which offers no hope of improvement must be endured with
stoical fortitude. But is it necessary to be quite so pessimistic?
What about civil disobedience as distinct from rebellion? If it
is impossible to overthrow the government, might it not be
possible to make it change its policies by a campaign of passive
resistance on the part of the subject groups. The obstacles to
mounting such a campaign are immense and in a country like
South Africa may well be insuperable so far as the immediate
future is concerned. But as a long-term goal to prepare and
work for, it affords scope for constructive action. Resigned
hopeless acquiescence in the *status quo* is therefore not inevitable.
The situation in the United States is, of course, very different
from that in South Africa but the effectiveness of well organized
and highly disciplined civil disobedience has been demonstrated
by the American Civil Rights Movement under the leadership
of Martin Luther King.

6. AN AMENDED VERSION OF THE PUBLIC INTEREST

According to Section 2, government is an essentially conservative institution. Every government is the government of an
individual self-sufficient society at a given time and place. Its
obligation is to promote the public interest in that society. But
it is not its business to try to change, much less to improve the
society's way of life. It must accept that way of life as it finds it
and concentrate on trying to identify and to secure the conditions necessary for it to be carried on successfully, having
regard to the limitations and the opportunities of the present
situation. But if this is what is implied by the idea of the public
interest, then so much the worse for that idea. Surely every
government has an obligation to do what it can to try to
improve its society's way of life and make it more adequate for
human beings?

A society's way of life is inadequate for human beings to the
extent that there are defects in its prevailing understanding.
But defects in understanding can be remedied only by improvements in understanding. How do these come about in the case
of a society's prevailing understanding? We have said that only

a minority of the members of each generation in a society are likely to try seriously to understand the world and human identity for themselves. The majority will be content to accept the understanding bequeathed to them by former generations. It is when the practical relevance of new ideas, beliefs and values becomes apparent that the conservative majority will come gradually to accept them without perhaps being fully aware that they are doing so. People are likely to be induced to change for the sake of practical not intellectual considerations.

It was also pointed out that different institutions and practices within the same way of life may involve different and even incompatible ideas, beliefs and values. In a complex society such as a modern nation the prevailing understanding is likely to be an amalgam of a number of different ways of understanding the world and human identity some of which are mutually inconsistent. When the conservative majority accept changes in their institutions and practices and come to think and feel in new ways, they probably will not abandon old ways of thinking and feeling in other areas of life, even when these old ways are inconsistent with the new. The emancipation of women was finally achieved in Britain largely as a result of the practical exigencies of the First World War. But while British men accepted it so far as education, careers and politics were concerned, many of them inconsistently continued to think and feel about women in the domestic and personal spheres of life in terms of the ideas, beliefs and values of an earlier epoch.

To return to our suggestion: the government's task is to do what it can to make its society's way of life more adequate. It must then decide what changes in existing institutions and practices will make an improvement in the prevailing understanding and do the best it can to bring them about. But what in fact is the best that it can do? Changes in institutions and practices are changes in the ways in which people think and feel, as well as act. A government can introduce reforms and innovations but these can only pave the way for such changes. Reforms deliberately introduced by a government must necessarily be in the form of deliberately enacted rules and deliberately formulated specific principles. If the desired changes in institutions and practices are to come about, the people concerned must learn to act in the spirit not the letter of the rules and to implement the specific principles intelligently. This will happen only as they come to think, feel and act in terms of the ideas, beliefs and values which are the rational grounds for the rules and principles. But that is something which no government can make them do. It can only provide them with necessary guidelines. Beyond this it may, through the tone of its conduct of affairs, contribute to a climate of opinion in which they will be more ready to make use of the guidelines, but that is all.

Consider the emancipation of women: a government can give them the vote. It can legislate to give them equal status as property owners with men and the same educational opportunities. It can set an example by employing women in its own service and giving them the same pay and opportunities as men. But while all this is necessary to pave the way, it is not the real thing. That will come about only as men, and for that matter women as well, come to think, feel and act in terms of the ideas, beliefs and values which the emancipation of women presupposes. *Mutatis mutandis* a government cannot end racial segregation. It may do something to hasten its end by repealing segregation laws and pursuing a policy of racial integration in public services and public employment, but racial segregation will come to an end only when men and women of different races come to think and feel about one another and act towards one another as fellow members of an integrated society with an open social order. To take one more instance: when a government sets up a state educational system or a national health service it is certainly introducing reforms and innovations. But intelligent co-operation from the teachers and from the doctors is a prerequisite for the success of these reforms. A government can draw up the necessary administrative blue-prints but it is up to teachers and doctors, and to parents and patients, to implement them and so bring about the actual changes in existing institutions and practices.

The most then that a government can do is to establish conditions in which improvements in its society's way of life may come about. Any initiative which it takes will be fruitful only to the extent that it meets with an appropriate response. But if this is to be forthcoming the desire for improvements must already exist. There must be some women who want to be emancipated, some members of different races who want to end segregation, some teachers and some parents, some doctors and some patients, who appreciate the desirability of a state educational system and a national health service. More generally: a society's way of life can be improved ony if there are some members who are aware of respects in which it is inadequate. There must be some whose understanding is better than the prevailing understanding. Moreover the members of the conservative majority who think and act in terms of the prevailing understanding must to some extent be dissatisfied with things as they are. Although not appreciating the defects in that understanding which make their way of life inadequate, they must feel sufficiently beset by problems and difficulties to be receptive to the idea of change. In other words: a government cannot directly improve its society's way of life. What it may be able to do indirectly will depend upon the potentiality for improvement which already exists.

But the baby must not be thrown out with the bathwater. Paving the way for improvements may often be something which only a government can do. There can be no state educational system and no national health service unless the government plans and organizes them: no emancipation of women, no ending of racial segregation without legislative and administrative action by the government. While government action can never be a sufficient condition for improvements, it may frequently be a necessary condition. Now if a government fails to take necessary action in a situation where the potentiality for improvement exists, improvements which might have come about will inevitably fail to materialize. The society's way of life will then be less adequate than it might have been, had the government made its indispensable contribution. Whether the government should be blamed is however another matter. Gauging the capacity for improvement in a society is a difficult matter and the government may be guilty of an error of judgement rather than a culpable sin of omission.

But be that as it may, enough has been said to discredit the idea that government is an essentially conservative institution. If there is any potentiality for improvement in a society's way of life much of it is likely to be wasted if the government is debarred from making its contribution. The idea that government is an essentially conservative institution betrays a defective understanding of human social living and of the part which government can play in it. It was derived from the idea of the public interest expounded in Section 2 and this idea clearly needs amending to take account of what has been said in this section.

What was said in Section 2 can be summarized in three steps:

A. The public interest is the corporate interest of a self-sufficient society in whose way of life private interests have a legitimate place.

B. This corporate interest is that of the members in the conditions necessary for their way of life to be carried on successfully.

C. These conditions, more precisely specified, are those which must be secured to enable all the members of the society to participate in its way of life on terms consistent with its established morality and social order.

So far as *A* is concerned no change is necessary but *B* needs amending because it implies satisfaction with the society's way of life and takes no account of any potentiality which there may be for improvement. The corporate interest must be an interest in the conditions necessary for the way of life to be as adequate as possible, not merely in the conditions necessary for it to be carried on successfully in its present form. This takes account of whatever potentiality there may be for improvement. More fundamentally: it recognizes that every self-sufficient society is a microcosm of mankind, a concrete embodiment at a given time and place of the universal human predicament.

What is wrong with *B* is brought out more clearly in *C*. It assumes that the established morality and social order are to be accepted uncritically and takes no account of the fact that to the extent that they betray a defective understanding, the society's way of life is inadequate. It also overlooks the fact that among the ideas, beliefs and values which underlie a given way of life there are likely to be latent ambiguities and contradictions. It assumes that a society's established morality and social order are all of a piece, that each is internally coherent and harmonizes with the other and that neither within nor between them are there any conflicting tendencies and strains. It therefore needs to be amended. The public interest must be in those conditions which need to be secured if all the members of a society are to participate in its way of life on terms consistent with what is enlightened in its established morality and social order than what is obscurantist. Those features are enlightened which reflect an understanding of the world and of human identity in which there is some appreciation of the nature of the human predicament and of the possibilities which human life affords. Those are obscurantist which lack this understanding and inculcate or foster attitudes and ways of acting which are opposed to it.

All this may be expressed by distinguishing between two ideas of the public interest: the conservative and the critical. The conservative idea is the one expounded in Section 2, the critical the amended version of the last two paragraphs. To repeat that amended version and sum up the critical idea: the public interest is the corporate interest of a self-sufficient society in whose way of life private interests have a legitimate place. This corporate interest is that of the members as human beings in the conditions necessary for the way of life to be as adequate as possible, not merely in those necessary for it to be carried on successfully in its present form. These conditions are those which must be secured to enable all the members to participate in the society's way of life on terms consistent with what is enlightened in its established morality and social order rather than what is obscurantist. The relation between these two ideas of the public interest is essentially that between critical humanism and social morality as levels of rational activity. The critical idea reflects the perspective of critical humanism, the conservative idea that of social morality. It follows that to the extent that a government goes about its work in the spirit of the critical rather than the merely conservative idea, it is in that respect at least, better as a government.

In Section 3 it was argued that the best form of government for a given society is that which harmonizes best with its established morality and social order. But this presupposes the conservative idea of the public interest. In terms of the critical idea that form is best which harmonizes best with what is enlightened rather than with what is obscurantist in the established morality and social order. In other words: that form is best for a given society which most facilitates and least obstructs the promotion of the public interest in terms of the critical idea. But it was also argued that one form of government is as such inherently better or worse than another, irrespective of whether it is the best form for a given society. Constitutionalism is inherently better than despotism, representative government than mere constitutionalism and democracy better than undemocratic representative government. If and when it becomes possible, the change from an inherently worse to an inherently better form would be an improvement in the way of life of the society concerned, but such a change is likely to come about only if government is being carried on in the spirit of the critical idea. If despotism is to give way to constitutionalism, the despot must want to make his society's way of life more adequate and must be willing when the time is ripe to abandon his despotic position. Where government is carried on in the spirit of the conservative idea, a society is likely to remain stuck fast with its existing form of government unless or until rebellion sweeps it away.

The main theme of this section has been the contribution a government can make to improve its society's way of life and the use of the potentiality for improvement which must already exist. But economic considerations will always impose limitations upon what a government can do. This is true whether the public interest is being promoted in the spirit of the critical idea or the conservative. The amount of human and material resources available is always finite. Not all the conditions which are in the public interest can be brought about at once. Governing is inevitably always a matter of determining priorities. But conditions outside a society no less than those within it affect its way of life. Governing is the pursuit of the national interest abroad as well as the public interest at home.

7. INTERNATIONAL RELATIONS: SOME ELEMENTARY
CONSIDERATIONS

The conservative idea of the public interest is different from the critical idea but in either case conditions abroad are relevant. The national interest abroad is complementary to the public interest at home. A nation with a developed industrial economy has for instance an interest in maintaining access to foreign sources of raw materials. But conditions abroad lie outside a government's jurisdiction for it can not give orders to the citizens of other nations. There are fundamentally only two methods by which it can promote the national interest abroad. One is to negotiate with other governments. The other is to coerce them, either by the threat or the actual use of force.

It may be objected that to use force except for purely defensive purposes is morally wrong. To promote the national interest by coercing other governments is aggression and aggression can never be morally justified. Some philosophers, notably Hobbes and Hegel, have thought that moral considerations can have no relevance in international relations. According to them there can be morality only within the framework of an organized society. The international world is not an organized society and hence moral considerations cannot have any relevance in international relations. This as it stands is incorrect. An established morality is an integral part of the way of life of every self-sufficient society. Embedded in every established morality is a theory of human identity. An established morality always includes ideas and beliefs about its society's place in the world and the significance of human life in the general scheme of things. Moral considerations are relevant to a given nation in its dealings with other nations in the sense that it ought to treat them in ways which are compatible with the theory of human identity embedded in its established morality. For the government of a nation in whose way of life the standpoint of critical humanism is substantially embodied, aggression is morally inadmissable as a method of promoting the national interest abroad. It knows that every other nation is like its own, a microcosm of mankind, that the members are fellow human beings and that fellow human beings, whether individually or collectively, ought not to treat each other arbitrarily.

To deny that moral considerations can be relevant in international relations is in effect to reject international co-operation.

Like every other form of co-operation, international co-operation can flourish only where there is mutual trust. There can be trust only where there is the mutual recognition of a moral obligation to deal honestly and to keep agreements. To reject international co-operation is to say that each nation should 'go it alone': that nothing can be gained from sharing of knowledge and skills or from collaboration across national frontiers in the discovery, dissemination, cultivation and appreciation of intrinsic values. From the standpoint of critical humanism, a government which bases its foreign policy upon such a view is betraying a manifestly defective understanding of the world.

But force has only too often been used for other than purely defensive purposes. War has been ubiquitous throughout human history; wars of tribes, of peoples, of kingdoms, of city states, of empires and during the modern era, of nations. How is this to be accounted for? To put it all down to human wickedness is too facile. The standpoint of critical humanism is essentially modern, reflecting as it does the sophisticated intellectual perspectives of modern scientific and historical knowledge. Its substantial embodiment in the ways of life of a number of Western nations has come about only very recently. Many human societies in the past thought and lived in terms of ethnocentric theories of human identity. Such theories did not allow for moral considerations in relations with supposedly inferior races. The adherents of religious cosmopolitan theories frequently believed themselves to be in possession of the ultimate truth and this belief encouraged monopolistic claims. Moral considerations tended to have little weight in dealings with infidels outside the faith and heretics within it.

Our ancestors did not think in terms of the standpoint of critical humanism. For the most part magical, religious and theological beliefs shaped their attitudes towards the world and human life. War and the aggressive use of force did not appear to them to be the evils which they can be seen to be from the standpoint of critical humanism. Rather they were indispensable methods of dealing with the innate inferiority and wickedness of many human beings. Before the advent of mechanized industry and scientific technology the material benefits of foreign trade and commerce were more limited and their disruption by war was less disastrous than it is today, war itself was far less destructive. It was always an evil but it has become so on a scale unimaginable to former generations. These considerations make our ancestors' ideas on the subject of the aggressive use of force intelligible, but also make it clear that those ideas will no longer do for us.

Appreciation of this is suggested by the existence of the United Nations Organization. This is not a world parliament, much less a world government. Rather it is an association of national governments, the basis of which is certain common interests which transcend national frontiers. The limitation of international conflicts, control of disease, co-operation in economic, scientific and cultural fields. Its *raison d'être* as an association is to establish working procedures through which these common interests can be successfully pursued. The rather chequered history of UNO during the last twenty years suggests that some of its member governments do not fully understand its basis and *raison d'être*. But those that do have good reason to maintain and strengthen UNO. Its failure would not be in the national interest of any of its members who share the common interests which are its basis.

But should a government's foreign policy be confined to promoting the national interest abroad and those common interests which it shares with other governments? If the answer is yes, then foreign policy becomes merely enlightened national selfishness. A government which promotes the public interest at home in the spirit of the critical idea will be concerned abroad with the conditions necessary for its own nation's way of life to become as adequate as possible. But it will not be concerned with what is necessary to enable the ways of life of other nations to be improved, so long as other nations do not menace its own national interest nor obstruct its efforts to promote it, it can afford to be indifferent to them. That millions of human beings abroad are living in poverty, squalor and wretchedness is none of its business. Its attitude is comparable to that of an individual engaged in the pursuit of his self-interest towards the interests of other people not connected with him. Enlightened national selfishness is something a good deal less than enlightened

K   289

humaneness and is alien to the cosmopolitan spirit of critical humanism.

It was argued in the last chapter that a rational agent has above everything else good reason to make the best contribution he can to the discovery, cultivation and appreciation of intrinsic values by as many human beings as possible, not merely by his fellow countrymen. The government of a nation in whose way of life the standpoint of critical humanism is substantially embodied, should, in its foreign policy, show concern about the lot of other nations and a readiness to help their governments improve their national ways of life. The initiative in this must rest with the governments concerned but outside help, in the shape of economic and technical assistance, may well be indispensable if existing potentialities for improvement are not to run to waste. Enlightened humaneness requires that a government which is in a position to give such help should provide it irrespective of whether any benefits are to be gained from doing so. A government ought to be its nation's agent in an enterprise in which, from the standpoint of critical humanism, all modern nations have good reason to join. This is to establish and maintain throughout the world conditions which will make it possible for human life everywhere to be enhanced and enriched. It is an enterprise which modern science and technology have brought within the realms of practical possibility. But there are enormous difficulties to be overcome arising out of the great disparities of wealth among the nations of the world, the problems created by cultural and ideological differences and the fear, suspicion and distrust which bedevil international relations.

PART 4

Freedom and Right in Perspective

Chapter 9

Freedom

1. FREEDOM AND CRITICAL HUMANISM

It was argued in Chapter 5 that to be free is to be self-determining. Personal freedom lies in the personal self-determination of the rational agent at the level of personal well-being: moral freedom is the moral self-determination of the rational agent at the level of social morality. Negative freedom, the absence of constraint by other people, is a necessary but not a sufficient condition for personal and moral freedom. As a form of human freedom, moral freedom is superior to personal freedom because it can in principle be universalized while merely personal freedom cannot. But there was a reservation about moral freedom arising out of the limitations of social morality as a level of rational activity. The moral freedom of the rational agent at this level is relative to his society's way of life. He tries to be socially responsible and just, deciding for himself how best to act in terms of these standards but his decisions are made within the framework of his society's way of life which he has to accept uncritically. He has no rational basis upon which to evaluate it. His conduct is thus being shaped by the beliefs underlying that way of life. These are determined for him, not by him, and his moral freedom is therefore something less than full self-determination. But the critical humanist decides for himself how best to meet the requirements of enlightened humaneness. In deciding he does not accept his society's way of life uncritically. He evaluates it from the point of view of its adequacy for human beings through a piecemeal critical appraisal of its prevailing understanding. He does not repudiate the demands of social morality. But he interprets them in the light of his decisions about enlightened humaneness. It follows that the generic human capacity for self-determination is more fully realized at the level of critical humanism than at the level of social morality. The critical humanist's conduct is not being shaped by ideas and values which have been determined for him rather than by him. He may accept much of society's way of life but only because he has satisfied himself that it reflects an adequate understanding of the world and of human life. He is therefore more free because more self-determining than the rational agent at the level of social morality. This freedom of the critical humanist may appropriately be called rational freedom because it is the freedom of the rational agent at the highest level of rational activity.

Only a minority in each generation are likely to become critical humanists. But this does not mean that rational freedom is open to the same objection as personal freedom, that it cannot be universalized. Personal freedom cannot be universalized because it involves an essentially pragmatic attitude towards morality. But there is nothing in the idea of rational freedom which in principle prevents its being achieved by everyone. It is not inconsistent with itself in the way in which personal freedom is. What makes it unlikely that rational freedom will ever be widespread is the empirical fact that most people tend to be conservative about their society's way of life. For the most part they are reluctant to call it in question and are content to accept the prevailing understanding bequeathed to them.

Moral freedom is universalizable in principle but not always so in fact. Where the social order is hierarchical those in the lower ranks will largely be confined to regularian morality. If all are to have moral freedom, all must be able to participate in the society's way of life on equal terms as rational agents at the levels of social morality and personal well-being. According to the idea of a free society in Chapter 5, all must have adequate opportunity for both moral and personal freedom. This means that it is only in a free society that moral freedom can in fact be universalized. But our earlier account of a free society was incomplete. It must be developed further, and in particular the implications of the last three chapters must be considered.

According to that account a free society must be a self-determining society, which was interpreted as meaning that it must have an independent existence in its own right with its own individual identity. This can now be amplified. A self-determining society must be a self-sufficient society: that is a society with a viable economy whose members intermarry and from generation to generation carry on a common way of life. But self-determination in this sense is merely a corollary of negative freedom. If a society is able to maintain any sort of way of life at all, and is free from external constraint, it is *ipso facto* a self-determining and hence a free society. But the way of life of a free society must have a distinctive and special character. It must be self-determining in the sense that all its members have the chance to become self-determining. But this self-determination was thought of only in terms of moral and personal freedom. It must be amended to take account of rational freedom. Since rational freedom is the freedom of the critical humanist the way of life of a free society must give potential critical humanists adequate opportunities for realizing their potential.

It may be thought that potential critical humanists can be left to take care of themselves. They are not dependent upon their society's way of life because they do not accept it uncritically. They emancipate themselves from it by trying to understand for themselves and subjecting it to criticism. But the standpoint of critical humanism is a sophisticated one. Whether potential critical humanists can become sufficiently acquainted with scientific and historical knowledge to be able to appreciate their perspectives will depend upon the character of their society's way of life and in particular on the educational opportunities which it affords. If they are to emancipate themselves from their society's way of life, that way of life itself must first adequately equip them intellectually and culturally. Left to take care of themselves many of them may fail to realize their potential.

Two questions set aside in Chapter 5 were: 'Is the way of life of a free society a possible one for human beings?' 'Is it better than any other way of life?' But the question of possibility is not an easy one. Who is to say what is possible for human beings? We might regard the idea of a free society as a standard for actual societies to approximate to and then ask: is it a possible standard? But this is still too general. Possible for whom, where and when? If, however, it can be shown that some actual societies have managed to approximate to it, then it is clearly a possible standard at least for those societies. It may be claimed that the ways of life of contemporary Western democracies largely exhibit the characteristic features distinctive of a free society.

The claim is a plausible one, especially looking at the legal and political institutions of Western democracy. But the way of life of an actual society is never all of a piece. Despite legal equality of status the social order may continue to be influenced by ideas of social hierarchy and hereditary status. Economic conditions may drastically affect the real opportunities which different members have for achieving the self-determination of which they are capable. Religious ideas and values may continue to be an important influence although the form of government is democratic: for instance in Roman Catholic countries like Italy and the Republic of Ireland. The most that can be allowed is that the Western democracies exhibit in their ways of life some of the characteristic features distinctive of a free society. In some respects such as law and politics they are in striking distance of the standard. But in many others they are far from approximating to it.

But this is enough to show that for the Western democracies the idea of a free society is a possible standard. What about the majority of mankind who live in societies which are neither Western nor democratic? It is not obvious that it is a possible standard for them, and it appears to have little relevance to the problems of poverty and technological backwardness which at present beset them. Changes in the present ways of life of these societies could bring them nearer to a free society. But are such changes desirable? What is the value of a free society's way of life? If and when it can be had, is it a good thing? More specifically: does it follow that the greater the extent to which a society's way of life approximates to the special character distinctive of a free society the more adequate it is for human beings?

We saw in Chapter 5 that a slave-owning society, a caste society and a theocracy can none of them be a free society. It was argued in Chapter 7 that the ways of life of these three types of society are inadequate for human beings. The institution of slavery betrays a defective understanding of what it is to be human. So do racial segregation, the wider institution of social caste and theocratic morality with its theological regularian foundation. What disqualifies these societies as free societies is what makes, or helps to make, their ways of life inadequate. Does it follow that anything in a society's way of life which disqualifies it as a free society necessarily betrays a defective understanding of the world and of human life? To put the same question the other way round: does it follow that the better a society's prevailing understanding, the greater the extent to which all its members will enjoy adequate opportunities for personal moral and rational freedom?

That it does follow in the case of personal freedom can be seen by recalling what was said in Chapter 7 about intrinsic values. It was said that if human beings are to give human life significance they must incorporate into it activities and experiences which are intrinsically valuable; also that there is a sense in which intrinsic values are empirical discoveries. That various sorts of activity and experience are intrinsically valuable is something which human beings can find out only by engaging in them. Now it is by pursuing his personal well-being as a rational agent and hence by becoming a free person that a man can best discover intrinsic values for himself and incorporate them into his individual life. If therefore all the members of a society are to give significance to their lives as human beings, they must all have adequate opportunities for becoming free persons. It does not follow that they will all be equally successful. But what matters is that they should all have an equal chance to try. In a society where this is understood, deliberate efforts will be made to organize its way of life so that all its members can enjoy adequate opportunities for personal freedom.

Equality of status is necessary if all are to have adequate opportunities for personal freedom. All must stand on an equal footing as members. There must be no division between first- and second-class citizens. But this is also necessary if all are to have adequate opportunities for moral freedom. Where there is a hereditary or racial social hierarchy, those in the lower ranks will largely be confined to regularian morality. Such a society betrays a defective understanding of what it is to be human.

A society whose prevailing understanding is adequate will have an open social order in which all the members have equality of status and therefore adequate opportunities for becoming free moral agents. It does not follow that all will in fact become equally socially responsible and just in their moral conduct. But once more what is important is that all should have an equal chance to try.

If there are to be adequate opportunities for rational freedom, there must be adequate opportunities for potential critical humanists to realize their potential. A society whose way of life embodies the standpoint of critical humanism and whose prevailing understanding is therefore adequate, will provide these opportunities. By the same token it will also provide adequate opportunities for moral and personal freedom. The more a society's way of life embodies the standpoint of critical humanism and hence the better its prevailing understanding, the more will its way of life have the special character distinctive of a free society. The answer to our second question is yes: it does follow that the greater the extent to which a society's way of life approximates to that of a free society, the better it is as a way of life for human beings. But two qualifications are necessary. The first is that it does not follow that an adequate way of life for human beings can be completely characterized in terms of the way of life of a free society. Other features such as those connected with 'higher intrinsic values' may not be clearly brought out by concentrating on the idea of a free society. The second is that the idea of a free society is not a possible standard for many societies. It is relevant only as a guide to the direction of future change. The way of life of a free society is better than that of any other but it may often be necessary to make do with something very much less.

2. THE SCALE OF FORMS OF HUMAN FREEDOM

Our conclusions so far may be expressed in a scale of forms of human freedom. In ascending order the forms in this scale are: negative freedom, personal freedom, moral freedom, rational freedom, and social freedom, that is the freedom of a free society. Negative freedom is the minimum form of human freedom. This is not only because the absence of constraint is a necessary condition for any sort of self-determination whatever but also because only someone capable of determining his conduct for himself can be subject to constraint. To be negatively free is to be vulnerable to constraint but not in fact to be subject to it and therefore to be in some measure self-determining. But this need only amount to some capacity for formulating and executing purposes of one's own. In personal freedom, the generic capacity for self-determination is more fully realized and we have already seen why moral freedom is superior to merely personal freedom, and rational freedom to merely moral freedom. But all these are individual forms of human freedom. Social freedom comes at the top of the scale because human life is necessarily social and in a free society all the members can make the most of their capacities for self-determination.

There is a sense in which each form in the scale includes those below it. One cannot be a free person, a free moral agent, or a critical humanist unless one is free from constraint. A free moral agent continues to promote his personal well-being within the framework of social morality. The critical humanist does not repudiate the demands of social morality. Nor does he neglect his personal well-being. But he interprets both in the light of the requirements of enlightened humaneness. Social freedom by definition includes rational, moral, and personal freedom. It also includes negative freedom in the sense that there can be no adequate opportunities if there is constraint. But each form nevertheless remains distinct. A man can be negatively free without being a free person, much less a free moral agent or a critical humanist. The degree of self-determination of which he is capable may be less than is necessary to enable him to pursue his personal well-being wisely and prudently. He can be a free person without being a free moral agent and he may be able to achieve moral freedom without being capable of rational freedom. He may succeed in realizing his potential as a critical humanist and in achieving rational freedom despite the fact that there are features in his society's way of life which disqualify it from being a free society.

The scale is also a scale of concepts of freedom. Each form is not only a way of being free but a concept or way of thinking of

freedom. The higher the place of a form in the scale, the better
it is as a way of thinking of human freedom because the better
the way of being free of which it is the concept. To think of
human freedom at all it is necessary to think of it as the absence
of constraint. But it is better to think of it as personal freedom
rather than merely as negative freedom, better again to think
of it as moral freedom, better still to think of it as rational
freedom, and best of all to think of it as social freedom. Each
form in the scale includes those below it and so does each concept. But just as each form remains distinct, so does each
concept. You cannot think of human freedom as personal
freedom without thinking of it as negative freedom. But you
do not have to think of it as moral, rational or social freedom.
If you think of human freedom in terms of any one of the concepts in the scale, you are committed to thinking of it also in
terms of the concepts which lie below it but not in terms of
those which lie above. There may often be good reason to think
primarily in terms of one of the lower concepts: for instance,
negative or personal freedom. But in doing so you are taking
a partial and incomplete view. An adequate theory of human
freedom must embrace the whole scale, which means thinking
of it in terms of social freedom.

In the positive theory of Green and Bosanquet, the distinction
between the internal and external sides of freedom is of central
importance. There is a sense in which this distinction is preserved in the scale of forms but it must be interpreted in terms
of self-determination not, as it was by them, in terms of the
ethical doctrine of self-realization. Each form in the scale has
both an internal and an external side. On its internal side, it
is the generic capacity for self-determination as this is realized
in the particular form. On its external side, it is the absence of
constraint in the shape of human interference with the realization of that form of self-determination. In negative freedom the
emphasis is all on the external side. The internal side is also
there: there must be some capacity for self-determination; but
it remains latent. In personal, moral and rational freedom the
emphasis is primarily on the internal side. Each form also has
an external side. There cannot be personal, moral or rational
freedom if there is constraint. But it is not in the absence of

constraint but the particular way in which the generic capacity
for self-determination is realized which makes each a distinct
form of human freedom. It is only in social freedom that both
sides are equally emphasized. If all the members of a society
are to have adequate opportunities to become self-determining,
they must be free from constraint. But they must also be endowed
with the generic capacity in the first place.

Freedom on its external side can be made an end of utilitarian
action. Sources of constraint can be identified and efforts made
to remove them. But this is not true of freedom on its internal
side. The generic capacity for self-determination cannot be an
end of utilitarian action, although the conditions favourable to
its realization may be. It is something which human beings
discover in themselves by exercising it. This has a bearing on
the sense in which social freedom can be a goal of political
action. Adequate opportunities for all to achieve personal,
moral, and rational freedom, may be adopted as the official
objective of government policy. But the policy can succeed only
to the extent that potentialities for internal freedom are already
present. People must be capable of using the opportunities and
must want to do so.

The emphasis on the internal side of freedom in personal,
moral, and rational freedom, calls attention to something
important. This is the mind and will of the rational agent at the
levels of personal well-being, social morality, and critical
humanism. A man becomes self-determining as a person and
achieves personal freedom by trying to promote his personal
well-being wisely and prudently. He becomes self-determining
as a moral agent and achieves moral freedom by trying to act
responsibly and justly as a member of his society. He becomes
self-determining as a critical humanist and achieves rational
freedom by trying to act with enlightened humaneness in every
phase of his life. What makes him self-determining and hence
free at each level is that he tries to act in it according to its
standards, deciding for himself how best to do so. How far he
is successful is another matter and does not affect the freedom
of his action. He may subsequently decide in the light of certain
features of the situation which at the time he overlooked, that
a different course of action would have been better: for instance

wiser or more just. But this does not mean that if at the time
he had taken them into account and adopted the different course,
his personal or moral freedom would have been greater. He
determined his conduct for himself at the time, albeit not as
wisely or as justly as he might have done. This last point needs
to be stressed. Freedom on its internal side is an integral part
of rational activity, but the two are not identical. Being rational
is something more than being self-determining, although the
latter is necessarily involved in it. Granted that in acting
rationally, a man must determine his conduct for himself, it is
another question how rational what he does is in terms of the
standards of a given level. It is not true that the greater the
rationality at a given level, the greater the freedom. But something else which is also true and which must not be confused
with this, is that each level of rational activity embodies a
different form of human freedom. The higher the level of
rational activity, the better the form of human freedom, because
the better the way in which the generic capacity for self-
determination is realized.

All this has implications for the criticism of human action.
Only a free man can be criticized for his conduct because he
must have determined it for himself if he is to be held accountable for it. There are two different grounds upon which he may
be criticized. The first is in terms of the standards of a given
level. This presupposes that he was trying to act according to
its standards and could have done better than in fact he did.
He could have been more socially responsible or prudent. The
second which is more fundamental especially in moral contexts,
is that he failed to act at the appropriate level at all. The
criticism is not that he tried to act according to its standards
and did not do very well but that he failed to try. This presupposes that he was capable of acting at the level in question
but was unwilling to make the effort. Admittedly criticism on
these grounds is a risky business. How can one be sure that he
could have tried? But in one's own case the difficulty does not
arise. I may know very well that on a particular occasion
although I could have done so, I did not attempt to act justly
because I wanted to avoid inconvenience or danger. I am open
to criticism not for showing poor moral judgement but for being

immoral: for failing to attempt what I knew I both could and should have attempted.

But to return to the scale of forms: why must it stop with social freedom? Is there no superior form above it which realizes the generic capacity in a better way? It may be thought that international or cosmopolitan freedom is superior to social freedom. But what would this be? A plausible suggestion is that it would be the freedom enjoyed by an international society all of whose members were free societies. But would this really be different from social freedom? Would it be a different way of realizing the generic capacity, involving something not contained in social freedom? The answer is surely no. It would still be social freedom, although on an international level and probably in some sort of federal form. It may be the case that if all human beings everywhere are to have adequate opportunities for personal, moral, and rational freedom, some sort of international federation will have to be brought into being. But if or when this happens, it does not mean that a new form of freedom will have been created. It means only that the implications of social freedom will have been more completely understood.

Does the scale of forms as it has been presented here cover all forms of human freedom? What about political freedom, economic freedom, religious freedom, and freedom of speech and expression? Where do they fit into the scale? Does it throw light upon them? We shall try to answer these questions so far as political, economic, and religious freedom are concerned in the course of the present chapter. The case of freedom of speech will be left to the next, where it can be more fruitfully discussed in connection with rights.

3. POLITICAL FREEDOM

It is often said that there can be no freedom unless the scope of government is limited. What is normally meant is that if the government can interfere in everything, if there is no limit to its meddling, little room is left for private life and for personal initiative and choice. This is of course true and it suggests one way of interpreting the idea of political freedom This is as a special case of negative freedom. It should be thought of as negative political freedom: that is, as freedom from constraint by government. No government can govern without using constraint, which means that negative political freedom is always partial, never complete. But this is not denied by the doctrine of limited government. Its point is that just because government involves the use of constraint, its scope should be limited.

Now according to the idea of the public interest, the scope of government is always limited. The task of the government is to promote the public interest, which means establishing and maintaining certain conditions in a society's way of life. It must do what is necessary to perform this task but has no business concerning itself with anything else. The public sphere, which is the proper concern of government, is always finite in extent. The private sphere, which falls outside its scope, is 'open-ended' and extends indefinitely. In other words, the idea of negative political freedom is built in to the idea of the public interest. But the public interest is often a problem not a datum. Some of the steps taken by the government to promote it may well be controversial. While the scope of government must in principle be limited, just what the limits should in fact be is by no means always clear. The public sphere is always finite, but just where the line should be drawn between it and the private sphere depends upon the circumstances prevailing at a given time and place. There is a sense in which negative political freedom is essentially residual in character. It can be encroached upon if the public interest makes this necessary. At the same time these encroachments do not have to be accepted uncritically. The government is a fallible human agency. It has no monopoly of wisdom or virtue. To challenge the government to show why the public interest requires a particular measure is in principle always justified.

But there must be freedom to participate actively in politics, to issue the challenge and put pressure on the government to answer it. This is the freedom which the members of the citizen body have under a representative form of government. Now being a member of a citizen body means being, or at least having the opportunity to be, self-determining as a citizen. To be a self-determining or free citizen is not to be like Sir Joseph Porter in H.M.S. *Pinafore* who:

> 'always voted at his party's call
> and never thought of thinking for himself at all'.

It is to make up one's own mind about political issues and acting in the light of the conclusions one reaches. This political self-determination of the free citizen involves something more than merely the absence of constraint by the government, although that is a necessary condition and may appropriately be styled positive political freedom. Citizenship falls within the scope of rational activity at the level of social morality, which means that there is a close connection between moral freedom and positive political freedom. If you are denied membership of the citizen body, your sphere of moral self-determination is correspondingly reduced. Being a member enlarges your opportunities as a free moral agent to act responsibly and justly as a member of your society.

Without positive political freedom, negative political freedom is insecure. This is the case under despotism. A despotic government is not subject to the rule of law. Its subjects may enjoy considerable *de facto* negative political freedom. But this is is always precarious. The despotic government can intervene in their lives when and where it likes and can arbitrarily subject them to constraint. In a sense negative political freedom is safe under constitutionalism. A constitutional government is subject to the rule of law and cannot arbitrarily constrain its subjects. But under constitutionalism without representative government, there is no way of seeing that the public interest is promoted intelligently. The scope of the government will certainly be limited, but will the limits be in the right place? It is possible for a society to be under-governed. It can suffer from too much negative political freedom rather than too little. In that case, much of the public interest may go by default. If the scope of government is to be what the public interest requires, still more if the public interest is to be promoted in the spirit of the critical rather than the conservative idea, there must be representative as well as constitutional government. If there is to be neither too little nor too much negative political freedom, positive political freedom is a necessary condition.

In negative political freedom, as with negative freedom in general, the emphasis is all on the external side. The latent internal side is not necessarily political. It is merely the minimum capacity for self-determination which is present in all negative freedom. Negative freedom is a necessary condition for higher forms of freedom, and the same is true of the special case of negative political freedom. You cannot be a free person or a free moral agent if you are subject to constraint by government. Positive political freedom is best thought of as a special case of moral freedom. This is its place in the scale of forms. As a concept of political freedom, it is superior to negative political freedom. It is better to think of political freedom in terms of free citizenship than merely as the absence of constraint by government. But thinking of it in the former way necessarily involves thinking of it in the latter way as well. There cannot be positive political freedom without the negative form. But there can be negative political freedom without the positive variety. The negative concept therefore needs to be distinguished from the positive. You can think of political freedom simply in negative terms without thinking of free citizenship and what it involves at all.

Where the form of government is democratic, the citizen body is co-extensive with the adult population, which means that all have adequate opportunities for positive political freedom. But where there is representative government without democracy, this is not so. There is inequality of status between those who are members of the citizen body and those who are excluded from it, and the latter are denied positive political freedom. They are 'second-class' citizens and their opportunities for moral freedom are less adequate than those of the 'first-class' citizens. This means that a society with an undemocratic representative form of government is something less than a free society properly so called. All its members do not have adequate opportunities for moral freedom because some are denied positive political freedom. It follows that a democratic form of government is a necessary condition for social freedom and that political freedom, both positive and negative, is part of social freedom. Negative political freedom is included in social freedom as a special case of negative freedom: positive political freedom as a special case of moral freedom. But both need to be distinguished from social freedom because both can exist without it. Positive political freedom is not however a necessary condition for rational freedom, although it certainly helps. A man may succeed in realizing his potential as a critical humanist despite being denied membership of the citizen body. His access to the necessary knowledge and experience will probably be made harder by his second-class status but it is not impossible. But a man who achieves rational freedom while being denied positive political freedom suffers in a real sense from social alienation, for his society is excluding him from a place in its way of life which he is pre-eminently qualified to fill.

A distinction was drawn in the last chapter between two senses of self-government. The second sense, with which we have been mainly concerned, is most fully achieved under democracy. It is an aspect of positive political freedom and is included in social freedom in the sense that a free society in virtue of having a democratic form of government, will be a self-governing society. But self-government in the first sense is also essential for social freedom. A free society must be a politically independent society. It must not be a colony or province of some other society. This idea of political independence calls attention to another meaning of political freedom: namely, freedom from alien political rule. This may appear to be simply negative political freedom in an international context but it is more than that. Political independence does not mean merely being free from constraint by foreign governments. It means not being subject to foreign governments at all. It is total, not partial, negative political freedom. But there is literally as well as metaphorically an internal side which may be called national political self-determination. A politically independent society is self-determining in the sense of being of itself sufficient for human life and having its own government.

When supporters of nationalist movements talk about freedom, they usually mean political freedom in the form of political independence. Some of them may also have ideas of positive political freedom and perhaps social freedom. Political independence is a necessary condition for social freedom but it is certainly not a sufficient condition for it. Political independence can be the deliberate goal of political action. Steps can be taken to persuade the colonial power to give up its hold. But the creation of social freedom is quite another matter. As we saw earlier in this chapter, it is only in a limited sense that it can be pursued as a deliberate aim. Some potentiality for rational, moral and personal freedom must already be present. All things considered, it is hardly surprising that in many newly independent countries the form of government is predominantly despotic in character. If they are to enjoy positive political freedom, they must discover its value and significance for themselves. It cannot be exported to them or made part of a foreign aid programme. But the fact that a society is not capable of democracy, or even constitutionalism, is not a good reason for withholding political independence. Unless there is political independence, they cannot begin to learn. What is necessary is that there should at least be the capacity for maintaining some sort of government and that if this is despotic it will not be too inhumane and may give some scope for pursuing the public interest in the spirit of the critical idea.

4. TOTALITARIANISM

The twentieth century has the dubious distinction of contributing totalitarianism to the stock of human political experience. A totalitarian government is an unlimited government. Its scope extends to everything. Economic life, the arts and sciences, sport and entertainment, religion, even family life and personal relations, are subjected to control and direction. This is different from despotism where there is at least a measure of negative political freedom however insecure. In Hobbesian language, where the despotic government is silent, the subject is free. But there is nothing about which a totalitarian government is silent. It pronounces upon everything. There is no escape from the all-embracing grasp of government, no negative political freedom, and consequently no other forms of freedom. There is no distinction between the public interest and private interests because nothing is acknowledged to be private. The hideous consequences of totalitarianism in practice are all too familiar. But what about the ideas behind it? What is it which makes totalitarianism seem plausible? If it is the antithesis of freedom, it is important to try to understand it, and in particular, to try to see what characterizes the totalitarian manner of thought.

As a first step, consider the case of a democracy engaged in total war: there is a single national end, military victory, which has absolute priority because national survival depends upon it. The government is in charge of the national effort to attain this end. Its task is to organize and direct the national effort. All the population have a single duty which takes precedence over everything else: to serve the national effort under the direction of the government. Both social responsibility and justice justify this absolute priority because of the threat to national survival. The national interest abroad has become concentrated in the single end of military victory. The public interest at home has become the corporate interest in the conditions within the society to mount the national effort as efficiently and vigorously as possible. It has ceased to be the public interest properly so called because in the face of the national emergency, private interests have virtually ceased to have any legitimate place. This means that the democratic government has in effect ceased to be a limited government. It has to do whatever the national effort requires and its scope must therefore be all-embracing. There are however two important qualifications. The first is that the extension of the government's authority is recognized to be temporary. It is for the duration only. The second is that the legacy of peace-time values, especially humaneness and compassion, serves to alleviate the rigour and sacrifice required by the national effort.

There are some obvious resemblances between this case and totalitarianism. Under totalitarianism there is a single national end which has absolute priority. It is to be reached by a national effort organized and directed by the totalitarian government and the population have an absolute duty to serve the national effort under the government's direction. But there is a vital difference. Under totalitarianism, the national end is not military victory. It is an ideal way of life envisaged by the totalitarian leaders: for instance, the way of life of a classless society, of a corporate state, or of an Aryan society of *Herronvolk*. This vision of an ideal way of life is an essential ingredient of totalitarianism. The promise of a nobler future which it holds out is the *raison d'être* of the national effort and of the sacrifices and hardships demanded by that effort. There is nothing comparable to it in a democracy at war where the inspiration for the national effort comes simply from the threat to national survival which only military victory can avert. What is looked forward to is a return to normal life, not something new and radically different.

But while military victory is not the final end under totalitarianism, it may well be considered an essential step on the way. It may be thought necessary to eliminate certain hostile foreign governments before the ideal way of life can be realized. But whether military operations are undertaken or not, the psychological atmosphere under totalitarianism is essentially that of total war. This is because the final end has the same absolute priority and is pursued with the same urgency as military victory. But there is no legacy of peacetime values to ameliorate the harsh demands of the national effort. Totalitarianism is orientated towards the future. It has turned its back on the past and does not want to preserve anything from the bad old days. Consequently expediency in relation to the final end is the only standard which is acknowledged. Other considerations such as humaneness and justice will have to wait until the ideal way of life has been realised.

Considered as a theory of government, totalitarianism contains some serious errors. The first is the idea that except in emergency conditions, such as total war, there is a single national end having absolute priority which is to be attained by a national effort organized and directed by the government. The public interest at home is always in a number of different ends, and so is the national interest abroad. Some of these ends are more important than others but none has absolute priority. The government has to decide upon their relative importance, and with this in mind it must take steps to attain them. But that is something very different from organizing and directing an overall national effort to which everything else is subordinate. It may be objected however that this misses the main point of totalitarianism which is that there is an ideal way of life which ought to have absolute priority as a national end. But this only draws attention to a second and more fundamental error. No way of life, however ideal, can be an end of utilitarian action even if that action is organized and directed by the government on a national scale and is given precedence over everything else. Particular conditions which are necessary for, or favourable to, a way of life can be ends of utilitarian action but not a way of life itself. That can come into being only as the members of a society come to think, feel and act, in terms of the ideas, beliefs and values which it presupposes. The most that a government can do is to pave the way.

This points to a false rationalism in totalitarianism. It lies in the failure to appreciate the scope and limits of utilitarian action. This in turn implies a defective understanding of the general character of rational activity. It is the false rationalism rather than the claim to have knowledge of an ideal way of life which is the fundamental flaw in totalitarianism. That claim is also significant because it contributes to some of the most notorious characteristics of totalitarian regimes. But it is important to see that even if the way of life envisaged by totalitarian leaders is a marked improvement over that which is at present being carried on in their society, totalitarianism as a theory of government is not redeemed. The cardinal error still remains: that of thinking that any way of life can be an end of government-organized and directed utilitarian action.

This cardinal error all too easily generates the idea that government action to bring about a new way of life is a kind of making or producing. The craftsman must have complete control of his materials. He must mould them according to a preconceived plan if he is to produce the finished article. The same is true of government. If it is to produce its finished article, a new way of life, it must have complete control of its materials, the human and material resources in its society. This is why a totalitarian government tries to control and direct not only the economy but the whole culture of its society. Essentially its subjects must be made to think and feel in terms of the values of the new way of life, and not be allowed to experience anything

311

alien to its ethos. The totalitarian leaders' conviction about the ideal character of this way of life fortifies them in their resolve to make their control comprehensive and to crush ruthlessly any opposition to it.

It may be thought that in practice totalitarian leaders are more likely to be interested in power than in bringing an ideal way of life into being. But it is still important to see that is wrong with totalitarianism as a theory to avoid being taken in by would-be totalitarian leaders. In particular, it is important to see why totalitarianism is the antithesis of human freedom. It is so in principle and not merely because wicked leaders pervert it for evil purposes. The false rationalism and the craftsman analogy with its ideas about shaping and moulding, mean that human beings are not being thought of as self-determining agents at all. They are materials to be worked upon, not persons to be worked for and with.

It follows from all this that the regime under democracy in total war is not totalitarian. There is no false rationalism. There is a single national end, military victory. But this is a finite objective and is an appropriate end of utilitarian action. Far-reaching government control and direction are necessary to bring it about but there is no question of trying to shape and mould the population by trying to make them think and feel exclusively in terms of certain ideas and values. Censorship will be for the sake of military security. Even in total war, a democratic government is still in principle accountable to the citizen body. Some of the normal democratic procedures may have to be suspended for security reasons but the government is still ultimately dependent upon popular support. A totalitarian government is not accountable to anyone. It is not subject to the rule of law. In these respects it has the attributes of despotism. But to describe it as merely an extreme form of despotism would be misleading. Despotism is a genuine form of government, albeit the most inferior. An enlightened despot can promote the public interest in the spirit of the critical idea. But totalitarianism, because of its false rationalism, is not strictly speaking a form of government at all. Rather it is a form of 'non-government', a political perversion.

The difference between despotism and totalitarianism is

important in the case of an 'underdeveloped' country. Its economic backwardness means that a programme of economic development must have top priority. Despotism is the best that can be managed in the way of a form of government and it may be thought that this must become totalitarian in order to carry through the programme. But this is a mistake. The programme can take the form of a series of targets to be attained over a given period of time. These targets are finite objectives and are appropriate ends of utilitarian action. Much of this action will have to be organized, co-ordinated and supervised by the government. There may be control and direction similar to that necessary in total war. But that is no reason for 'going totalitarian' and trying to impose new ideas, beliefs and values upon the society by compelling the members to think and feel exclusively in terms of them. Cultural changes will come about in any case as the programme of economic development proceeds. A government which promotes the public interest in the spirit of the critical idea may be able to do something to foster and facilitate these changes. But to think that there is a short cut, and that if the government has total control of the whole way of life, it can speed up cultural changes by imposing it from above, is to fall into the false rationalism characteristic of totalitarianism.

Finally, a word is necessary on the subject of Communism. Stalin's Russia exhibited all the characteristics of totalitarianism. What is now going on in China under the name of the 'cultural revolution' suggests that the thought of Chairman Mao, if not the practice of Chinese Communism, is totalitarian in character. But classical Marxism is not totalitarian, nor is there much evidence of totalitarian tendencies in Lenin's theoretical writings. There is some evidence to suggest that in post-Stalinist Russia, and still more in some of the Eastern European Communist régimes, there is a movement away from the totalitarian manner of thought. These régimes are certainly still despotisms but that is at least better than being totalitarian and it means that future developments towards constitutional-ism and eventually of democracy are at least possibilities. Communism must not therefore be equated with totalitarianism although it has often degenerated into it.

5. ECONOMIC FREEDOM

Wherever limited resources with alternative uses have to be allocated among competing ends there is an economic problem: how to allocate them efficiently. This suggests that economic freedom lies in the economic self-determination of the rational agent at the level of utility. A man becomes self-determining as an economic agent and achieves economic freedom by trying to use his personal resources as efficiently as possible in bringing about the particular conditions necessary for the execution of his ulterior purposes, and more generally, to provide for his needs. It follows that economic freedom is a necessary ingredient of personal freedom in the sense that if a man is to be self-determining as a person, he must be self-determining as an economic agent. He must manage his personal economy for himself, allocating his personal resources according to his own judgement about how they can best be used to promote his personal well-being. But if he is to have a personal economy to manage, he must have resources with alternative uses, and must be in a position to choose between different ways of using them. How much he has and what choices are open to him will depend upon the economy of his society and upon his position in it.

A society's economy is its allocation of its human and material resources among the activities which make up its methods of production and distribution. The activities which they comprise are utilitarian, consisting as they do in the producing of goods and the rendering of services for consumption by its members. Each of these activities involves an economic cost. It uses a certain quantity of the society's finite human and material resources which therefore cannot be used in other productive and distributive activities. The more land used for urban development, the less available for agriculture. If more people are employed in service industries, fewer can be employed in manufacturing industry.

A self-sufficient society must have a viable economy, maintaining an overall balance in its commercial dealings with the rest of the world. There is a parallel between a society's economy and an individual man's personal economy. If a man is to be self-determining as a person, he must have a viable personal economy maintaining an overall balance between his expenditure and income. It is tempting to conclude from this that the parallel holds all the way. If an individual man is to be self-determining as a person, he must manage his personal economy for himself. If a society is to be self-determining and hence free, it must manage its economy. The government, as the agency authorized to act on behalf of the whole society, must do the managing.

From this conclusion it is a short step to another. The government must use its society's human and material resources as an individual man uses his personal resources. The individual man, as a self-determining economic agent, decides upon his particular ends and upon their relative importance, and organizes and allocates his personal resources as efficiently as he can to attain them. The government must do the same. It must decide what kinds and what quantities of goods and services are to be provided, and must organize and allocate its society's human and material resources as efficiently as possible to bring about this social end. But the outcome to which this logically points is a régime which, if not totalitarian, is at least comparable to that required in total war. Such a régime is likely to severely restrict personal freedom. It implies rationing, direction of labour and the control of private property. The paradoxical conclusion is that in a self-determining society, the members will be hardly, if at all, self-determining.

The paradox arises from the tacit assumption that a self-sufficient society is an individual man 'writ large'. The assumption is plausible because of the parallel between the economic situations of a society and an individual man *vis-à-vis* the rest of the world. Both must have viable economies. But the parallel does not hold all the way, and to assume that it does is a fundamental error. There is nothing in the case of an individual man which corresponds to the internal situation in a society. Its population consists of individual men and women. While from an economic point of view, they are its human resources, they are no way comparable to a man's personal resources. They are the society's members who share in its way of life and participate in its methods of production and distribution as self-conscious agents and persons, not merely as units of labour power. To think that the government of a free society must manage its economy in the same way in which a man as a free person manages his personal economy is to betray a radically defective understanding of freedom, of government, and of the economic dimension of human life.

It may be thought that a free society must have what is known as a free economy. There is an official doctrine of the free economy derived from classical economics. According to this doctrine, a free economy is a competitive market economy. Production and distribution are carried on by private enterprise in response to and in anticipation of, consumer demand. Consumers are free to spend their money as they think best. There is freedom for commercial, industrial and financial enterprise. There is an open labour market in which there is freedom to employ and to enter into employment at wages and salaries fixed by mutual agreement. There is an open capital market in which there is freedom to borrow and to invest according to private estimates of profitability. It follows as a necessary corollary that there must be no monopolistic control of any market and no restriction upon entry to it. There must also be a high degree of mobility of labour.

Another corollary is what is known as the 'nightwatchman' theory of the state. According to this theory, the government is the custodian of the market place but it must not interfere with the transactions which go on there. Its job is to protect the premises and keep them fit for business but not do business itself. In other words: in a society with a free economy, the public interest is confined to the protection of person and property, the enforcing of contracts freely entered into, and the prevention of monopolistic practices. Apart from securing these conditions, the government's economic policy should be one of *laissez faire*. The assumption is that given these conditions, the competitive market will operate autonomously. There is no need for government organization and direction. The economic sphere is the legitimate sphere of private interests. At first sight, the freedom envisaged looks like negative freedom, and especially negative political freedom. But further consideration suggests that what is intended is personal freedom, not merely negative freedom. Men and women are supposed to enter the market as free persons engaged in the enlightened pursuit of self-interest. Each is responsible for his individual personal well-being and as a consumer, worker, or enterpreneur, is expected to act rationally in promoting it. So much for the official doctrine but before considering its implications for social freedom something else must be taken into account.

A man's personal resources and choices will depend upon his society's economy and his position in it. A society's economy is geared to its methods of production and distribution. A modern industrial economy is very different from an agricultural economy with domestic industries. It makes available a much greater quantity and variety of goods and services, and a worker in a modern society has a much wider range of choices open to him than his own pre-industrial ancestors or an Asiatic peasant. A man's personal economy depends not only upon the total output of the social economy but upon the share of the total which he can command. It is one thing to be an industrial worker, another to be a 'top executive': one thing to be a peasant, another a landowner. It may be thought that a man's share depends upon his personal talents. This might to some extent be true if certain conditions are satisfied: an open market, full employment, adequate educational opportunities for all to discover and develop their personal talents. The less these conditions are satisfied, the less the truth in the suggestion. In an agricultural economy they are not satisfied. Hereditary status rather than personal talents will be the decisive factor in a man's occupation. If he is lucky, his place in the social economy may offer him some scope for using his personal talents, for instance as a craftsman. But these talents will not affect his place in the social economy which will be settled for him by his birth.

There are three main reasons why a free society must have a modern industrial economy. The first is that the low productivity of an agricultural economy will mean that many people will be too poor to achieve much in the way of economic self-determination. Sheer poverty will deny them adequate opportunities for personal freedom. The second is that in an agricultural economy, there will be a largely closed social order based on hereditary status instead of equality of status in an open social order and so inadequate opportunities for all to achieve either moral or personal freedom. The third is that there can be adequate opportunities for rational freedom only if potential critical humanists can realize their potential. They will largely be unable to do so in a society with an agricultural economy because the absence of scientific technology will mean that the scientific perspective and its practical relevance is not understood. But a society with a modern industrial economy is obviously not *ipso facto* a free society. Other features in its way of life may disqualify it. While it is not a sufficient condition for social freedom, a modern industrial economy is a necessary condition.

But must the industrial economy of a free society be a free economy in terms of the official doctrine? Must the government confine itself to the role prescribed for it in the 'nightwatchman' theory of the state? The answer turns on whether certain conditions which are in the public interest in a free society are likely to be forthcoming if the government pursues an economic policy of *laissez faire*. They include those just mentioned in connection with the development of personal talents: an open labour market, adequate educational opportunities and full employment. They will also include: the maintenance of balance of payments abroad and prices and incomes at home; minimum incomes for the rational pursuit of personal well-being; adequate medical services for all; the maintenance of efficient systems of transport and communications; provisions for scientific and technological research. These will be more fully discussed in another section.

Are these conditions likely to be forthcoming in a free economy where the government acts according to the 'nightwatchman' theory of the state? Experience suggests that they are not, or at least not to the extent necessary. In those societies which have come within striking distance of social freedom, *laissez faire* has been abandoned in favour of a policy of deliberate government intervention. This is hardly surprising. According to the official doctrine, the economic sphere is the sphere of private interests. We saw in the last chapter that it is a mistake to think that the public interest and private interests are essentially complementary. There is no pre-established harmony which guarantees that the enlightened pursuit of self-interest by everyone will spontaneously furnish all that the public interest requires. According to the official doctrine, all are to participate in the market as free persons. But no account is taken of what is necessary to enable them to become free persons in the first place, still less of what is necessary for rational and moral freedom.

The upshot is that a free society will have a mixed economy, that is an economy in which there is both private and public enterprise. There will be an initial presumption in favour of private enterprise. Trade and industry will be left in private hands except where the public interest pursued in the spirit of the critical idea requires intervention by the government. It will be required on a fairly considerable scale, partly in the shape of regulation and control by fiscal and legislative measures: partly in the shape of direct public enterprise in particular fields. But it will always be relevant to challenge the government to show why the public interest requires intervention in any given case. Hence the importance for social freedom of positive political freedom under a democratic form of government. In the scale of forms, economic freedom is intermediate between negative freedom and personal freedom. Like personal freedom, it must be adapted to the requirements of higher forms of freedom. It is included in social freedom in the shape of the partial economic freedom of the mixed economy.

6. RELIGIOUS FREEDOM

It was argued in Chapter 5 that in a free society religious diversity would be an open possibility. Churches would be voluntary associations and people would be free to join any or none and to work out their religious position for themselves. This was endorsed in Part 3, where it was argued that an adequate theory of human identity must not be geared to the particular tenets of any one religion. This did not mean that the more secular a society's way of life the better. Rather it meant that the more mature the understanding of the religious dimension of human experience displayed in a society's religious practices the better; that the more religious diversity is accepted and the greater the religious toleration the better. But while 'toleration' is an appropriate term to express the attitude of one religion to another in a free society, it is not strictly appropriate to express the attitude of the society towards religion as such. Toleration implies orthodoxy. What is tolerated is heresy from the standpoint of the orthodox. But in a free society there is no religious orthodoxy and consequently no heresy. One religion may be better than another because reflecting a better understanding. But none can be literally true so far as its particular tenets are concerned. Hence 'religious freedom' rather than 'religious toleration' is the appropriate term to express the attitude of a free society towards religion.

Like political freedom, religious freedom has both a negative and a positive form. Negative religious freedom is simply freedom from constraint in all religious matters. You do not have to join any church if you do not want to. You can take your pick among the existing religions or start a new one or ignore the claims of religion altogether. Positive religious freedom means self-determination in the sphere of religion. A man achieves it to the extent that he works out his attitude towards religion for himself and bases his practice upon the convictions he has reached rather than allowing his religious position to be settled for him by social custom or convention. In the scale of forms, negative religious freedom is part of negative freedom: positive religious freedom is part of personal freedom. It follows that negative religious freedom is a necessary but not a sufficient condition for positive religious freedom. You must be free from constraint in matters of religion if you are to be self-determining. But the fact that you are free from constraint does not mean that you will in fact be self-determining. You may simply ignore religion or follow fashion without thinking. In a free society, there must be complete negative religious freedom and adequate opportunities for all to achieve positive religious freedom.

But are there to be no limits to negative religious freedom in a free society? Should nothing be forbidden which is done in the name of religion, provided that it does not harm or inconvenience those not taking part? Consider an extreme case:

a religion which involves ritual human sacrifice. Suppose that it is the religion of a tiny minority and completely voluntary. No one is compelled to participate in its gruesome rites. Its sacrificial victims are all adults who offer themselves enthusiastically, convinced that such a death is the consummation of life. Ought the practice of this religion to be allowed in a free society? The case that it ought is briefly this. Its prohibition would be a breach of positive religious freedom and hence of personal freedom. If people want to sacrifice themselves in its name, why shouldn't they? It is a purely private matter which concerns only its devotees.

But ought it to be treated as a purely private matter? Two considerations strongly suggest that it ought not. The first is that death is final and irrevocable. The sacrificial victims are taking a step upon which there is no going back. The second is that such a religion by no means displays a mature understanding of the religious dimension of human experience. On the contrary, it exhibits a marked degree of ignorance and superstition as do these who practise it. Out of ignorance and superstition, the sacrificial victims are taking an irrevocable step. If they are prevented from taking it, they may come to think differently. Enlightened humaneness therefore requires that they should be prevented. They must be saved from the disastrous consequences of their own folly. When folly leads people to destroy themselves, it ceases to be a purely private matter. It may be objected that in a free society, paternalism can never be in the public interest. But granted that it is paternalism, the objection does not follow. Paternalism can sometimes be in the public interest in a free society. It is in the public interest that all should have adequate opportunities for personal, moral and rational freedom. It is therefore in the public interest that people should be prevented from foolishly destroying themselves in the name of something which can fairly be branded as error compounded with delusion. Preventing them means preserving their opportunities for personal, moral and rational freedom, albeit against their will.

It may be objected that to prevent people from pointlessly destroying themselves is to curtail their personal freedom. But this objection confuses personal freedom with merely negative freedom. To be prevented from pointlessly destroying yourself is to be subjected to constraint, or more accurately, to restraint. But personal freedom is not merely the absence of constraint and restraint. It consists in personal self-determination achieved through rational activity at the level of personal well-being. Pointless self-destruction is no part of rational activity at this level. The devotees of the sacrificial religion are not free persons properly so called. They embrace it voluntarily but this voluntary action can hardly be described as genuine personal self-determination. They are moved not by any wise conception of personal well-being but rather by a vague amalgam of superstitious hopes and fears. Nor can they be said in any meaningful sense to be achieving genuine religious self-determination. The case of a ritualistic sacrificial religion shows that even in a free society negative religious freedom, like negative freedom in general, can only be partial not total. In fact it is highly unlikely that in a free society anyone would choose to embrace such a religion.

Most religions have traditionally associated a specific body of moral teaching with their particular tenets. On many matters there is common ground between different religions. But on some, they lay down conflicting moral precepts: for instance, Christianity and Islam on the subject of polygamy. This also happens within what is nominally the same religion. The various Christian denominations do not all agree in their moral teaching on subjects such as divorce, suicide, birth control, abortion, gambling and drink. Some religions claim that their specific moral teaching is applicable to everyone. This claim is a natural one for a world religion with a cosmopolitan theory of human identity to make. According to Islam: there is one God; Allah is his name; Mahomet is his prophet. In principle therefore all mankind ought to live by the prophet's teaching. Christianity claims to be in possession of ultimate truth. Everyone should be a Christian and live according to Christian moral teaching. Most Christian denominations and sects claim to be the repository of ultimate truth and claim that all should live according to their interpretation of Christian moral teaching.

Religious diversity in the same society may give rise to difficulties. Disputes occur when different religions lay down

conflicting moral precepts and claim that everyone should observe them. These disputes will come to a head when it is in
the public interest to legislate uniformly for the whole society
on matters like marriage and divorce, religious education and
abortion. One solution is for legislation on contentious matters
to reflect the religious moral precepts of the majority of the
population. This may be thought in some sense democratic.
But the majority solution has implications for the negative
religious freedom of the minority. They are being compelled to
conform to certain moral precepts of a religion to which, from
the standpoint of their own religious convictions, they have no
reason to conform. Their negative religious freedom is being
curtailed while that of the majority is not since the majority
have a religious duty to conform anyway.

If this majority solution is adopted, the society is something
less than a free society. Religious moral universalism is incompatible with social freedom. Social freedom means the same
negative religious freedom for all, and adequate opportunities
for all to achieve positive religious freedom. That means that
each religion and denomination must abandon its claim that its
specific moral reaching applies to everyone. But what is the
alternative to the majority solution in cases where religious
moral precepts conflict and where it is in the public interest
to legislate? Where are the principles of this legislation to come
from, if not from the religion of the majority? The answer is:
from the standpoint of critical humanism. If there is to be a free
society, it is this standpoint, not the tenets of any one religion,
which must be the basis of its way of life.

Consider marriage and divorce. What is to count as marriage
must be legally defined, as must the conditions under which a
marriage can be terminated. This legislation will necessarily
embody ideas about the nature and purpose of marriage and its
place in human social living. In a free society, these ideas will
reflect the understanding of the world and human identity
specific to critical humanism, not that which is contained in the
particular tenets of any one religion. Their basis will be the
standard of enlightened humaneness together with considerations of social responsibility and justice interpreted in the light
of that standard. It is not possible here to work out these ideas

in detail, but it is safe to say that while they would emphasize the intrinsic value of life-long monogamous marriage, they would also recognize that there are circumstances in which divorce is the lesser evil if not the greater good. In a free society, therefore, there would be legal provision for divorce.

What are the implications of legal divorce for the religious freedom of those who are opposed to it on religious grounds? Neither their negative nor their positive religious freedom is impaired, for they do not have to avail themselves of divorce. They can continue to treat marriage as a life-long union in accordance with the moral precepts of their religion. Even in a mixed marriage where one spouse objects to divorce, there is no serious difficulty. For the objecting spouse it is not divorce but separation and so long as he or she does not remarry, the religious moral obligation has been fulfilled. The negative religious freedom of Roman Catholics is not impaired if contraceptives are legally available. They do not have to avail themselves of them. But the negative religious freedom of non-Catholics is being impaired if contraceptives are legally forbidden. They are being subjected to constraint by a religion to which they do not subscribe. It makes no difference whether Catholics are in the majority or minority. It may be true that if contraceptives are legally available, Catholics will be tempted to use them, but in a free society, the law must not be used to enforce discipline upon the members of any church. That is a matter between the church and its members.

Abandoning religious moral universalism means that religious moral precepts become the private moral rules of voluntary associations. They are obligatory for the members of the particular church, but not for anyone else. This is a necessary condition for social freedom. It makes possible both negative and positive freedom on equal terms for all. Like all types of voluntary association, churches must adapt themselves to the requirements of the public interest in a free society. But within this framework, the members of each church can achieve religious self-determination according to its particular tenets, while those who wish to ignore religion, or come to terms with the religious dimension of human experience in other ways, are free to do so. No doubt this implies a fundamental change in the particular idea of themselves held by some religions. But it is a change at one and the same time in the direction of social freedom and of a better understanding of the religious dimension. The established morality of a free society must be humanistic not theological. It must reflect the standpoint of critical humanism which means that it must not be geared to the tenets of any creed or faith. It must be a human morality properly so called.

7. REPLIES TO OBJECTIONS

According to Cranston, a man who announces: 'I am free!' is not saying very much. It is necessary to know what he is free from. According to the modified positive theory of this book, the statement amounts to: 'I am capable of self-determination and I am not subject to any form of constraint.' This can certainly be a significant utterance. The speaker is saying that he is in a position to decide for himself what course of action to follow, and proposes to do so. But what is it to be self-determining? In what context is it possible? Why is it important? These are the questions we have been grappling with. Cranston has not shown that they are illegitimate and the fact that his perspective excludes them points to the limitations of his 'new analysis'.

It is true that the scale of forms does not necessarily reflect what English speakers ordinarily mean by 'freedom' in social, moral and political contexts. But why should it? Some difference from everyday habits of thought and speech is only to be expected since in everyday life people do not ask such questions as: What can and ought to be meant by 'freedom' in these contexts? What are the best ways to think of it? How are they related? At the same time there are no linguisitc improprieties in the theory. Grammatical and logical rules have not been violated. The system of interrelated concepts summed up in the scale of forms does not involve a complete break with everyday ideas about freedom. They are its point of departure and it elicits and develops the meanings which they suggest but do not explicitly convey. The resulting conceptual synthesis has been expressed in terms drawn from ordinary language, the terms selected being those most appropriate to the subject-matter. The resources of ordinary language are there to be exploited in the interest of advancing understanding, and communicating any advances made.

It has been argued in this chapter that the more a society's way of life approximates to the special character distinctive of a free society, the more adequate it is as a way of life for human beings. Does this justify Berlin's charge of rationalism? According to Berlin, rationalists think that there is only one right way for human beings to live and that it can be discovered by human reason. The standpoint of critical humanism seems to be a rationalist standpoint in his sense. But if it is, the dire consequences alleged by Berlin do not follow. There is nothing in the scale of forms or in the account of political freedom which justifies attempts to 'force people to be free' or to coerce them into social freedom. The criticism of totalitarianism based on the standpoint of critical humanism exposed the fundamental error in all such attempts. The fundamental flaw in totalitarianism is its false rationalism. To think that any way of life no matter how ideal can be an end of utilitarian action is to betray a defective understanding of rational activity in general and of utilitarian action in particular.

There are really two separate indictments in Berlin's charge of rationalism. One is false rationalism, and the modified positive theory of freedom in this book is not guilty of that error. The other is the error of thinking that there is one right way of life for human beings and that it can be discovered by human reason. According to Berlin this is a mistake because it rests on the false assumption that all human values must in principle be compatible. Experience shows that the human values are many and diverse and that they can and do conflict with one another. There is no pre-established harmony which guarantees that they can all be fully and equally realized. The idea that there is, is not supported by experience. It fails to take account of what Berlin calls 'an inescapable characteristic of the human condition' which he says is: 'the necessity of choosing between absolute claims'. But does it follow that there can be no good reason for giving preference to one claim rather than to another?; that because all human values cannot be fully realized, there can be no rational order of priority which would justify realizing some fully and others partially? According to critical humanism, these conclusions do not follow. There are good reasons for subordinating the claims of personal well-being to the demands of social morality, and for revising and modifying both in the light of considerations of enlightened humaneness: good reasons again for setting limits to personal freedom for the sake of social freedom. Much of this book has been devoted to showing what these reasons are and why they are good ones.

There is a sense in which critical humanism is rationalistic. It offers a standpoint for the rational evaluation of the ways of life of actual societies and defends it on rational grounds. But the evaluations take the form of judgements that in certain specific respects, a society's way of life is inadequate for human beings and indicate what sorts of changes would be an improvement. This is something less than laying down a blue-print of the one right way of life for human beings. It may be thought that my concept of social freedom is a blueprint. I have contended that the more the way of life of a society approxi-mates to a free society, the better that way of life. But while in a sense social freedom is a blueprint, there are two things to remember about it. The first is that it is not a possible standard for all societies everywhere. The most that is claimed is that changes in the direction of it are desirable if and when they become possible. The second is that social freedom does not profess to give a final and all-embracing account of the most adequate way of life for human beings. It claims only that an adequate way of life would at least have the special character distinctive of a free society and gives some account of what that special character is. New knowledge and understanding will disclose new ways in which human life can become more adequate and the concept of social freedom leaves the way open for them.

It may be thought that despite what was said in the intro-duction, this book involves a through-going commitment to free will as against determinism. But does it? It was argued that a man's action can be rationally criticized on two different grounds. The first is in terms of the standards of a given level of rational activity. It presupposes that he was trying to act according to these standards and could have done better. The second is in terms of levels of rational activity. He is criticized not for doing badly at a given level but for failing to act at the appropriate level. This presupposes that he knew what the appropriate level was but was unwilling to act according to it. In one sense this implies free will. It presupposes that there is such a thing as rational activity and *a fortiori* that there is a generic capacity for self-determination with which human beings are naturally endowed, albeit unequally. But the limited sense in which there is free will, implies a limited sense in which there is determinism. Generic capacity is a natural endowment; the precise extent to which any man is endowed with it will be determined by genetic factors. The most that a man can do is develop and exercise this generic capacity to the full. His success in this may be prevented by other factors outside his control; in childhood experiences, inadequate educational, cultural and economic opportunities. But these factors are not wholly beyond human control. Something can be done about them and social freedom includes the recognition that this is so.

Chapter 10

Rights

1. RIGHTS AND CRITICAL HUMANISM

We saw in Chapter 5 that rights are essentially social in character, that there is a difference between the rights which are actually recognized in a society and the rights which its members ought to have, and that the right to freedom is of special importance because it must be recognized if there are to be any other rights at all. It was suggested that natural rights might be interpreted normatively as human rights: that is, as the rights which human beings always and everywhere ought to have, irrespective of whether they are recognized in actual societies or not. But it was argued that this ran headlong into the problem of moral relativism. The argument of Part 3 of this book, however, points to a slightly different interpretation which does not involve moral relativism. Human rights are not the rights which human beings ought to have always and everywhere. Rather they are the rights which all the members would have in a society whose way of life was adequate for human beings. But if this idea of human rights is to be significant, two questions must be answered. The first concerns the rights themselves. What are they? How far is it possible to specify them? The second concerns what appears to be their hypothetical character. No actual society has a way of life which is fully adequate for human beings. What can be the relevance of rights which the members would have, in a society which nowhere exists, to the rights which members of actual societies ought to have?

The argument of the last chapter has a bearing on these questions. A way of life which is adequate for human beings will have the special character distinctive of a free society's way of life. Among the rights which all its members would have will therefore be those which all the members of a free society would have. The account which has been given of social freedom suggests that it is possible to say what the more important of these rights would be. So far as their relevance to actual societies is concerned, it will presumably be the same as the relevance of social freedom as a standard for actual societies. Two other points should be noted. One concerns the necessary place of rights in social freedom. All the members of a free society must have adequate opportunities for personal, moral and rational freedom. It is through the medium of rights that these opportunities can be secured for them. The other concerns the sense in which every right itself embodies a measure of freedom. You are entitled but not obliged to do something, or to have something done. You can be self-determining with respect to the exercise of the right. But in deciding whether or not to exercise a right, moral considerations are of special relevance. This is because social morality is the rational ground for the claim to have a right. Each right is therefore a particular case of moral freedom. This is its place as a limited embodiment of freedom within the scale of forms.

If there are to be any rights at all, there must at least be the right to freedom, that is, to be free from arbitrary constraint. The right to freedom is one which all the members of a free society would have. It secures them the necessary negative freedom without which there can be no higher forms of freedom. But it is not merely one more human right among others. In an important sense, it is the primary human right since without it there can be no others. There is also no difficulty about specifying the more important of the political rights which the members of a free society would have. A free society must have a democratic form of government. All its adult population must have equal status as members of its citizen body. Membership of that body necessarily carries with it certain political rights of which the most important are: the right to vote, to stand at elections, to form and to join political associations, to criticize and oppose the government of the day, and to express opinions on all political matters. These democratic political rights are necessary if all the members of a society are to have adequate opportunities for positive political freedom as distinct from merely negative political freedom. They are therefore human rights because they are rights which all the members of a free society would have. They would have them in addition to the right to freedom, which as a political right is simply the right to negative political freedom. The obligation correlative to this last right is an obligation upon the government and its officials to observe the rule of law. The obligations correlative to democratic political rights are obligations upon the government and upon all members of the citizen body not to interfere with anyone in the exercise of his democratic political rights.

But suppose that the best that a society can manage as a form of government is despotism. Democratic political rights cannot be rights which its members ought to have. Strictly speaking the question of what rights they ought to have cannot even arise. This is because under despotism there can only be what may be called 'quasi-rights'. A despotic government is not bound by the rule of law. Its subjects may enjoy considerable *de facto* negative political freedom. But this is always at the caprice of the despotic government which can interfere in their lives when, where, and how it likes. It is only under constitutionalism that there can be the right to freedom and hence rights properly so called. Have democratic political rights then any relevance in a society with a despotic form of government? Yes, as something to aim at. As matters stand, they are not rights which the members ought to have. But things would be better if they were. Despotism must give way to constitutionalism so that the right to freedom can be secured. This is a prerequisite for subsequent developments towards democracy and the rights which it involves.

What is true of democratic political rights is true of human rights in general. They serve as a yardstick for estimating whether a society is within striking distance of social freedom and indicate the direction of desirable social change. But apart from the right to freedom and democratic political rights, we have still to see what other human rights there are. That means exploring further the implications of social freedom. But social freedom is not the whole story about a society whose way of life is adequate for human beings, or as we may henceforth call it, an enlightened society. The way of life of an enlightened society will embody the standpoint of critical humanism and its prevailing understanding will therefore be adequate. The theory of human identity specific to critical humanism should therefore also throw light on the rights which the members would have, light which should illuminate the insight gained from social freedom. But first something must be said about two other topics. One concerns the relation between the idea of rights and the idea of the public interest: the other, the implications of the cosmopolitan spirit of critical humanism for the idea of human rights.

In an important sense, the idea of rights and the idea of the public interest are complementary. It was argued in Chapter 5 that the rights which the members of a society ought to have are those necessary to enable them to participate in its way of life on proper terms. It was argued in Chapter 8 that the public interest, according to the conservative idea, is the interest which the members of a society have in the conditions necessary to enable all of them to participate in its way of life on terms consistent with its established morality and social order. It is therefore in the public interest that the rights which the members of a society ought to have should be given legal recognition and protection, apart from special cases where this is not in accord with the principle of net advantage. It is also in the public interest that any discrepancies between the rights actually recognized and those which the members ought to have should be removed by legislative action. There is an important corollary. There can be no rights against the public interest. More precisely: if something is against the public interest, it cannot be a right which any member of a society ought to have. Something is against the public interest if it undermines or threatens conditions which it is in the public interest to secure. No one can therefore be morally justified in claiming to be entitled to do or to have done, anything which conflicts with these conditions.

But to say that rights are subordinate to the public interest would be misleading. The point is rather that the question of what rights people ought to have cannot be answered in isolation from the wider question of what the conditions are which it is in the public interest to secure. Deciding what the public interest requires means deciding among other things what people ought to be entitled to do and to have done. Consider the right to freedom: it is the right to be free from arbitrary constraint. Now the use of constraint to enforce the law is not arbitrary. The right to freedom must be the right to freedom under the law. The provisions of the law therefore set limits to the negative freedom to which there can be a right. But what should the provisions of the law be? The answer turns on what the conditions are which it is in the public interest to secure. Hence decisions about the public interest involve decisions about what the scope and limits of the right to freedom ought to be.

The government is the custodian of the public interest. It is therefore the task of the government to decide what are to count as rights so far as legal recognition and protection are concerned. This means that it is the government's responsibility to keep the body of rights actually recognized in its society under constant review, to identify discrepancies between these rights and those which the members ought to have, and to take steps to remove them. But so far we have considered only the conservative idea of the public interest. What about the critical idea? According to it: the public interest is in the conditions necessary for a society's way of life to become as adequate as possible, not merely in those necessary for it to be carried on successfully in its present form. How does this affect the responsibility of the government in relation to rights? What difference does it make if the public interest is promoted in the spirit of the critical idea?

The short answer is that in deciding what rights are to be recognized and protected, the government will take account of any potentiality for improvement which there may be. While government action can never be a sufficient condition for improvement, it may frequently be a necessary condition. This necessary legislative action may well involve the conferring of rights: for instance, giving women the vote. But if in a situation in which there is some potentiality for improvement, the government confines itself to the conservative idea, the necessary legislative action will not be forthcoming and much of the potentiality will run to waste. The society's way of life will then be less adequate than it could have been.

In Chapter 5 we saw that if the members of a society are to agree about the rights they ought to have, there must be widespread agreement among them about the fundamental character of their way of life. In a divided society disputes about rights are insoluble. They simply register the fact of social conflict. But if there is widespread agreement, can there be any potentiality for improvement? Yes, but only if there are some members who to some extent think in terms of critical humanism rather than social morality. The relation between critical humanists and the conservative majority is not like that between the conflicting groups in a divided society. The critical humanists share in the widespread agreement but with important reservations. Their attitude is that while they accept much of the existing way of life and do not want to change it wholesale, they nevertheless think that there are important respects in which it could be improved. While they agree with the conservative majority about many rights, there are others not acknowledged by the conservative majority, which it would be better if members had.

In our interpretation of the idea of human rights, we have not questioned the conclusion that rights are essentially social in character. They are the rights which all the members of an enlightened society would have. But the cosmopolitan spirit of critical humanism with its emphasis upon the enjoyment of intrinsic values by human beings everywhere prompts second thoughts. It suggests that every human being is at least entitled to be treated as a self-conscious agent and a person irrespective of race, nationality, colour, or creed: or rather, that it would be better if every human being had the right to be so treated. The idea of such a right is not vacuous. It would be a composite of at least two rights: the right to freedom, and the right to have promises kept. Treating someone as a self-conscious agent and a person means not subjecting him to arbitrary constraint. It also means keeping your word to him unless to break it is the lesser evil. The standpoint of critical humanism furnishes the rational basis for deciding in principle what constitutes arbitrary constraint and what counts as the lesser evil.

But granted that it would be better if all human beings had this right, is it a non-social right? Is it not rather a right which human beings would have in virtue of membership of a universal human community? Mankind has not yet become a single self-sufficient society. But each self-sufficient society is a microcosm of mankind in the sense of being a concrete embodiment of the universal human predicament. That predicament, just because it is universal, is the rational basis of a universal human community. The idea of such a community is morally acknowledged in the attitude of many national governments towards refugees. Refugees are stateless persons. But they are properly regarded as fellow human beings with the right to be treated as such. The idea of an international political community is acknowledged in the treaties, conventions, and diplomatic practices which together make up international law. Or perhaps it would be truer to say, that the recognition that these constitute international law is at the same time the recognition that the nation-states of the world in principle constitute an international political community.

2. THE RIGHT TO LIFE

So far nothing has been said about the right to life. It may be thought that the right to freedom can be held to include it. If you are entitled to be free from arbitrary constraint, you are entitled to go on living unless there is a morally good reason for you to be killed. But this will not do. I may be justified in using force against someone without being justified in killing him. To kill him is not merely to subject him to constraint. It is to annihilate him. The right to life must be discussed apart from the right to freedom. It is important to distinguish between the right to life and the duty to preserve life as such, your own as well as other people's. Locke failed to draw this distinction. According to him, such a duty rules out suicide. He did not see that if suicide is ruled out, so is the right to life properly so called, because the right to life must include the right to commit suicide. You are entitled but not necessarily obliged to go on living. Others have an obligation not to take your life and you have one not to take theirs. But you are not forbidden to take your own. Suicide may sometimes be morally justified.

Locke defended the idea of a duty to preserve human life as such on theological grounds. What God has given, only God ought to take away. But this cannot be taken literally. Human life is a natural phenomenon in the sense that it is one of the innumerable forms of life which have emerged in the course of evolution. An individual human life is a human creation in the sense that human reproduction is a natural process which has to be initiated by human action. If then human life is to be regarded as a gift at all, it must be as a gift from your parents since it is they whom you have to thank for your individual existence. But is it a gift at all? Surely not: a gift must have a recipient as well as a donor, and it must be possible for the recipient to decline what is offered. These conditions are not satisfied in the case of human life. You cannot decline to be born. All human life is finite. Death sooner or later is inescapable for everyone. What is important is not mere biological survival but worthwhile human life. A man may sometimes have good reason to take his own life. When, for instance, in old age he is faced with the prospect of a lingering and painful death, why should he wait for it to occur as a natural event? Locke's prohibition against suicide rests on theological dogma alone and is contrary to enlightened humaneness. In an enlightened society there will be the right to life but not the duty to preserve human life in Locke's sense. The right to life, that is to say, is a human right. It implies a correlative obligation to refrain from taking any one else's life but not necessarily to refrain from taking your own.

But the exercise of the right to life, like every right, is justified only when it does not conflict with the demands of social morality. It cannot justify evading these demands when they involve personal danger. You cannot justifiably excuse yourself from military service in wartime simply on the ground that you may be killed. If there is a clash between your rights, and your duty as a citizen, it is your duty which ought to have priority. You can exercise your right to life, as it were negatively, by committing suicide. But you are justified in doing so only if you are not being socially irresponsible or unjust. It is not merely a matter of what is wise or prudent according to your presumably gloomy estimate of your future prospects of personal well being. The presumption behind the right to life is not that suicide will often be justified but only that there are occasions on which it is, and that the possibility of resorting to it ought therefore not to be morally excluded. It is necessary to distinguish between rational and pathological suicide. Many suicides are the outcome of mental illness not rational reflection. A victim of severe depression is not in a fit state to exercise his right to life and it is not violated if he is prevented from committing suicide. On the contrary, enlightened humaneness requires that he should be prevented, and that steps should be taken to alleviate his pathological condition. The right to life concerns only rational suicide.

Is the obligation correlative to the right to life unconditional, or is the intentional killing of other human beings sometimes justified? Murder, that is intentional killing without a morally good reason, is the apotheosis of injustice. It is not merely to treat the murdered person's claims and interests as unequal to your own but is to disregard them altogether. But not all intentional killing is murder. In certain circumstances it may be the lesser evil and hence morally justified. If I am the victim of an unprovoked attack and can save my life only by killing my assailant, I am morally justified in doing so. He has shown by his action that he does not respect my right to life. In the circumstances, his death at my hands is a lesser evil than mine at his. These considerations also justify killing by the police, to protect the right to life of innocent people. It follows that the obligation correlative to the right to life cannot be unconditional. There are morally good reasons for disregarding it if to kill is the lesser evil. One might conclude from this that killing can be the lesser evil if two conditions are satisfied. The first is that the person to be killed must have already morally forfeited the right to life: the second that his death is necessary to protect the right to life of others.

But there are cases of intentional killing that might be justified where these two conditions are not satisfied. Consider euthanasia or 'mercy-killing'. It may sometimes be simply suicide 'by proxy'. A dying man, for whom life means only the prolongation of suffering, wants to die. In response to his request, a close friend puts him out of his misery. He is co-operating with the dying man to enable him to exercise his right to commit suicide. In the circumstances the exercise of the right is neither socially irresponsible nor unjust, and enlightened humaneness justifies the co-operation. But suppose that the dying man has not expressed a wish to commit suicide. Is his friend justified in acting on his own initiative? If the dying man is no longer capable of deciding one way or the other, enlightened humaneness justifies releasing him from futile suffering. Is his death by euthanasia an evil at all? Surely not. What is evil is the suffering involved in the natural process of his dying and his euthanasia cuts short this suffering. While his death cannot be regarded as a positive good, it is neither an intrinsic nor an extrinsic evil. It follows that in some circumstances, intentional killing can be morally justified without being the lesser evil because not an evil at all. Its justification is that in the circumstances, it best meets the requirements of enlightened humaneness. It may be objected that pain-killing drugs can eradicate suffering until death comes about naturally. But while this may be true, is there any reason for maintaining mere biological survival when all capacity for significant human experience has gone for ever?

What about the more controversial case of euthanasia in the form of infanticide? A new born infant cannot exercise the right to life for himself. Until he becomes able to do so, it is the duty of his parents to protect and care for him. If infanticide is not to be murder, there must be a morally good reason for disregarding this duty. What could such a reason be? Suppose that an infant is born so grossly deformed that his prospects for worthwhile human life are nil. Enlightened humaneness suggests that quick and painless infanticide is justified. There is a certainty that prospects are nil where severe brain damage has doomed the infant to a merely vegetable existence devoid of all significant human experience. But in many cases certainty is impossible. There may be no doubt that the infant is condemned to a life plagued by frustration and pain, but not necessarily one utterly devoid of all significant human experience. In such cases infanticide is an evil because it entails the risk of preventing worthwhile human experience. But it may be a lesser evil than the pain and frustration caused by such a life. Judgements of the lesser evil must always be made in the light of individual circumstances and therefore cannot be brought under any single rule. When they concern intentional killing, the overriding consideration must be what will best meet the requirements of enlightened humaneness in the individual circumstances.

The legal recognition and protection of the right to life means the legal prohibition of murder. But unless all intentional killing is to be treated as murder, a distinction must be drawn between lawful and unlawful intentional killing. This is straightforward enough in the case of self-defence. The two conditions together furnish a simple test which can be used by a court in all instances to decide whether the intentional killing was the lesser evil. But euthanasia, especially in the form of infanticide, presents difficulties. There is no simple test. Medical evidence may conflict. There is a real danger that abuses may go undetected. It may be possible literally to 'get away with murder' under the pretext of euthanasia. In view of this it is doubtful whether it can ever be in the public interest in an enlightened society to legalize euthanasia.

An argument frequently put forward against legalizing abortion is that it violates the right to life of the unborn child. What is contended is that so far as the right to life is concerned, there is no difference between a new-born infant and an embryo. Abortion is therefore infanticide. Those who hold such a view usually support it on theological grounds. But apart from theological doctrine, is there any reason to think that it is true? Surely there is not. Infanticide is the taking of a human life. It can occur only after the natural process of human reproduction has been completed. Abortion is the deliberate termination of that process before it has been completed. It is properly described not as taking a human life but as preventing one from beginning. It cannot therefore violate the right to life since no life is taken. Those who oppose abortion on theological grounds will not be convinced and the sincerity of their belief is not in question. But in a free society, theological doctrine cannot be the basis for legislation.[1] The question is whether it is in the public interest to legalize abortion. Talk

[1] See Chapter 9, Section 6.

about the right to life of the unborn child only confuses matters.

3. RIGHTS AND PUNISHMENT

Punishment concerns rights in two ways. One has to do with the legal protection of rights: the other with its effect on the rights of the person punished. But what is punishment and why should there be punishment? There is punishment properly so called only when a penalty is inflicted upon an offender for an offence, by an agency authorized to inflict it by the system of rules against which the offence was committed. The penalty must be something unwelcome to the offender and its infliction must be a deliberate act, not the merely natural consequences of his offence. But why should there be punishment at all? More especially: why should legal offenders incur penalties, as distinct from being made to compensate those they have harmed?

There is a ready answer in what is called the retributive theory of punishment. Legal offenders should be punished as a matter of justice. They have done wrong and justice requires that wrong-doing as such should be punished. But is this true? Does the fact that a man has done wrong of itself constitute relevant grounds for subjecting him to differential treatment in the form of punishment? Perhaps it does by depriving him of material benefits gained by his offence, as well as compelling him to make reparation. But in neither case is this to punish him. It is to annul some consequences of his wrong-doing, not to inflict a penalty upon him. Justice does not require that wrong-doing as such should be punished. Nothing human is perfect and no human agency is justified in arrogating to itself the task of punishing wrong-doing as such. For the government to do so would be presumptuous in the extreme. The government's business is to promote the public interest, not to try to be a moral tribunal. But this does not mean that the punishment of a legal offender is unjust, still less that there should be no such thing as punishment. It means only that relevant grounds for it must lie in something other than merely the fact of wrong-doing.

It is in the public interest to prevent legal offences. Punish-

ment deters many would-be offenders. The threat of a penalty
is for many people a sufficient disincentive to law-breaking,
provided that the penalty is known, most offenders are caught,
and the penalty is actually inflicted. But it is not sufficient in
all cases. Only people capable of forethought can be deterred.
Some, for whom the threat is insufficient, may be deterred from
further offences after they have once been punished. But others
are undeterrable and, in spite of being punished, go on committing offences. The only way of preventing them is by physical
means. There are two ways of doing this. One is to imprison
them for life: the other is to kill them. The penalty in the first
case is the loss of negative freedom. They are subject to
permanent restraint. In the second case, it is the loss of life
itself. The purpose of punishment ought to be to prevent legal
offences by deterrence if possible but by physical means if
necessary. It is in the public interest to prevent legal offences
and thus there should be punishment. It protects society from
the harm done by legal offenders and so protects legally
recognized rights. Punishment is not the only way of preventing
legal offences but it makes an indispensable contribution.
Without it, the number of offences would vastly increase.

But what about justice to the offender? Five conditions must
be satisfied. The first is that he must in fact be an offender, that
is, he must have committed an actual offence against an existing
law: the second, that at the time he both could and should have
known that he was committing an offence; the third, that he
was responsible for his actions and could have refrained from
doing what he did; the fourth, that the penalty inflicted is an
appropriate one for his particular offence; the fifth, that the law
he has broken, while not necessarily a good one, is at least not
so bad that breaking it is morally justified. If these conditions
are all satisfied, there is no injustice. There are relevant
grounds for subjecting the offender to differential treatment in
the form of punishment. They are: that it is in the public
interest to prevent legal offences; that punishment is necessary
to prevent them; and that the offender has knowingly and
intentionally committed an offence. While the purpose of
punishment is preventive, there is a retributive element in its
nature. The offender has done wrong, and while that is not in

itself a sufficient reason for his being punished, he has no rational grounds for complaint since the public interest requires it. The trouble with the retributive theory is that it does not distinguish between the nature and the purpose of punishment. It is in part at least, right about the nature but wrong about the purpose.

If the penalty for a particular offence is to be appropriate, it must contribute effectively to preventing offences of that kind. But what form it should take and how severe it should be, whether primary importance should be given to deterrence or to physical methods of prevention, are questions which must be answered in the light of empirical evidence about the nature and prevalence of such offences. There is however one consideration of the utmost relevance: enlightened humaneness to the offender. He may have made others suffer. But that is not a good reason for making him suffer more than is necessary for the preventive purpose of punishment to be fulfilled. Consideration should be given to possibilities of reform when deciding the penalty. An effective way of preventing the offender committing more offences is to turn him into a law-abiding citizen. Reform however must not be confused with punishment. To reform a man is not to penalize him but to benefit him. It may be possible to reform while punishing but punishment is not as such reformative.

Punishment normally involves constraint. Whether they want to or not, offenders are compelled to pay fines, to go to prison, to endure corporal punishment, or suffer death. But provided that the penalty is an appropriate one for the particular offence, this constraint is not arbitrary. The offender's right to freedom is not violated. But what about his other rights? Capital punishment extinguishes them altogether by extinguishing him. Imprisonment means that he is effectively deprived of political rights, and that his other rights are seriously curtailed. But if the penalty is an appropriate one, he has no cause to complain. This is especially so if his offence is a crime, consisting in the knowing and intentional violation of someone else's rights. The claim to have rights is morally justified only if the obligation to respect the rights of others is acknowledged and he has failed to acknowledge it. But enlightened humaneness requires that the deprivation or curtailment of his rights should not be greater or for longer than is necessary.

Can capital punishment ever be an appropriate penalty? The argument that it is appropriate for murder because the murderer has morally forfeited his right to life will not do. While he cannot rationally complain if his own life is taken, it does not follow that it ought to be taken. Death is the extreme penalty because it is irrevocable. If it is to be the appropriate penalty for murder, it must be shown that there is no less drastic alternative which will both deter potential murderers and prevent convicted murderers from murdering again. A similar case must be made out for any other type of crime for which death is proposed as the appropriate penalty. But can this ever be shown beyond reasonable doubt? Can the assertion that no alternative will suffice, ever be justified? The evidence of the deterrent effect on murder of the death penalty is inconclusive. The murderer can be prevented from murdering again by imprisoning him until there is good reason to believe that it will be safe to release him. The same is true of other crimes such as treason. It is doubtful, to say the least, whether enlightened humaneness to the criminal can ever be reconciled with the death penalty. Is lifelong imprisonment as inhumane as the death penalty? In captivity, a man's opportunities for a worthwhile human life are certainly enormously restricted. But they are not necessarily abolished altogether. The death penalty abolishes them once and for all. Why shouldn't the decision be left to the offender? If life imprisonment is the appropriate penalty, and if the prospect is intolerable, let him have the alternative of committing suicide. If this proposal is felt to be distasteful, that could be because contemporary thinking about suicide is confused.

Finally a word must be said about the limits of the present discussion. They are set by the third condition necessary for punishment. The offender must have been responsible for his actions and could have refrained from doing what he did. There are undoubtedly offenders of whom this is untrue. But what has been said here applies to rational not to pathological offenders. Pathological offenders need remedial treatment and, if they are dangerous, must be kept under restraint. But whatever is done for them is not properly described as punishment. It may well be the case however that rational and pathological offenders are at opposite ends of a spectrum. In between are many others of whom it is difficult to say whether they are sufficiently responsible to be held accountable for what they have done. But responsible or not, the public interest requires that they should be prevented from committing offences. The presumption can only be, unless there is convincing evidence to the contrary, that the offenders could have refrained from law-breaking and are liable to legal penalties. At the same time, there is everything to be said for trying to rehabilitate convicted offenders and, if latent pathological tendencies come to light, for turning to remedial rather than punitive treatment.

4. ECONOMIC RIGHTS

In the mixed economy of a free society, production and distribution are left to private enterprise except where it is in the public interest to introduce regulation and control, or to initiate public enterprise. There is an initial presumption in favour of private enterprise but there is also the recognition that the public interest is not always best served by it. The economic rights of the members will be those which they would have under a system of private enterprise. But the scope and limits of these rights will be modified by the conditions necessary for social freedom, these being conditions which it is in the public interest to secure. Two of them are of special importance: the right to private property and the right to work. Taking the right to private property first: according to the French socialist Proudhon, 'Property is theft'. This cannot be literally true because theft presupposes property. You can steal only what does not belong to you. But it serves to emphasize the importance of the concept of ownership.

Property and ownership are complementary concepts. All property is owned and only what is capable of being owned can be property. Ownership may be personal or corporate, depending upon whether the owner is a single person or some kind of social group. Personal ownership is always private ownership. Corporate ownership is private when the social group is a voluntary association. If something is my private property, it is for me and no one else to decide what is done with it. As its owner, I have the right to dispose of it as I think fit. I can keep it, or get rid of it by selling it, exchanging it, giving it away, or destroying it. If I keep it, I can either make use of it or simply hoard it. I am entitled to do what I like with it but I am not obliged to do anything in particular. When corporate ownership is private, the members of the social group have the same right in their corporate capacity. It is for 'us' the members, to decide what 'we' will do with what 'we' own.

The obligation correlative to the right to private property is an obligation not to steal, and more generally, not to interfere with private owners in disposing of their property. But neither the right nor the obligation can be unconditional. The right to private property is a particular application of the general right to freedom. Private owners are entitled to dispose of their property as they think fit and are therefore entitled to be free from arbitrary constraint in disposing of it. But the right to freedom is the right to freedom under the law. The provisions of the law set limits to the negative freedom to which there can be a right and hence to the negative freedom of private owners to dispose of their property. Whatever else they do, they must at least keep within the law. If what they do with their property is illegal, the obligation not to interfere ceases to hold.

Public property is property which is owned by some kind of public body: a municipality, a public corporation, or the state itself. Public bodies must have discretion in the use which they make of their property but it is misleading to call this discretion a right. This is because of a fundamental difference between public and private ownership. Provided that they keep within the law, private owners are accountable to no one but themselves for what they do with their property. If they waste it, or use it foolishly, that is their business. But public bodies are not in this happy position. They exist to give public service. They are therefore not entitled to do what they like with what they own but have an obligation to do something in particular with it: namely to use it efficiently in giving public service. Their discretion is within the framework of this obligation. They are therefore not accountable only to themselves because it is in the public interest that their discretion should be exercised wisely and competently. The difference may be summed up by saying that private ownership confers a right while public ownership imposes a responsibility. But it is a responsibility which rests upon the officials of the particular public body and they must not be molested or impeded in their day-to-day discharge of it. The obligation not to steal and not to interfere applies to public property no less than to private property. Although not in this case correlative to a right, it is none the less an obligation.

The right to private property must include the right to acquire it as well as to dispose of it. You cannot dispose of what you have not got. This is implicit in what has been said already. If I have the right to sell or give away what I own, others must have the right to buy it or to receive it as a gift. Admittedly this points to a loose end. I can acquire private property legitimately in the first place only by buying it or being given it. Those from whom I have acquired it must themselves originally have acquired their property from others, and so on *ad infinitum*. Nothing has been said about the origins of private property and how the right to it first came to be recognized. Historical and anthropological research suggests that the primeval form of property was communal rather than private or public. The tribe as a corporate group owned most, if not all, of the meagre resources out of which its members extracted a bare subsistence. The existence of private property presupposes a relatively sophisticated way of life in which private interests are recognized to have a legitimate place. How these ways of life developed, how private and public property grew out of primeval communal property, is a story which cannot be told here. Undoubtedly much of it is the story of violence and theft. Proudhon is not wholly wrong. Our concern however is not with origins but with implications, once private property is in being and the right to it is recognized.

Without the right to private property, there could be no such thing as private enterprise in economic life at all. Under private enterprise, production and distribution are initiated and carried on by entrepreneurs acting individually and in voluntary associations. They act in anticipation of, as well as in response to, consumer demand. Consumer demand presupposes the right to acquire and dispose of private property in the form of personal possessions. The activities of entrepreneurs presuppose the right to acquire and dispose of it in the form of capital and land. This suggests that since private enterprise is an integral part of the mixed economy of a free society, the right to private property is a human right. It is one which all the members of a free society would have. We have still to see how the scope and limits of the right to private property are affected by the conditions necessary for social freedom. We must also discuss the implications for the right to private property of the typical modern form of large-scale business enterprise: the limited liability company. But first something must be said about the other important economic right, the right to work.

Socialists have sometimes interpreted this right as the right to have work provided. They have seen it in terms of protection against the evil of unemployment. There is something in this as we shall see later. But as an account of what the right to work is, it will not do. The essentials have been missed. Having the right to work means that you can take any job you can get. But you are not obliged to take any job in particular, or for that matter, any job at all. You are entitled but not obliged to work. The right to work also includes the right to become an entrepreneur. You are not limited to working for other people but can set up in business for yourself. There is an important corollary. Under private enterprise, the right to work must include the right to give work: you are entitled to become an employer.

The obligation correlative to the right to work is an obligation not to restrict entry into any job, occupation, or field of business enterprise. But here as elsewhere, neither the right nor the obligation can be unconditional. Like the right to private property, the right to work is a particular application of the general right to freedom and is subject to the provisions of the law. These provisions should reflect the public interest. This means that the obligation more precisely specified is an obligation not to impose arbitrary restrictions upon the work which people can do: that is, restrictions which cannot be justified as being in the public interest. Thus it is not arbitrary to deny entry into an occupation to those who lack necessary professional competence or technical skill. But subject to these limitations, the right to work entitles you to work at anything you like, for anyone who will employ you, and on the other side, to employ anyone who will work for you. Without the right to work, there can be no open labour market and no entrepreneurs. It is as necessary for private enterprise as the right to private property, and like it, is a human right. All the members of a free society would have the right to work as well as the right to private property. The two rights are co-ordinate and interdependent. Neither is worth anything without the other.

There is another aspect of the necessary role of private enterprise in a free society. Economic freedom is an ingredient of personal freedom. Having adequate opportunities for personal freedom, means having adequate opportunities for economic freedom, which in turn means having the right to private property and to work. In a modern industrial economy without private enterprise, production and distribution would have to be centrally organized and planned. Rationing and the direction of labour might not be openly resorted to, but the rights to private property and to work would certainly be drastically curtailed. If there are to be adequate opportunities for economic self-determination, if the right to private property and to work are not to shrink to insignificance, there must be scope for private enterprise. Not only are the rights essential for private enterprise, some scope for private enterprise is essential if the rights are to amount to anything.

Private enterprise is market enterprise but markets are public not private institutions. This is recognized even in the 'nightwatchman' theory of the state, according to which it is in the public interest to prevent monopolistic control of any market, or the 'cornering' of a market by private interests. The public character of markets has implications for the right to private property in a free society. If this right is to be a human right, if all the members of a society are to have it, all must have equality of status as consumers. This does not mean that all must have equal incomes. But it does mean that there must be no arbitrary restrictions upon their entry into any market as consumers. This in turn means that retailers and all purveyors of services have an obligation to serve all *bona fide* customers. They must not discriminate among them: for instance, refusing to serve coloured people. As retailers, they have the right to enter any market and sell what they like but not to pick and choose to whom they will sell. Similar considerations apply to the right to work as a human right. We have already seen that it involves no arbitrary restrictions upon entry into any occupation. If all are to have the right, all must stand on an equal footing in the labour market. There must be no discrimination in employment either by employers or trade unions on irrelevant grounds such as race, colour, or creed. The right to work entitles you to work at anything you like and for anyone who will employ you. But it does not entitle you to pick and choose with whom you will work. You must accept them if they are suitably qualified. The same goes for employers. Their choice of whom they will employ must not be capricious. They have an obligation to take account only of relevant qualifications.

A word is necessary about trade unionism in relation to the right to work: particularly the right to strike and what is called the 'closed shop'. The right to strike is vital to trade unions as an ultimate sanction in their efforts to improve the pay and working conditions of their members. On the face of it, the right to strike is not incompatible with the right to work and indeed may be interpreted as an extension of it. You are entitled but not obliged to work and are therefore entitled to withdraw your labour. Admittedly a strike is not the withdrawal of labour by individual workers acting without reference to one another. It is the withdrawal of labour by a group of workers acting consciously and deliberately together. But this does not make any difference provided that two conditions are satisfied. The first is that no one should be compelled to join a strike. The right to strike must be a right in the proper sense of the term. You are entitled but are not obliged to go on strike. The second is that employers should have the right to impose a lockout. The right to employ is a corollary of the right to work and it means that employers must not be compelled to employ people on terms which they regard as unacceptable. Given these two conditions, the right to strike may fairly be regarded as a consistent extension of the right to work.

At first sight, the closed shop looks like a monopolistic restriction imposed by a trade union. But there is a case for it which briefly is this. All the workers in a trade, not merely the union members, enjoy the better pay and working conditions secured by union action. To take the benefits without contributing to the cost of securing them is unjust. All the workers in the trade ought therefore to join the union. They can be made to do so if the trade becomes a closed shop. This restriction upon entry into the trade is not arbitrary because it prevents injustice. But what about the position of the employers? Why should they undertake to employ only union members? The closed shop restricts their right to employ and weakens their bargaining position, giving the union a decided advantage. Justice in industrial relations requires that in determining the scope and limits of rights, equal weight should be given to the claims of unions and employers. Neither side should receive favoured treatment at the expense of the other. The case against the closed shop is that it does precisely this. It favours the unions at the expense of the employers and involves an arbitrary restriction upon the right to employ. Hence it is unjust.

According to the case for the closed shop, it prevents injustice. According to the case against, it perpetrates it. There is however a decisive consideration in support of the case against. A trade union does not need the closed shop in order to carry out its task effectively. It needs widespread loyalty and support from its members but that cannot be secured by compulsion. It must be spontaneously forthcoming. It is therefore not in the public interest in an enlightened society for closed shop agreements to be given legal recognition. This is not to deny that the workers in a particular trade may well have a moral obligation to join the union. It is only to deny that they should be compelled to join, which is what legalizing the closed shop would amount to. Whether people have a moral obligation to do something is one question: whether it is in the public interest to compel them to do it is another.

It was said earlier in this section that corporate ownership is ownership by a social group and that it is private ownership when the group is a voluntary association. The modern limited liability company is a social group and is a voluntary association in the sense that no one is compelled to work for it or to invest in it. But its owners, the shareholders, are not a social group. They are a set of persons who are probably unknown to one another and who have in common only the fact that each of them owns shares in the company. It is the management, not the shareholders, who decide what is done with the company's property, and more generally the policies and operations of the company. For practical purposes, that is to say, it is the management who are the real owners. For the most part, they are accountable only to themselves since so far as the shareholders are concerned, the company is simply a source of income. The management must keep the shareholders reasonably satisfied with what they get out of it but that is all. The policies and operations of large modern companies however have repercussions throughout the economy. They affect prices, wages, salaries, employment, and the balance of payments. It does not follow that what is best for the company is always best from the standpoint of the public interest in a free society. What the management does cannot be a purely private matter which concerns itself alone. Its policies and operations are inevitably 'tinged with public interest'. In some respects, modern companies are more like public bodies than voluntary associations. The interest of the company must be interpreted in the light of the public interest which is to say that the management must exercise the right to private property in the light of the requirements of social responsibility. That means not only accepting but co-operating constructively with government measures of regulation and control.

Public enterprise is the other side of the mixed economy of a free society. It is carried on by public corporations or other agencies deliberately set up by the government and authorized to carry on production and distribution in particular fields such as fuel and power, transport, and communications. It is frequently in the public interest for a public enterprise to be a public monopoly: for instance in the case of electricity supply, or railways. This means limiting the scope of the rights to work and to private property. But there should be no confiscation.

Private owners of capital and land must be paid fair compensation when an industry or service is 'taken into public ownership'. Once having been set up, public agencies must respect the rights to work and to private property. They must go into the labour market to recruit the workers they need, on level terms with other employers and must purchase their materials and equipment at market prices as ordinary customers. No one should be compelled to work for a public agency or to sell to one. The fundamental economic rights to private property and to work are as essential in the public sector of the mixed economy of a free society as they are in the private sector. Their scope and limits will be affected by the requirements of the public sector and also by the need to regulate and control, but their character as rights remains unimpaired.

5. RIGHTS AND THE 'WELFARE STATE'

In the last chapter reference was made to certain welfare conditions which in a free society would be in the public interest: full employment, adequate educational opportunities, adequate medical services, and a minimum level of income. It may be thought that in a free society the members would have rights to these conditions. But this is a misleading way of putting the matter. In any society it is in the public interest that so far as possible the rights which the members ought to have should be given legal recognition and protection. But it does not follow that because something is in the public interest, it is for that reason something which the members ought to have as a right. The relation between rights and welfare conditions needs clarifying.

Consider the case of full employment. The right to work is not worth much if there is no work to be had. Is there a right therefore to have work provided? Presumably this means that if I am unable to find work for myself, I am entitled to demand it from the government, and that the government is under an obligation to provide it for me. But does it also mean that the government must provide me with the kind of work which I want? If so, there can be no such right. It is ruled out on economic grounds. It could never be in the public interest for the government to attempt the impossible task of giving anyone who asked for it the kind of work he requested. If on the other hand what is meant is that anyone who is unemployed would have the right to turn to the government for help in finding work, in re-training and in moving to a new job, this is something different from the right to have work provided. The members of a free society would have the right to such help. But it would be the right to help in finding work from among the alternatives available, not the right to have work specially created irrespective of its economic justification. This does not rule out programmes of public works organized by the government. But these programmes must be shown to be in the public interest on economic grounds. They must not consist simply of 'made' work. The conclusion to be drawn from all this is that while full employment is in the public interest in a free society, it cannot in any meaningful sense be a right. Rather it is a necessary condition if certain rights, notably the right to work, are to be realities and not merely formalities.

To say that in a free society there would be a right to education is misleading. Taken literally, it implies that parents would be entitled but not obliged to have their children educated, whereas the opposite is the case. They would have a duty. The relevance of rights is within a system of education. There can be rights to different kinds and levels of education. But no one can have a right not to be educated at all. But if parents are to fulfil their duty, appropriate educational institutions must be available and this is the government's responsibility. There cannot however in any meaningful sense be a right to such institutions. The position is rather that a good educational system is a necessary condition if there are to be any rights in the sphere of education. What is in the public interest is that there should be such a system and that within it there should be rights which will secure adequate educational opportunities to all. This does not mean that in a free society education would be a state monopoly. Some scope for private enterprise in education is desirable for the sake of innovation and experimentation. If people in a free society want to run schools at their own expense, why shouldn't they? But private educational ventures must satisfy criteria laid down by the government.

While these criteria should leave room for innovation, they must specify the fundamental requirements which have to be met to qualify for recognition as a school. Subject to these requirements, there would be the right to run private schools and a correlative obligation on the government to give official recognition to private schools which satisfy its criteria. The government's task must be to see that the educational system as a whole, both state and private, gives adequate educational opportunities to everyone.

On the face of it, as far as rights are concerned, there is an important respect in which the case of medical services differs from the case of education. No one can have a right not to be educated at all. But in a free society, everyone must have a right to refuse medical treatment. To compel a man to submit to medical treatment against his will is a gross violation of his right to freedom. It is the apotheosis of arbitrary constraint. But it is not arbitrary constraint to isolate a man suffering from a highly infectious virulent disease, although it would be to force him to undergo treatment for it. Nor is it arbitrary to place certain mental patients under restraint for the sake of protecting both society and themselves; nor to induce them to take sedatives, since they are incapable of rational thought and decision. Finally certain public health measures which are in the public interest and which it is necessary for all to accept, cannot properly be regarded as violating the right to refuse medical treatment. There cannot be a right properly so called against the public interest. What is important is that the individual should not be compelled to suffer bodily interference against his will because in the opinion of doctors his personal health requires it. As a free person, that is something which he must be left to decide for himself. The right to refuse medical treatment is the negative side of the right to have it. You are entitled but not obliged to receive medical treatment. But if the right is to be more than a formality, there must be adequate medical services to which all have access. In a free society it will be the government's responsibility to see that there are. This does not mean that medical services will be a state monopoly. While there should be scope for private medicine and therefore a right to engage in private practice and to have private treatment, this must not be at the expense of an adequate medical service for all.

In a free society it is in the public interest that no one's income should fall below a minimum level. The minimum must be sufficient to enable a man to provide the essentials of life for himself and his dependants. 'The essentials of life' must cover the food, clothing, and shelter, necessary for physical and mental health, not merely for bare subsistence. A man's income may fall below the minimum owing to unemployment, illness, old age, or simply because in current market conditions his earning capacity is insufficient. His poverty may be due to bad luck, to his own folly and improvidence, or to a combination of both. But whatever the reason, the fact that his income is below the minimum means that neither he nor his dependants have adequate opportunities for personal freedom. Enlightened humaneness requires that his income should be brought up to the minimum, and it is in the public interest to provide for this to be done out of public funds. Does this mean that in a free society there would be a right to a minimum income? Yes, in the sense that if a man's income in relation to his needs falls below the minimum he would be entitled to the financial assistance necessary to bridge the gap. Insurance may enable many people to keep their incomes above the minimum without having to resort to assistance from public funds. It is in the public interest in a free society to encourage private insurance schemes and to organize and support public insurance. But over and beyond this, the right to receive assistance from public funds is essential as an ultimate protection against the evil of poverty.

Welfare measures involve taxation but so does all government activity. Taxation enables the government to pay for what the public interest requires. Hence it is in the public interest for taxation to be on a scale sufficient to yield the necessary revenue. But this revenue has for the most part to come out of what is earned by private enterprise. There is therefore an upper limit to the level of taxation. It must not be so high that private enterprise becomes unprofitable. But how high must it get before this happens? Clearly no precise answer is possible. It is often said that taxation is too high if business efficiency is penalized and the incentive to work hard and take on responsibility is weakened. No doubt this is true but it still leaves uncertain just what the breaking point is. Much probably depends upon habits and expectations, and much also upon the government's ability to impress upon people the requirements of the public interest and the need to pay for them. The question of what level of taxation is appropriate is essentially a political matter which the government must decide and for which it must take responsibility.

The fact that taxation is a political matter emphasizes the justice of the well-worn slogan: 'No taxation without representation!' In a free society, this is provided for. The democratic citizen body to which the government is accountable is also the body of tax-payers. The payment of taxes is a social obligation. The democratic citizen has the right to exercise the government's judgement of the public interest and the policies by which that judgement is implemented. But he must pay the taxes which the government imposes whether or not he approves of its policies. He has his chance at the next election to express his disapproval. Nor can he justifiably claim exemption from taxation on the ground that he does not make use of certain welfare measures. People sometimes argue that if they send their children to private schools, they should get tax relief in proportion to the cost since they are not making use of the public education system. But this misses the point. The public system is provided as a social service and as a member of society a man has an obligation to contribute to its cost. He has the right not to use it and to educate his children privately but that does not affect his obligation as a citizen to pay his share of the cost of the public system. But while the paying of taxes is a social obligation, it must be justly apportioned. In a free society, there would be progressive taxation, the rate being paid being related to earnings. How steep the rate of increase should be, like the question of the overall level, is, however, a political matter. There is room for controversy about its detailed application but not about the inherent justice of progressive taxation.

A free society may fairly be described as a welfare state in the sense that it is in the public interest that certain important welfare conditions should be established and maintained. Our theme in this section has been the relation between these conditions and rights. We have seen that it would be misleadnig to say that the members have rights to these conditions. The position is rather that they make it possible for the members to have certain rights and that these are rights which are themselves justified on the score of social freedom. But subject to this qualification, they may be summed up under the comprehensive title of 'welfare rights'. It follows that welfare rights are human rights properly so called since all the members of a free society would have them. Finally two points: the first is that economic conditions necessarily set limits to what can be done in the way of welfare provisions. The more prosperous the society, the better the provisions which it is possible to make. The second is that no matter how adequate the welfare provisions, there are likely to be some people who will benefit little from them. Welfare rights based on well-organized public welfare services can provide the opportunities necessary for personal, moral and rational freedom, but they cannot guarantee that advantage will be taken of the opportunities. Some people will make a mess of their lives no matter how much they receive. What matters is that no one should be prevented from succeeding because of circumstances beyond his control which could be remedied by social organization.

6. THE RIGHT TO FREEDOM OF SPEECH

Democratic political rights include the right to criticize and oppose the government of the day, and to express opinions on all political matters. The right to freedom of speech in politics is therefore a human right. But what about other spheres besides the political? There is an apparently straightforward answer. The right to freedom of speech is a particular case of the general right to freedom. I am entitled to be free from arbitrary constraint. I am therefore entitled to say what I like, where and when I like, in whatever way I like, provided that I do not violate any restrictions which it is in the public interest to impose. But I am also entitled to keep silent. I am not obliged to express any opinion, make any statement, answer any questions, unless once more it is in the public interest to compel me to speak. The scope and limits of the particular right to freedom of speech are the same as those of the general right to freedom. They are set by the requirements of the public interest. But while this is true so far as it goes, it evades the main question. When, if at all, is it in the public interest in a free society to restrict what people can say, and to compel them to speak against their will?

A free society must provide adequate opportunities for all its members to achieve personal, moral, and rational freedom. Moral freedom includes positive political freedom, which is why democratic political rights are human rights. They provide the conditions necessary for all the members of a society to be self-determining as citizens. In particular, the right to political freedom of speech secures a necessary type of negative freedom: the absence of constraint upon political expression and communication. Adequate opportunities for rational freedom mean adequate opportunities for potential critical humanists to realize their potential. That means among other things negative freedom in the shape of the absence of constraint upon expression and communication, in all fields of activity which contribute to human beings' understanding of themselves and the world. In particular, it means no restriction upon the scope of critical inquiry and discussion, and upon art. The importance of this 'cultural' freedom of speech as we may henceforth call it was understood by Mill, despite the fact that in *Liberty* he was ostensibly writing as a Utilitarian. His case for it in the second chapter has deservedly become a classic.

It is therefore in the public interest in a free society for there to be cultural and political freedom of speech. What about other areas of public communication: for instance advertising, journalism, and entertainment in all its forms? If there are to be adequate opportunities for personal freedom including economic freedom, must there not be freedom of speech in these areas? This suggests that in a free society it is in the public interest for there to be what may be called 'commercial' freedom of speech, as well as cultural and political freedom of speech. Does that mean that there should be no restrictions at all? Not necessarily: but it does mean any curtailing of freedom of speech must be shown to be the lesser evil from the standpoint of the public interest. Any sacrifice of cultural, political, or commercial freedom of speech, must be more than outweighed by the evil which is prevented.

There is a distinction implicit in Mill's argument which has a bearing on our present discussion. This is between the content of what is said in speech, writing, or any other form of public expression, and the foreseeable consequences of its being said. Mill's case against censorship is in effect a case against censoring purely on the ground of content. That something is believed to be false or evil is no justification for banning it. On the contrary, it should be exposed to public discussion so that the reasons for its alleged falsity or evil can be critically examined and people can make up their own minds about it. Mill bases his case on human fallibility. No one has a monopoly of truth or virtue. He is surely right. It can never be in the public interest in a free society to censor, or in any other way to curtail freedom of speech, solely on the grounds of the content of what is said. To attempt to do so is always the greater evil. To fail to appreciate this is to betray a defective understanding of human freedom and of the vital role of independent criticism in questions of truth and value. If freedom of speech is to be curtailed at all in a free society, it must be because the foreseeable consequences of what is said are contrary to the public interest.

But doesn't the content always affect the foreseeable consequences? Not necessarily: the decisive factor so far as the public interest is concerned may be the time, place, and manner of expression, a political demonstration held in city streets at a busy hour will dislocate the traffic and cause general inconvenience. There is good reason in the public interest to control the demonstration, confining it to certain routes and times. But this is to regulate the free expression of opinion, not to suppress it. Suppose however that the political demonstration is over a highly controversial issue about which there are passionate feelings and that the foreseeable consequences of its taking place are violence and civil disorder. It will then be in the public interest to ban the demonstration. This suggests that foreseeable consequences which justify curtailing freedom of speech are due to the content of views and opinions, not merely to the time, place, and manner of their expression. No doubt this is true but it does not affect the main point. Granted that if the content had been different the foreseeable consequences would have been different, it is because these consequences are what they are, not because the content is what it is, that the curtailing of freedom of speech is justified.

Some further illustrations may be helpful. In Britain, public comment upon legal cases which are *sub judice* is effectively silenced by the threat of contempt proceedings. There is good reason to think that in a free society this restriction upon freedom of speech would be in the public interest. The foreseeable consequences of public comment would be to make it difficult for juries to approach their task with an open mind. This in turn would prejudice legal justice. The restriction undoubtedly involves some sacrifice of commercial freedom of speech and perhaps also of cultural and political freedom of speech. But this is the lesser evil from the standpoint of the public interest in a free society. A similar conclusion applies to laws against libel and slander. The foreseeable consequences of allowing libellous statements and slanderous attacks would be that innocent people would be harmed through damage to their characters and reputations. The restriction upon freedom of speech imposed by libel and slander laws is therefore the lesser evil. A restriction of a very different sort is that which is imposed upon scientific publication in the name of military security. This undoubtedly involves some sacrifice of cultural freedom of speech. But provided that the restriction really is necessary for military security, the sacrifice is the lesser evil. The military security of a free society is necessary for its continued existence and scientists must give priority to their duty as citizens to help defend it.

So far we have considered only restrictions upon freedom o speech. What about the use of compulsion to make a man speak? At first sight, the distinction between content and foreseeable consequences seems to have no relevance. If a man is silent, there is no speech and hence neither content nor consequences. But why force a man to speak unless it is thought that what he says might be significant? This suggests that it is the prospective content of his speech which is the decisive factor. In a free society however this cannot by itself justify forcing him to speak. To force him to speak is to violate his personal freedom, and more especially, his freedom as a speaker, to decide for himself when and about what to speak. In view of this, is forcing a man to speak ever justified in a free society? The answer is yes, if the foreseeable consequences of leaving him to decide for himself whether or not to speak are contrary to the public interest. Thus in a free society there is good reason to compel witnesses to testify in court and to give evidence to quasi-judicial tribunals, since if testifying and giving evidence was a voluntary matter, many witnesses would fail to put in an appearance and the administration of justice would be seriously handicapped. In the case of compulsion therefore, no less than in the case of restriction, it is the foreseeable consequences not the content which is the touchstone in curtailing freedom of speech.

But to return to restrictions: is it always clear when the foreseeable consequences are contrary to the public interest? What about pornography, blasphemy, and racist propaganda? Publications of these types are morally offensive to many people. Does this mean that the foreseeable consequences of such publications are contrary to the public interest in a free society? Ought a book, play, or film, to be banned if many people are likely to be disgusted, outraged, or insulted by it? In support of a ban, it may be argued that there is no reason to be indulgent towards the pornographer, the blasphemer, or the racist. They contribute nothing to the arts and sciences, to democratic politics, or to decent entertainment. There is no sacrifice of cultural or political freedom of speech, and while there is some sacrifice of commercial freedom of speech, this is the lesser evil.

But this misses the point. The foreseeable consequences of any publication or other public statement, are contrary to the public interest in a free society, only if there is good reason to think that they are of such a character as to undermine or threaten any of the conditions which are necessary for all the members to have adequate opportunities for achieving personal, moral, and rational freedom. Now the fact that people are shocked, offended, or outraged by a book or a television programme does not mean that their opportunities for personal, moral, and rational freedom, are being impaired. In a free society, they do not have to read the book or watch the programme. If having started to do so, they find it offensive, they can stop. Nor do they have to accept what they read or watch uncritically. They can express their objections, point out what they consider to be obscene, irreligious, or racist, and suggest that publishers and producers show better taste and judgement in future. Moreover cultural and political freedom of speech may well be curtailed if an attempt is made to ban what people are likely to find morally offensive. Books, plays and films which attempt to deal seriously with sexual and racial themes may come under the ban because ignorant or prejudiced people object to any candid discussion of these matters and take passages out of context as instances of obscenity or racism.

But what about the alleged tendency of pornography to deprave and corrupt, and of racist propaganda to incite racial hatred? By 'deprave and corrupt' is presumably meant the encouraging of sexual promiscuity, of sexual deviance and perhaps also of sexual violence. The contention is that there is a causal connection between pornography and undesirable sexual behaviour. Is there empirical evidence to support this contention? Probably all that can be safely said is that pornography does nothing to foster good sexual behaviour. There is also the problem of determining what is to count as pornography. Is it anything which arouses sexual desire, or only what encourages sexually undesirable behaviour. If the latter, we are back where we started: if the former, much literature, drama, to say nothing of advertising, contains a pornographic element. Similar difficulties arise in the case of racist propaganda. Admittedly in a situation where racial tension already exists, the foreseeable consequences of virulent racist propaganda are unlikely to be in the public interest. But that is because such propaganda fans racial hatred which is already present, not because it causes it in the first place. A society in which there is serious racial tension is in the nature of the case something less than a free society. The conclusion to which all this points is that in a free society the public interest will be best served by leaving pornography and racist propaganda to be dealt with by open public criticism rather than by resorting to any kind of literary or political censorship. The same is true of blasphemy which would be condemned by a discriminating public opinion as a breach of good taste.

To summarize our discussion so far: we have been investigating the limits of the right to freedom of speech as a human right. The only relevant consideration so far as these limits are concerned is the foreseeable consequences of what is said, or on the other side, of keeping silent. The right entitles you to say what you like or to keep silent provided that in each case the foreseeable consequences are not contrary to the public interest in a free society. If these consequences are injustice, a breach of the peace, or of military security, it is in the public interest to impose specific restrictions and compulsions. In these cases, any sacrifice of cultural, political, and commercial freedom of speech, is the lesser evil. Whether there are any other cases of which this is true is questionable. There is a correlative obligation on the government to protect the right to freedom of speech. That means protecting cultural, political, and commercial freedom of speech from all attempts to arbitrarily curtail it, or to victimize those who express unpopular opinions. It also means protecting the right to keep silent, through legal safeguards against compulsory interrogation by ambitious reporters and publicity-seeking politicians.[1] There is also a corollary right which the government has an obligation to protect: the right of people to decide for themselves what they will read, watch, or listen to, without being interfered with by would-be private censors or over-zealous local councils. Finally while the government has a duty to regulate the time, place, and manner of the exercise of the right to freedom of speech when this is necessary in the public interest, such regulating must not become a veiled curtailing of freedom of speech. While the public interest justifies banning a public meeting when civil disorder appears inevitable, the threat of possible violence should not be made the pretext for a ban. The meeting should be protected against the threat and called off only in the last resort.

There is also a correlative obligation on every member of a free society to respect the right to freedom of speech of all the

---

[1] As exemplified by the notorious activities of the late unlamented Senator McCarthy during the 1950s.

other members. This means not preventing people either as individuals or as groups from expressing whatever views they like, and also not victimizing them for the particular views which they express. Victimization may take the form of economic sanctions: refusing a man promotion, or sacking him because of his political views which in no way affect his working efficiency. It may take the form of social discrimination or even ostracism. But the obligation to respect the right to freedom of speech is not an obligation to support or in any way to condone what is said. 'I disagree with everything you say but I will defend to the death your right to say it' puts the matter succinctly if somewhat melodramatically. It in no way inhibits the right to attack what is said with the utmost vigour. But an important qualification must be added. The obligation not to victimize is not an obligation to refrain from judging a man by the content of his public pronouncements. If he goes on record in support of stupid, misguided, or evil causes, you are justified in regarding him as someone who at the very least is lacking in knowledge and understanding of the issues involved. More generally: a man's public pronouncements are evidence of his character and intelligence and he cannot justifiably complain if people use this evidence in forming their opinions of him. To deny this is in effect to undervalue freedom of speech, since it is to hold that what a man says should not be taken seriously and that he should not be expected to stand by it.

It has been argued many times in this book that one is justified in claiming rights only if one acknowledges the obligation to respect the rights of others. It may be thought that this has implications for the position of anti-democratic political parties in a democracy. Consider the case of the Communist Party. The evidence of Communist régimes points overwhelmingly to the conclusion that under communism freedom of speech is very drastically curtailed. There is no political freedom of speech, very little cultural freedom of speech, and by definition no commercial freedom of speech since there is no private commerce. From this it seems reasonable to conclude that a communist party in a democracy does not acknowledge an obligation to respect the right to freedom of speech of other people in general and other political parties in particular. They pay lip-service to the obligation because it is politically expedient to do so, and in any case they are not in a position to deny other people freedom of speech. But if they ever came to power, they would behave like Communist régimes everywhere. Political freedom of speech would be one of the first casualties when they took over. They are therefore not morally justified in claiming the right to political freedom of speech for themselves in a democracy and a democratic government need have no scruples about denying it to them. Indeed it may be thought that it is in the public interest for a democratic government to outlaw the Communist Party since it is availing itself of the facilities of democracy in order to destroy democracy. This is a plausible argument especially so far as the moral issue is concerned. No doubt the Communist Party, and for that matter every would-be despotic party, is not morally justified in claiming the right to freedom of speech. But does it follow that it is in the public interest to deprive them of it and to outlaw them? The answer, at any rate so far as a free society is concerned, is a most emphatic no! It is not in the public interest to try to outlaw the Communist Party or to treat it differently from any other party so far as the right to freedom of speech is concerned. This is because to do so would mean political censorship, and political censorship based on the content of political opinions. The right to freedom of political speech would have to be limited to the expression of non-Communist opinions, since otherwise the Communist Party would be able to reconstitute itself under another name and continue as before. But how are communist opinions to be identified? There is at least some common ground between Communist and non-Communist ideas. The outcome of trying to impose such political censorship would be gravely to weaken political freedom of speech, to threaten democracy, and to move away from rather than towards social freedom. Communists may not be morally justified in claiming the right to political freedom of speech. But it is in the public interest in a free society that they should have it. 'Toleration' is the appropriate term to express the attitude of a free society towards Communists and other anti-democrats.

It was suggested earlier in this chapter that human rights can serve as a yardstick for assessing how far a given society is within striking distance of social freedom. The right to freedom of speech is an especially useful measuring rod. The relevant question is to what extent the limits upon it are those which would be placed upon it in a free society. To the extent that they are not, to the extent that there is, for instance, some degree of literary censorship, this is evidence that the society is something less than a free society properly so called. There is an important sense in which the right to freedom of speech is a moral as well as a legal right. It and its correlative obligations must be an integral part of a society's established morality before it can be given effective legal recognition and protection. This is because the obligation not to victimize is an obligation to act in a certain spirit rather than according to the letter of a rule. That the right to freedom of speech as a human right is embodied in a society's established morality so that the great majority of the members accept it as a constituent feature of public and private life is convincing evidence that the standpoint of critical humanism is substantially embodied in that society's way of life.

7. RIGHTS AND THE INTERNATIONAL WORLD

Nations can have rights only as members of an international community of states. But there is one right which must be recognized if there is to be any international community at all. This is the right of already existing nation-states to political independence. It does not mean that nation-states are eternal entities but only that changes in the identity and composition of existing nation-states must come about through mutual agreement. We saw earlier in this chapter that as a member of a universal human community, every human being would have the right to be treated as a self-conscious agent and a person irrespective of nationality, race, colour, or creed. This human right is a composite of two others: the right to freedom, and the right to have promises kept. There is a sense in which the right to political independence is this composite human right 'writ large'. If a nation-state is to be politically independent, it must have the right to freedom from interference by other states. That means freedom from aggression and from outside meddling in its internal affairs. It must also have the right to have treaties respected and international agreements honoured. If there is to be an international political community, all nation-states must meet the obligations correlative to these rights.

But can the right to political independence and its correlative obligations be unconditional? Changed circumstances may mean that treaties and international agreements have become out of date. When this happens, there is good reason to re-negotiate them or perhaps to dissolve them. There is no problem in principle about this. A state is entitled to have a treaty observed but it does not have to insist on it. The exercise of every right is morally justified only if it is compatible with moral demands and the right to have treaties observed is no exception. In this case the relevant moral demands are the responsibilities of membership in the international political community. For the sake of international co-operation, it may be a state's duty to waive its treaty rights, to re-negotiate them, or to accept the dissolution of an international agreement. But what about the right to be free from external interference and the correlative obligation to refrain from it? It may be thought that in the nature of the case, these must be unconditional.

But suppose that a government is committing hideous atrocities against a section of its own population: as for instance the Nazis did to the Jews. Does the obligation not to interfere in the internal affairs of another state still stand? It may be that to intervene would be a greater evil because it would result in a world war. But it is important to distinguish between questions of political prudence and of moral principle. International responsibility may justify giving priority to considerations of political prudence if the alternative is a world war. But that does not mean condoning the atrocities under the pretext of respecting the right of a state to be free from external interference in its internal affairs. There is no obligation upon other states to refrain from condemning what is happening in the strongest possible terms, nor is there an obligation to prevent or obstruct clandestine efforts by private groups to undermine the offending government by underground resistance financed and supplied from abroad. On the contrary there is a duty to do everything

possible unofficially as well as officially short of world war to
end the atrocities. While the idea of an international political
community does not presuppose that all the member states are
enlightened societies, it does presuppose that they are at least
in a minimum sense human societies. It is the idea of a universal
human community in a political form and the presumption is
that none of the member states will resort to blatantly anti-
human practices at home or abroad. If any of them do, they are
attacking the universal human community and all other states
have a duty to take whatever steps they can to defend it.

There is an obligation correlative to the right to political
independence to give diplomatic recognition to the legitimate
government of a state. What is the situation when an insurgent
government takes over after a successful revolution? Should
recognition be withheld from it and still be given to the deposed
legitimate government as a 'government in exile'? The objection
to this is that it amounts to meddling in the internal affairs of
another state. To continue to recognize the deposed government
is in effect to take sides in the revolution. On the other hand it
may also be claimed with some plausibility that to recognize
the insurgent government is also to take sides. It is this
problem which is the justification for the distinction between
de facto and *de jure* recognition. It is a useful expedient until
things have settled down after the revolution. It is sometimes
said that there is a right to revolution. Taken literally this
sounds like a contradiction in terms. It is certainly not a right
which for obvious reasons could ever be given legal recognition
and protection. What is of course meant is that there are
occasions on which revolution against a legitimate government
is morally justified. and as we saw in Chapter 8, this is true in
the sense that revolution may sometimes be the lesser evil.
But so far as other states are concerned, the people of a given
state are entitled but not obliged to continue to respect their
legitimate government. If they decide to rebel against it, that
is their affair, and other states have an obligation not to interfere
one way or the other unless there are humanitarian grounds for
interfering.

In nationalist propaganda, an appeal is sometimes made to
what is called 'the right to national self-determination'. It may

be thought that this right is a corollary of the right to political independence but it is most emphatically not. The right to political independence is a right which already existing nation-states have. It is the right to continued political independence, not the right to become politically independent in the first place. Can there in any meaningful sense be a right to national self-determination? To say that there is, is to say in effect that any social group within an existing state which can claim to have a national identity is *ipso facto* entitled to become a nation-state if its members want to do so. It is to say also that there is a correlative obligation upon the government of that state to allow the group to detach itself if the members decide to exercise the right. But what justifies the claim to this right? The group may have had an independent national existence in the past. But that is not in itself a good reason for becoming a politically independent nation today. If the members of the national group are treated as second-class citizens, the claim for national political independence is a strong one. But it does not follow that because a particular group has a separate national identity, its members are *ipso facto* second-class citizens. While nationalist movements are sometimes morally justified, there is no moral right in any intelligible sense of 'right' to national self-determination. The concept of a right is not an appropriate one for the expression of nationalist aspirations well-grounded though these aspirations may be in certain cases.

It was suggested earlier that the right to political independence could be regarded as the composite human right 'writ large'. Does this mean that the right to political independence is itself a human right? There are good reasons for not so regarding it. Human rights are the rights which the members of an enlightened society would have. But the international political community of today is something a good deal less than an enlightened society. It is not clear that an adequate political expression of the idea of a universal human community would take the form of a community of nation-states. It may be the case that if all human beings everywhere are to have adequate opportunities for personal, moral and rational freedom, the system of nation-states will have to be superseded and replaced by a federation of 'supra-national' political communities. We saw in Chapter 6 that nations are not eternal entities. They have emerged historically out of other types of community and are likely themselves to give way to others in the future. In the nature of the case we cannot know today what the character and structure of an enlightened world political community would be. Hence we cannot now know if the right to political independence would be of any relevance in such a community. The most that can be said is that it is an essential feature of the present international political community and that because it is a right in the proper sense of the term, it makes possible the eventual transformation of that community into something better. All things considered, it is best to confine the idea of human rights to the rights of individual human beings.

I have left to the end what is perhaps the most important aspect of the right to political independence. The right to be free from aggression includes the right to resist it and resisting it usually means resorting to war. There is no need to enlarge on the horrors of nuclear war. But it is necessary to acknowledge that as things stand today, the resort to war in order to stop aggression can be a morally justified exercise of the right to political independence. It is being exercised against a state which has failed to fulfil its obligation to respect the right. But there is a most important condition. The war must be a limited one, confined to stopping the aggression. In the age of nuclear weapons, no state can have the right to resort to unlimited war, even if the alternative is national defeat. A limited war may sometimes be the lesser evil but a general war cannot be. The exercise of the right to political independence is morally subordinate to the responsibilities of membership of the international political community, and the most fundamental of these responsibilities is the preservation of world peace.

8. RETROSPECT AND CONCLUSION

The human rights discussed in this chapter do not make up a complete list. My contention is only that in an enlightened society, all the members would have at least these rights. In the 'United Nations' Declaration of Human Rights there is a long list of what in the opinion of the signatories are human rights. I do not know whether all of them would count as human rights according to my interpretation. The purpose of the UN declaration is practical, not theoretical and critical. There is implicit in it a view of what some of the features of an enlightened society would be. But whether this is a coherent view, whether if so there are good reasons for accepting it, and what counts as good reasons are further questions. Perhaps this book can help to answer them. The idea of human rights is not however the only way in which rights can be thought of. In Chapter 5 a distinction was drawn between the rights actually recognized in a society's law and established morality, and the rights which its members ought to have on the basis of its current way of life. This points to three distinct ideas of rights. They can be thought of:

A. As the rights which people actually have: that is as recognized rights.

B. As the rights which they ought to have: that is as morally justified social rights.

C. As the rights which it would be better if they had: that is as human rights.

The idea of recognized rights is clearly indispensable if rights are to have any practical significance in the day to day life of a society. But its perspective is limited to the *status quo*. The attitude of mind is regularian, not rational and critical. Moreover the fact that some rights are recognized in a society's established morality but not in its laws points to the idea of morally justified social rights. This idea makes room for criticism and change. But there are also limitations. The perspective is that of social morality and the spirit is that of the conservative idea of the public interest, not the critical. In the idea of human rights, these limitations are overcome. A society's existing way of life is no longer accepted uncritically. Potentialities for improvement can be capitalized. The spirit is that of the critical, not the conservative idea of the public interest.

All this may be summed up in terms of a scale of forms of the idea of rights: the forms in ascending order being recognized rights, morally justified social rights, and human rights. Each lower form in the scale has a place in the one above it. This is obvious in the case of morally justified social rights, where the idea of recognized rights is preserved in the contrast between the rights which people actually have, and those which they ought to have. It may be thought that the idea of human rights implies no reference to any actual society and can be taken on its own. But that would be to miss its main significance which is as a yardstick for estimating the extent to which an actual society is within striking distance of social freedom and hence on the way to becoming an enlightened society. That means estimating the extent to which the rights which people ought to have as members of a given society are those which it would be better if they had. Changes in recognized rights can be made by removing discrepancies between them and morally justified social rights. But these changes will represent an improvement only to the extent that morally justified social rights and human rights coincide. In a fully enlightened society, recognized rights, morally justified social rights, and human rights, would completely coincide. But no actual society is ever a fully enlightened society. Hence the distinction between the three forms of the idea of rights and the relations between them are always relevant.

There is a sense in which one human right is always both a recognized right and a morally justified social right. This is the right to freedom, which is necessary if there are to be any other rights at all. In an actual society, the scope and limits of the right to freedom both as a recognized right and as a morally justified social right, may well be different from what they would be in a free society. This is also likely to be true of other human rights which have a place both as recognized rights and as morally justified rights in an actual society: for instance, economic rights and the right to freedom of speech. The difference between the three forms is sometimes a difference, not between what counts as a right, but over the scope and limits. It may also be a difference about the range of persons who have a right, as with political rights under a representative but undemocratic form of government.

In the introduction to this book, I said that its aim was to see freedom and rights in perspective and to try to discover what the perspective should be. According to my argument, it should be the perspective provided by the standpoint of critical humanism together with the theory of government based on the idea of the public interest. The view of freedom and of rights which this perspective gives is summed up in the two scales of forms: the one of human freedom; the other of the idea of rights. I also described this book as an essay in philosophical synthesis. A philosophical synthesis always contains a personal element. It is one man's attempt to understand the meaning and relevance of certain general ideas and inevitably bears upon it the stamp of his personal idiosyncrasies and limitations. It therefore needs to be subjected to independent criticism so that its merits, if any, can be revealed and its defects exposed. It can never be more than an individual contribution to the continuing critical discussion through which philosophical understanding is advanced. Its author can at least hope that others will be stimulated to improve on it.

Sources of Quotations in Part 1

In the following table the numbers in brackets refer to those given in the text after each quotation. In some of the passages quoted, I have made minor alterations in punctuation in order to incorporate them more smoothly into my own text.

Chapter 1

Section 1. A. John Stuart Mill
From J. S. Mill. *On Liberty*. Basil Blackwell, Oxford, 1946.

(1) p. 5	(4) p. 9	(7) p. 11	(10) p. 17
(2) p. 8	(5) p. 9	(8) p. 14	(11) p. 50
(3) p. 9	(6) p. 9	(9) p. 18	

Section 1. B. T. H. Green and Bernard Bosanquet
From T. H. Green. *Lectures on the Principles of Political Obligation*. Longmans Green and Co., London, 1941.

(1) p. 3	(3) p. 2	(4) p. 2	(5) p. 2
(2) p. 2			

From Bernard Bosanquet. *The Philosophical Theory of the State*. Macmillan, London, 1951.

(6) p. 125	(9) p. 118	(12) p. 134	(15) p. 119
(7) p. 125	(10) p. 133	(13) p. 118	
(8) p. 128	(11) p. 134	(14) p. 118	

Section 2. A. Maurice Cranston
From Maurice Cranston. *Freedom. A New Analysis*. Longmans Green and Co., London, 1953.

(1) p. 33	(5) p. 27	(9) p. 34	(13) p. 42
(2) p. 2	(6) p. 28	(10) p. 36	(14) p. 43
(3) p. 3	(7) p. 30	(11) p. 43	(15) p. 43
(4) p. 27	(8) p. 29	(12) p. 42	

Section 2. B. Sir Isaiah Berlin
From Isaiah Berlin. *Two Concepts of Liberty*. Oxford, Clarendon
Press, 1958.

(1) p. 8	(5) p. 30	(9) p. 52	(12) p. 54
(2) p. 12	(6) p. 28	(10) p. 52	(13) p. 59
(3) p. 19	(7) p. 32	(11) p. 53	(14) p. 59
(4) p. 18	(8) p. 36		

Chapter 2

Section 1. Thomas Hobbes: John Locke
   A. Thomas Hobbes
From Thomas Hobbes. *Leviathan*. Basil Blackwell. Oxford.

(1) p. 82	(3) p. 84	(5) p. 84	(7) p. 84
(2) p. 82	(4) p. 86	(6) p. 83	

   B. John Locke
From Joh Locke. 'Second Treatise on Civil Government', in
Social Contract. World's Classics, O.U.P., 1946.

(1) p. 17	(5) p. 6	(9) p. 8	(13) p. 24
(2) p. 17	(6) p. 71	(10) p. 8	(14) p. 32
(3) p. 5	(7) p. 12	(11) p. 24	(15) p. 33
(4) p. 5	(8) p. 7	(12) p. 24	(16) p. 71

*Section 2. Jeremy Bentham: D. G. Ritchie: Margaret Mac-
donald*
   A. Jeremy Bentham.
From Jeremy Bentham. 'Anarchical Fallacies', in *Collected
Works*. Edited Bowring. Volume 2. William Tait. Edinburgh,
1843.
(1) p. 501
From Jeremy Bentham. *Introduction to the Principles of Morals
and Legislation*. Oxford. Clarendon Press, 1876.

(2) p. 18	(4) p. 2	(5) p. 24	(6) p. 224
(3) p. 1			

   B. D. G. Ritchie
From D. G. Ritchie. *Natural Rights*. George Allen and Unwin.
London, 1952.

(1) p. 78	(6) p. 88	(11) p. 98	(16) p. 103
(2) p. 78	(7) p. 87	(12) p. 98	(17) p. 103
(3) p. 79	(8) p. 94	(13) p. 101	(18) p. 104
(4) p. 80	(9) p. 94	(14) p. 101	
(5) p. 81	(10) p. 98	(15) p. 103	

C. Margaret Macdonald

From Margaret Macdonald. 'Natural Rights' in *Philosophy, Politics and Society*. Editor Laslett. Basil Blackwell. Oxford, 1956.

(1) p. 37	(4) p. 39	(7) p. 39	(10) p. 48
(2) p. 39	(5) p. 44	(8) p. 40	(11) p. 49
(3) p. 39	(6) p. 44	(9) p. 47	(12) p. 53

Section 3. *H. L. A. Hart: A. I. Melden*

A. H. L. A. Hart

From H. L. A. Hart. 'Are there any Natural Rights?' in *The Philosophical Review*. Volume 64, 1955.

(1) p. 174	(6) p. 178	(11) p. 185	(16) p. 188
(2) p. 174	(7) p. 183	(12) p. 187	(17) p. 190
(3) p. 175	(8) p. 183	(13) p. 187	
(4) p. 177	(9) p. 183	(14) p. 187	
(5) p. 178	(10) p. 184	(15) p. 188	

B. A. I. Melden

From A. I. Melden. *Rights and Right Conduct*. Basil Blackwell. Oxford, 1959.

(1) p. 1	(6) p. 10	(11) p. 49	(16) p. 78
(2) p. 5	(7) p. 11	(12) p. 61	(17) p. 84
(3) p. 5	(8) p. 42	(13) p. 62	(18) p. 85
(4) p. 2	(9) p. 49	(14) p. 74	(19) p. 86
(5) p. 2	(10) p. 49	(15) p. 77	(20) p. 86